Walk Good

Travels to Negril, Jamaica.

Roland Reimer

Printed in Victoria, Canada

National Library of Canada Cataloguing in Publication

Reimer, Roland Thomas
    Walk good / Roland Thomas Reimer.

ISBN 1-55369-871-1

    1. Jamaica—Description and travel. 2. Reimer, Roland Thomas—Journeys—Jamaica. 3. Negril Region (Jamaica)—Description and travel. I. Title.

F1872.2.R43 2002	917.29204'6	C2002-903930-4

TRAFFORD

This book was published *on-demand* in cooperation with Trafford Publishing.
On-demand publishing is a unique process and service of making a book available for retail sale to the public taking advantage of on-demand manufacturing and Internet marketing. **On-demand publishing** includes promotions, retail sales, manufacturing, order fulfilment, accounting and collecting royalties on behalf of the author.

Suite 6E, 2333 Government St., Victoria, B.C. V8T 4P4, CANADA
Phone	250-383-6864	Toll-free	1-888-232-4444 (Canada & US)
Fax	250-383-6804	E-mail	sales@trafford.com
Web site	www.trafford.com	TRAFFORD PUBLISHING IS A DIVISION OF TRAFFORD HOLDINGS LTD.	
Trafford Catalogue #02-0684	www.trafford.com/robots/02-0684.html		

10   9   8   7   6   5   4   3

Dedication

This book is dedicated to my Dad, who never got a chance to see it but had a lot to do with it.

Acknowledgements, thanks and praises. . .

To JohnnyCakes, who saved me from embarrassing myself.

To my wife, for putting up with me spending so much time on this project.

To the 'boardies' of Negril.com and Rob Graves, who are bountiful cornucopias of information on Jamaica and from whom I drew daily inspiration.

And thanks to Bob . . thank you, thank you, thank you . .
Rastafari!

Author's Note

Walk Good is a work of fiction.
Many of the events, characters, objects, organizations and locations depicted within are entirely conjured from the author's imagination. Where real persons, places, things or institutions are incorporated into the story, they are used fictitiously to create the illusion of authenticity.

Walk Good
Walk good, walk good.
Noh mek macca go juk yu,
Or cow go buck yu.
Noh mek dog bite yu.
Or hungry go ketch yu, yah!
Noh mek sunhot turn yu dry.
Noh mek rain soak yu.
Noh mek tief tief yu.
Or stone go buck yu foot, yah!
Walk good, walk good.

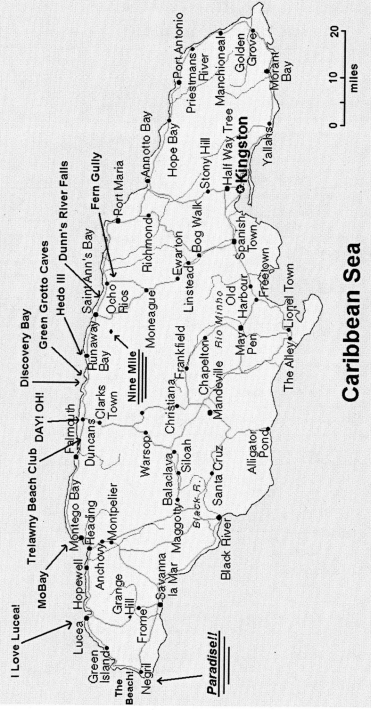

Jamaica

Caribbean Sea

I Love Lucea!

The Beach!

Paradise!!

Negril
Green Island
Lucea
Grange Hill
Frome
Hopewell
MoBay
Anchovy
Montego Bay
Reading
Montpelier
Savanna la Mar
Maggotty
Siloah
Balaclava
Christiana
Black R.
Black River
Santa Cruz
Alligator Pond
Warsop
Duncans
Falmouth
Clarks Town
Trelawny Beach Club
DAY! OH!
Discovery Bay
Green Grotto Caves
Hedo III
Dunn's River Falls
Runaway Bay
Nine Mile
Moneague
Frankfield
Chapelton
Mandeville
Rio Minho
May Pen
Old Harbour
The Alley
Lionel Town
Freetown
Spanish Town
Bog Walk
Linstead
Ewarton
Richmond
Saint Ann's Bay
Fern Gully
Ocho Rios
Port Maria
Annotto Bay
Hope Bay
Stony Hill
Half Way Tree
Kingston
Yallahs
Port Antonio
Priestmans
River
Manchioneal
Golden Grove
Morant Bay

0   10   20
miles

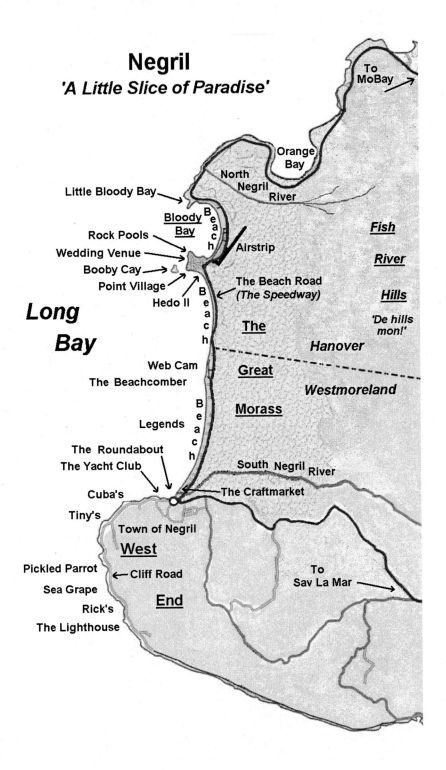

The Pickled Parrot

'We run t'ings, t'ings noh run we.'
Jamaican Proverb

 I creep tentatively to the edge of the cliff, my toes clutching mightily at the rough cement pathway. There's a circular platform at the edge of the drop-off. I crouch down and lean forward to peer over the precipice. Thirty-five feet below are the sparkling blue waters of the Caribbean.

It looks more than thirty-five feet to me, much more. The water is crystal clear and I can see down to the sandy bottom another twenty feet below the surface. When the height of the cliff is added to the depth of the water and my six feet are thrown in, I'm looking sixty feet straight down, but even from this height the water looks so very inviting, and in spite of the slight vertigo that I'm feeling, I really do want to jump.

It's calm today. The sun, high in a cloudless sky, massages my shoulders, already brown from weeks under its hot gaze, with familiar, comfortable heat. I look through the spangles of sunlight sliding over the surface of the water to the bottom. It's mostly light colored sand, broken by the occasional darker patch of eelgrass and the pink of coral heads.

I'm standing on the cliff diving platform at The Pickled Parrot; a restaurant nestled in the belly of Pirate's Cove in Negril, Jamaica. Amy and I had come here to swim, have a few Caribbean cocktails and catch the sunset. The Pickled Parrot is our favorite spot for watching Negril's glorious sunsets.

I retreat a step from the drop-off, turn and, for the third time, read the cautionary sign propped against the seaward-facing wall of the thatch covered, gazebo style restaurant-bar. In bold white lettering on a bright red background it proclaims;

**CLIFF
JUMPING
IS DANGEROUS
DO AT OWN RISK**
Pickled Parrot

I recall the words of the young rope swing attendant when I asked him about jumping off the cliff. "Keep yu feet togedder," he said (I had already thought of that). "Hit de water feet first," he told me, "doan belly flop or yu split yu belly wide open." Not exactly words of encouragement but it's nice to know what you're getting into.

I look across the cove to the diving platform at the Pirates Cave, another cliff-side restaurant about one hundred yards away. The drop there is forty feet. A young Jamaican man executes a perfect swan dive from the platform. He knifes into the water with hardly a splash. A few seconds later he bobs to the surface, lets out a war cry and gives his dreads a shake. It looks easy enough from here.

Except on days when the water is too rough, which are few and far between in this nook of paradise, there are always a few tourists who dare to jump the cliff. It's fun and provides a sideshow for the patrons of the restaurant. There's a rope swing too, and I'd done that quite a few times, bellowing like Tarzan as I arced out over the water. But the rope swing is situated on a lower terrace and the drop doesn't look anywhere near as scary as does my present view from the cliff top. Two days ago Amy had finally gotten up enough nerve to go off the rope swing. She squealed when she let go of the rope, limbs flailing like propellers. She crashed into the water making a surprisingly big splash for someone her size. When she came back to the surface she was minus her bikini top.

Today we had watched several cliff jumpers, and as usual, every one of them survived the plunge. There was one kid, who looked to be about fifteen, who jumped. He took a long time out on the platform, but he finally did it. He survived too. It makes me wonder if the odds are for me or agin me. That's how it all got started. After the kid surfaced I said, "If that young buck can do it, then so can I."

"Go ahead Hon, jump! You'll be fine," Amy urged.

"Ahhh . . . not today, maybe next time," I said, immediately regretting my comment about the kid.

"Oh, you always say that but you never jump! Go on, do it . . . I dare you!"

How many people have jumped, dived, climbed or otherwise gone to their ultimate demise as the result of a dare? Quite a few, I'd wager. And that's how I ended up here, standing at the edge of a cliff thirty-five feet above the water. I peek back over the edge; the water is mesmerizing. I feel myself sway forward a little.

In my younger days I was a skydiver, an adrenaline junkie. I logged ninety-three minutes in free-fall before I packed my rig for the last time. That was the day that a friend of mine, an experienced jumper, inexplicably delayed too long before opening her parachute.

The lowest altitude that I jumped from was 2200 feet, the highest 13,000. This 'little cliff' is a mere 35 feet. Maybe it's the intervening years, or the lack of a comfy parachute strapped to my back, but this comparatively little jump is giving me a lot more pause than any skydive ever did.

I'm keenly aware that several people are watching me, waiting for me to take the plunge; I can feel their eyes on my back. I look over at Amy, sitting at a table under a thatched awning on a lower outcropping of cliff, camera in hand. She's smiling tentatively, but I can tell she's not entirely sure about this either. I shrug my shoulders and put my hands out to my sides, as if to ask her final permission. She nods and brings the camera up. The photo may come in handy when we present our case to the medical insurance adjuster.

It's now or never, but in fact I was committed the moment I stepped up to the plate. I would never live it down if I backed out now. Foolish male bravado!

I look up from the water and out to the horizon, it's easier that way. I take a big gulping breath and squeeze my nose shut with one hand; with the other I reach down and cup my 'boys'.

I hesitate a moment, then move my right foot out over open space, and push off with my left . . . .

Babylon by Bus

'Lang road draw swet, shaat cut draw blud.'
Jamaican Proverb

There's 'Road to Negril' chatter on the message board of the 'Negril.com' web site and some are saying that the rebuilding of the infamous road to Negril is almost complete! Yeah, and I just put your check in the mail too pal.

Even during my first visit to Negril in 1976 there was a lot of talk about rebuilding the road, and that was a quarter of a century ago. But maybe this time it *is* different, maybe a miracle has happened. I'll check the road first-hand when I get to Jamaica in twelve days.

In anticipation of my trip, I've been visiting the Negril.com message board every day; many, many times a day in fact. I literally cannot wait to get to Negril. I've got a bad case of Pre-Negril-Syndrome. Reading the message board eases my PNS symptoms and at the same time gets me cranked up for the trip.

Apart from the sun and the sand and the sea and the surf, and the people that live there, one of the things that I look forward to on my regular visits to Negril is the trip from Montego Bay (MoBay) to Negril on the dreaded and legendary 'Road to Negril'. The Negril souvenir shops sell T-shirts boasting 'I Survived the Road to Negril', depicting a battered old bus jouncing along a pot-holed road with luggage tumbling off the roof rack and shocked-looking, wide-eyed tourists gaping out the windows. But the drive really isn't that bad. Granted, there are a lot of potholes and big washouts after a rain, and those who travel the road do get bounced around a lot, but Jamaica is a third world country. If I wanted an island experience with smooth roads, I'd go to Hawaii. The surface of the road to Negril, with all of its imperfections, is immaterial. It's what is seen and experienced along the roadside that's important.

Einstein posited that with the right kind of vehicle, one could stretch time. Well I've found a way to do it without a fast starship; I just book a trip to Negril. The moment I close the deal, time starts to slow down. The closer that I get to departure, the more it slows. The last two weeks are interminable. How can time drag so? I feel as if I'm back in a stifling grade school classroom on a warm spring day, watching the clock, waiting for the home bell. Every day drags on, seemingly endless. Tick............Tick...........Tick, even the seconds pass in slow motion. It's as if some tiny invisible time-devil has grasped the second hand on the clock and is holding it back, sneering and snickering at me as I wait for the time to pass.

Then, about two days before departure, the time-devil stops holding back the second hand and starts to push on the hour hand. I find myself in a flurry of wrapping things up at work, buying last minute items, washing and packing and going over lists to make sure everything is in readiness. I inevitably run out of time and leave for the airport feeling rushed and certain that I've forgotten something important, or perhaps left the garage door open.

Ultimately, I end up sitting in the plane. A contented feeling, tinged with excitement, washes over me. It's as if I'm going home; and in a way I am. We're headed for the Montego Bay airport located in the northwestern part of the island. Montego Bay is the smaller of Jamaica's two international airports; the other is located in Kingston, the capital, on the eastern side of the island.

Jamaica, with a population of approximately 2.5 million, is the largest English-speaking island in the Caribbean. The vast majority of Jamaicans are descendants of African slaves. Other groups include East Indians, Chinese and Europeans. This ethnic diversity is recognized in Jamaica's national motto, *"Out of Many, One People."*

Today is Saturday. The first week of my stay in Jamaica will be my last week as a single man. Amy, my fiancée, will be coming down next Saturday and six days later we'll be married on the beach. A group of family members will also be coming to the island to help us celebrate our wedding. I'm looking forward to getting everybody together. Sometime during the next week I have to make sure that the wedding preparations are in place. Other than that my agenda is clear. This week is my time to reacquaint myself with Negril, a place that is never far from the forefront of my mind.

The Airbus 330 slows and descends between heaping mounds of cumulus clouds. Out the window I catch glimpses of the blues and greens of the Caribbean. The sea is spotted with white caps and the occasional long wake that trails behind a ship. There's a reggae beat coming over the airplane's sound system and the mood on board is upbeat and anticipatory, happy chatter punctuated with bursts of laughter fills the cabin. Although this is a regular Toronto – MoBay scheduled flight, it feels like a holiday charter. Soon every window has a head blocking it. I watch the sea go by below us; we're much lower and are getting very close now. I stomp my feet, they're tingling with anticipation, I can hardly sit still. We begin our final turn into the MoBay airport. Through the window I see a sun-drenched island, rows of palms line the roadsides and in the distance a regiment of green hills overlook the airport.

With a landmass of 4,411 square miles, Jamaica is the third largest of the Caribbean islands. It's 146 miles long and varies in width from 22 to 51 miles. The island is very mountainous. Almost half of its land mass lies above 1,000 feet, and Blue Mountain Peak, the highest point on the island, stands at 7,402 feet above sea level.

We bump down onto the runway. Sporadic applause echoes through the cabin. It's a short taxi to the ramp. Momentarily the doors of the aircraft, front and rear, are opened. The heat and humidity of the island waft languorously through the cabin, and thankfully, the scent of the sea quickly disperses the stale bum smell left by 225 people who have just gotten up out of their seats after the four-hour flight.

I emerge from the cabin onto the deck of the old fashioned roll-up stairs. The MoBay airport does not have the luxury of modern loading fingers, but there is a lot of construction around the terminal building and I expect that the new additions will include them. I'll be sorry to see the old stairs go. I step out of the plane into the dazzling tropical sunshine. It's hot! I squint into the deep blue sky. Tall clouds crown the tops of the green hills to the east. The tropical sun licks my skin and the breeze off the sea flaps my shirt.

I consider stepping onto the hot tarmac at the MoBay airport the official beginning of my vacation. It is so nice to be back! What is it about this island that makes me feel so at home? Weeks of sun, sand and the warm Caribbean stretch enticingly ahead.

While walking through the terminal on the way to clear customs, it's a habit of mine to check out the people who are in the departures area waiting to board their flights home. At the MoBay airport the arriving passengers pass by the departing passengers just before the turnoff for customs. They look deeply tanned and relaxed, sitting there with their woven hats and packages of rum. But they look more than relaxed, there's something else. It's in their faces and in their body language. Even the children traveling with their parents have the look. After many trips to Jamaica I think I've figured out what it is. Their vacations in the sun have drained them of the karmic sludge that builds up in those of us who live in the cold, drab cities of the northern climates. Their psyches have been given the once-over. Plucked out, de-gunked, cleaned and polished and put back in, imbued with new life. In Jamaica the Rastafarians have a word for it, 'ital', meaning wholesome, natural, vital. Ital is also used to describe a way of life. The people waiting to board their flights back to reality look rejuvenated . . . they look ital.

In the short hallway before customs we're greeted by a group of Jamaican folk singers and dancers. The ladies are dressed in multicolored, multi layered, crinoline dresses and they're wearing traditional headdress. A couple of men are strumming on guitars. They sing and sway as we pass by on the way to the immigration hall.

I join one of the lineups. The MoBay immigration hall is perpetually hot and stuffy, perhaps the agency thinks they can sweat out the interlopers or maybe they haven't discovered air conditioning yet. The customs and immigration agent is quick and polite, if a little stiff, "Where are you going?" Stamp, stamp. "Hold on to this paper," he hands it to me. "Have a nice stay in Jamaica." He beckons to the next person in line.

I descend a flight of stairs to the baggage claim floor, clear customs and finally walk into the airport arrivals area; it's a hubbub of activity. Like most airports, there are several bored looking people standing around holding up signs bearing the names of arriving passengers. But these signs are different, they show the names of exotic hotel destinations or tour companies and some of them are painted with hibiscus blossoms. Each one holds the promise of an exciting tropical stay. I'm surprised to see my own name on a sign being held up by a nice looking Jamaican lady in an Air Canada Vacations uniform.

I approach her, "You're looking for me?" I ask, curious as to why she wants to talk to me.

"Mr. Reimer?" I nod. "Your hotel, ah," she checks a sheet of paper, "Sam Sara, is overbooked, so we are sending you to another hotel on the beach - - Legends." She looks at me for a reaction. Legends, I know the place, it's the sister hotel to Sam Sara. I've walked past it on the beach hundreds of times, but have never stopped in, not even to visit the bar.

"Legends is on the beach," I said. The accommodations in Negril can be categorized as those on the beach and those on the cliffs to the west of town. Sam Sara is on the cliffs and I had been looking forward to a stay on the cliffs this trip.

Yes, and it's an upgrade too!" the agent replies, mistaking my response for enthusiasm. She opens a brochure and points to some promo photos of Legends.

This does nothing to appease me, as my experience with brochure photos versus reality has been universally disappointing.

"An upgrade?" I said, still unsure about the change in plans.

"Yes, and we are going to refund you two nights stay," she added, as if it was unimportant.

"Oh, now you're talking!" I said, my British blood awakening.

Smiling, she nods and hands me an envelope then points me toward the door to the airport's bus yard, happy to have me on my way without incident. They say that change is opportunity, so I shrug my shoulders and thank her.

I'm halfway across the floor when she comes running after me. "Mr. Reimer!" What now, I wonder, hoping for additional refunds. "You are also entitled to a free dinner at Legends for your trouble. Just tell the restaurant manager who you are."

"This gets better and better," I tell her. An upgrade, a free meal, the beach, things are already starting to get interesting and I haven't even left the airport.

I duck into the men's room to doff my golf shirt and change into a light tank top. I had already changed into sandals and shorts in the stinky little bathroom on the plane. Someday soon I'll arrange my affairs so as to live in a climate where I can spend the rest of my days dressed in a wardrobe that consists entirely of shorts, sandals and a large variety of T-shirts and tank tops.

My luggage consists of a tote bag that is stuffed to capacity and one large, baggage-smasher proof, hard-shell Samsonite. It is densely packed with wedding essentials and is very heavy. I trundle it through the door to the bus parking lot and I'm immediately descended upon by a phalanx of red-capped, uniformed porters. I've been here before, so I'm ready for them. Two of them lunge for the handle of my big suitcase, but I put my shoulder down and use my high school football open field running skills to deftly dodge both of them. Another one comes at me from my right. His eyes are wide, he's compact and looks powerful. He makes a grab and his hand locks momentarily onto the suitcase. I pull it hard to the left and dip. He loses his grip and I make a final short dash to the curb, the unofficial goal line. Touchdown! Triumphant, I feel like slamming my tote bag onto the hot asphalt and doing a stupid dance.

The baggage porters at MoBay can be pretty aggressive. On one trip Amy and I were dropped of in front of the departures area and when I emerged from the bus about 20 seconds behind her I was surprised to see her engaged in a fierce tug-o-war with a porter who had nabbed her suitcase. It's true, blondes really do have more fun.

The tropical sun is glaring harshly off the glass and chrome of the many busses and vans in the lot. I pop on my shades, my island ensemble now complete. I ask directions and eventually track down my ride to Negril. I see the driver standing beside the small bus in the shade of a big potted ficus tree. I introduce myself, the tag on his shirt declares that his name is Lassive. Many people in Jamaica have names that conjure up images of past colonial times. I throw my tote bag onto the front seat of the bus, reserving the best seat for the trip to Negril. Lassive is a big sturdy guy about six feet tall. He has close-cropped hair, an easy smile and a deep voice. He obviously works out, his pecs and deltoids strain at the seams of his crisp white driver's shirt. He's a lady-killer, if Amy was here she would be swooning, and not because of the heat or humidity. Lassive grabs my big suitcase and easily manhandles it into an open window at the rear of the bus.

Several other passengers are standing around beside the bus, their ghostly blue-white limbs poking out of shorts and tank tops that haven't been worn for months. I look at my own forearms, I'm so pale and the sun is so intense that I'm sure I can see the blood coursing through my veins. The other passengers look happy to be here but they still have an uptight air about them. I probably look the same to them. A couple of days in the sun will do wonders for us all.

Lassive consults his checklist and then gives us the signal to board the bus. "OK, lets go to Negril," he says. I jump into the front seat. The bare skin of my shoulders burns as it makes contact with the hot leatherette upholstery. Lassive cranks up the motor and the radio comes on at full volume, blasting the interior of the bus with reggae music from IRIE 107.7, Jamaica's coolest radio station.

"Sorry 'bout dat!" Lassive yells. He turns the volume down, but only a little. He reaches under the driver's seat and pulls out a little clear plastic bag filled with pieces of cut sugar cane. He turns around and holds the baggie up to the passengers, "Have you tried sugar cane?" he asks. "Jus' chew on it an' suck it, it's sweet," he says. The baggie makes the rounds and everybody gets a couple of pieces. "But don't spit it on my floor," Lassive adds. The woman in the seat behind me finishes sucking the sweet juice out of the cane. She asks Lassive where she should put the stringy pulp that she's holding in her hand. "Jus' t'row it out de window!" he replies.

Jamaicans, while fervently proud of their country, have not yet fully embraced the concept of putting trash in its proper place.

On a good day, Negril is an hour and a half down the road, but depending on road construction, it can take much longer than that. We leave the airport and head into MoBay. At the exit to the airport we pass a long, low concrete sign, the large bas-relief letters, painted in a vibrant pink, call out;

'WELCOME TO MONTEGO BAY'

Shortly thereafter, a more conventional sign urges us to;

'Drive, Ride and
Walk Good'

Seeing these signs drives home the fact that I am finally, actually, and blessedly here.

We proceed on the left-hand side of the road of course, which feels strange, but only for the first few minutes. Jamaica used to be a British colony and the practice of driving on the wrong side of the road has been carried forward into modern times. The speed bumps here are called 'sleeping policemen', as they are in England.

Soon, another sign points the way to Negril and proclaims;

'Negril 72 Km'

Measuring distances in kilometers is another vestige of British heritage.

We drive along the coast on the 'Hip Strip' where most of MoBay's tourist establishments are located, passing the Breezes resort and a string of souvenir and jewelry shops. We pass the Margaritaville nightclub and the Doctor's Cave Beach, MoBay's only real beach.

There's a twist in the road ahead, we approach it and slow down to navigate the curve. A group of young men are loitering on the corner. I pull my arm in the window, take off my watch and slip it into my tote bag.

Lassive looks at me, "Why you takin' off your watch mon?" I suddenly realize he thinks that I'm afraid it's going to get ripped off my arm by someone we pass on the street. But it's not that at all, I have a habit of getting rid of the watch soon after I arrive on vacation. On top of that, it's a $39.95 Timex Explorer so it really has little value.

"As of now I don't care what time it is," I tell him, "all I have to know is whether it's day time or night time." For some reason, Lassive finds this extremely funny. He puts his head back and roars deep laughter, then looks back at the road still shaking his head and smiling.

This area of MoBay is commercially developed, we pass a McDonalds and a Kentucky Fried Chicken outlet, the Colonel's smiling face beaming out at us as we roar by. There's a long smooth concrete wall, about six feet high that corrals the commercial yards on the inland side of the road. It runs along for a fair stretch. Like a long extended billboard, it's painted in sections with advertisements for commercial establishments; plumbing and electrical services, drug stores, tour companies and all manner of other businesses.

We pop out at the end of the Hip Strip at a big roundabout, another British colonial artifact. Here there's another road sign informing us that Negril now lies 82 kilometers distant. It seems that, for our efforts in traveling the five kilometers from the airport, we have somehow regressed by 10 kilometers on the road to Negril.

Immediately beyond the roundabout Lassive slows the bus down to a crawl. Ahead of us, taking their time as they saunter across the road, is a straggling herd of cows. The cows in Jamaica come complete with horns. Big, impressive, long, sharp horns . . . just the way they were meant to be. These cows, perhaps emboldened by their bony outgrowths, are totally oblivious to the traffic. Lassive maneuvers the bus through a space between a couple of them and we are again on our way.

The road straightens out but the surface is uneven. The traffic is thinner and we pick up speed. As we do the bus starts to rock from side to side. A car pulls out to pass us, music thumping from the inside. As it roars by the horn sounds, but not with a beep, instead it plays the first bar from *'I wish I was in Dixie'*. The car has been hand-painted in the Rasta colors of red, green and yellow. The driver's arm is out the window, waving as he passes. Lassive beeps the horn in response. Across the rear window of the car, in large glittering stick-on letters, is written, *'Not Skeered'*. Many Jamaican car owners decorate the darkly tinted windows of their vehicles with names or slogans. Other accessories, like big fuzzy dice hanging from the rear view mirror, are also common.

The road to the south of MoBay around the bay is in pretty good shape, but there's not much to see here, the high ground to the left, the sea to the right. We pass a big sewage treatment plant to the seaward side of the road just before we turn to the west.

There's evidence of the fabled roadwork along this part of the road. Long tracts of land paralleling the road have been expropriated and are in the process of being cleared of bush. We slow down, the traffic is lined up ahead of us. At the point where we approach a flagman there's a collection of heavy equipment and dump trucks parked helter-skelter across the road. The trucks look as if they've had a hard life. One of them, its box loaded high with gravel, sits hunched forward, disabled by a front tire that has gone flat. Several men are standing around, hands on hips, looking resignedly at the tire.

Here a new bridge is under construction over one of the many small creeks that make their way down to the sea from the hills above. We get detoured off the main road through a small hamlet called Anchovy. A sign posted on a telephone pole proclaims that the 'Miss Anchovy Pageant' will take place next week. The narrow road that winds through the village is extremely rough, no doubt made worse by all the traffic that has been re-routed over it. Everything in the bus shakes and rattles with a vengeance, it's impossible to carry on a conversation amid the clatter.

Soon we are back on the main road and free of construction.

Lassive puts the hammer down and gets the bus careening down the narrow road. He sees me eyeing the speedometer.

"Don't worry mon, every 'ting is under control," he assures me, "I drive dis trip t'ree times a day," he says, holding up three fingers. I wish he would keep both hands on the wheel. We zoom past a truck parked on the left side of the road with only inches to spare, a shock wave of air blasts into the open window. I pull my arm in from the window again. Someone once described driving on Jamaican roads as 'a near death experience', I understand exactly what he meant.

Abandoned at the side of the road, almost completely covered in vegetation, is a derelict power shovel, it's rusted and everything that is remotely useable has long ago been stripped from its carcass.

Lassive seems to know everybody that passes in the opposite direction, beeping and waving at them as they go by. In fact, since we left the airport, he has used the horn continuously, and so do the other drivers on the road. The trip thus far has been punctuated by *'Beep!'* from our bus and ***Beep! Beep!*** in response from passing vehicles. To Jamaican drivers the horn is not an accessory; it is a vital necessity, more important and used more frequently than the brakes. I've heard that the first thing to go on a Jamaican car is the horn. The automobile horn repair and replacement shops here must do a thriving business.

We cross another new bridge at Great River. Just beyond, as we start the climb to Round Hill, I look back at MoBay. The view is spectacular! The blue ocean, the hills of the city dotted with buildings, the sweep of Montego Bay and the whole scene drenched in brilliant sunshine, it's gloriously and totally Caribbean.

The further we get from the city, the more the road surface deteriorates. There are more potholes and narrow portions, especially when we pass through built up areas, but as the road gets worse the roadside gets correspondingly more interesting.

The first town we enter is Hopewell. The main street hugs the sea. On one corner blue tarps cover the stalls of a small produce market. Cars and people clog the street.

Just beyond Hopewell we pass one of the many seaside bars that literally line the roadside between MoBay and Negril. This one, called 'The Old Steamer Beach Bar and Grill', is located on the narrow strip of land between the road and the seashore and fronts a small stretch of sandy beach. The skeletal wreck of an old coastal steamer lies in the water offshore, its rusted boiler and ribs poking up out of the water. Local folklore has it that this particular steamer was run by a certain Captain Groome from the town of Rio Bueno on the north shore. Captain Groome reportedly used his ship to run guns to Cuba.

We roar past the exclusive Tryall golf club, situated on land that was originally an expansive sugar plantation. To the left of the road is a large water wheel, built by slaves in the early 1800's and restored in the 1950's, that used to be part of the old sugar mill that was located here.

Next is the town of Sandy Bay. The town has been misnamed, there's no beach here and the coast runs relatively straight, so there is no bay either. However, it's an industrious looking town. There are quite a few buildings that are under construction and on a long gradual slope overlooking the sea is a large Jockey underwear manufacturing plant.

A big woman in a colorful dress is walking down the side of the road, balancing a basket filled with laundry on her head. Many Jamaicans still wash their laundry in rivers and streams. Lassive deftly avoids the lady then swerves back to hug the left side of the road as a truck coming from the other direction angles toward us to avoid a big pothole. This doesn't phase Lassive, but it scares the hell out of me. Lassive turns around in his seat and asks if anyone wants to make a stop. If that truck had come one inch closer I would have had to make a stop at the nearest restroom. One of the guys in the back yells that he's "really, really thirsty and needs a drink". Then he asks Lassive where he can get rolling papers for the ganja that he bought at the airport. 'Ganja' is the most common of the many Jamaican colloquialisms for marijuana, others are 'herb' and more infrequently, 'bread'. We pull over across from a roadside stop.

Thirsty and his woman disappear into the darkness of the bar, which is a rudimentary structure clad in unpainted, weathered boards. The outside is festooned with colorful liquor and beer advertising posters. There's one of a dapper looking Jamaican man smiling and holding up a frosty bottle of Heineken. I almost change my mind about going into the bar. Soon Thirsty and woman emerge, he with an armful of Red Stripes (a popular Jamaican beer) and she clutching a pad of Rizla rolling papers, distinctive by its red packaging. They get back on board and Thirsty immediately bends to the task of rolling his first 'in-country' ganja joint, more commonly referred to as a 'spliff' in Jamaica. Rizla papers are big, much larger than regular cigarette rolling papers. I'm not sure about this, but I suspect they are sized with spliffs in mind.

We get back underway, a couple of chickens burst from the bush ahead and dash for the other side of the road. They barely escape with their lives.

There is a nice open stretch of road here and we make good time. To seaside, a pelican swoops low over the water, looking for lunch.

Inland, cows graze on verdant slopes below high jungle hills.

Ahead, the decaying stone ruins of an old sugar mill rise above the vegetation. The coastal area stretching south of MoBay and was once home to many large and prosperous sugar plantations that were constructed by the forced labor of imported African slaves. Due to frequent and violent slave uprisings, the land here is stained with the blood of Jamaica's ancestors. We roll past crumbling foundation walls and the skeletal remains of a windmill tower, standing as a mute witness to past times.

Scattered here and there along the side of the road are ramshackle stands selling coconuts, woodcarvings and assorted crafts. We pass one with a neat row of conch shells lined up like soldiers on parade, proudly showing their gleaming pink insides to all that pass.

Thirsty finishes rolling his spliff, gives it a lick and holds it up to admire. It has a tapered cone shape with a blunt end and its sides are smooth. He's done a pretty good job considering he did it in the back of a rocking bus. He lights it up and takes a big noisy hit. The pungent ganja smoke coils through the bus.

I look at Lassive, he seems cool with it, but he asks Thirsty to pop open the window vent. Soon the spliff is making the rounds of the passengers, some decline but most partake. Most seasoned visitors to Jamaica, and Negril in particular, take marijuana at its face value, a mild intoxicant that does no apparent harm. The herb has a mellow, fresh, green smell to it. We roll down the road, there's a quiet ebb of conversation in the bus. The music from IRIE FM fills the gaps, resonating with a full rich sound. A feeling of happy tranquility settles over me, I'm almost home. We roll past fields of vibrant green. All is right in our world.

We round a corner and there before us is Miskito Cove. The unique spelling of the name, 'Miskito' rather than 'mosquito', stems from misspelling on old maps. It was named after Indians who traveled from the Musquito Shore on the eastern coast of modern Nicaragua. They used the cove as an entry point when on raiding parties to attack Jamaica's native Arawak Indians. Miskito Cove is home to a small fishing village but equally important is its topography. It's a narrow inlet, nearly a mile long, that's sheltered by a substantial reef that lies relatively close to shore. When high seas and hurricanes threaten, many of the local boat operators, including those from Negril, make a run for the protection of Miskito Cove.

Beyond Miskito Cove we get on to a lengthy stretch of straight road. Here there are signs of recent roadwork, the ground has been scraped bare and there are a couple of dusty bulldozers parked at the side of the road, baking under the hot sun. The ground rises a little along this stretch and we can see far out to sea. Lassive gets the bus rocking again. Suddenly he reaches down to his CB radio, which has been chattering quietly since we left the airport, and turns it up a little. I listen, between the static and crackling I can make out the word 'Babylon' being repeated several times. A tour bus passing in the opposite direction flashes its lights at us, the Jamaican warning for "watch out, police ahead". We slow down to what seems like a crawl. Around the next corner there are several police cars parked by the side of the road in the shade of some tall trees. An officer is standing beside one of them, pointing a radar gun at us. I'm a bit surprised, I didn't expect to see radar traps on Jamaican roads. We cruise by at regulation speed. Once past, Lassive smiles at me and says, "Babylon not gonna get I."

There are more signs of construction along the way. At one ravine crossing there are several huge concrete bridge spans stacked along the embankments. I recall seeing them there last year, and the year before that. It looks like it will be a serious bridge someday, when someone finally gets around to building it.

A big brown sow wanders out into the road directly in front of the bus, Lassive jerks the wheel just in time to miss her but the right front wheel slams into a gaping pothole. The bus lurches and a woman in the back lets out a yelp. Lassive pounds his fist on the steering wheel and mutters something in patois that I can't make out.

We approach the high headland that overlooks Lucea Harbour. There's a roadside beer stand and a hand-painted sign that claims;

Best View - Check it Out!

Partway down the slope of the headland are three large cylindrical tanks. At first glance they look like oil storage tanks, but in fact they serve as molasses reservoirs for National Rums Ltd. Each time I pass the molasses tanks I experience an inexplicable warm, fuzzy feeling in the pit of my stomach.

One of my favorite spots along the road to Negril is just ahead, 'The Ganja Bridge'. This part of the road reminds me of sections of the famous 'Road to Hana' in Maui. We come around a tight left turn high above the sea and then the road dives steeply to the bottom of a hill. The road is very narrow, with space for only one-and-a-half cars. There's a high cliff to the left that is overgrown with tropical vegetation and to the right a sheer drop-off to the sea. At the bottom of the hill there's a tight turn and a single-lane bridge. Road traffic must come almost to a complete stop to cross it. The resident entrepreneurs, taking advantage of this, have set up a small refreshment stand just before the bridge.

Every time that I've crossed The Ganja Bridge, be it day or night, there's a guy that comes out waving a big bud of ganja. Today I look around and sure enough, I see a dreadlocked man coming up to the bus, a large cellophane-wrapped bud in his hand.

"Best on the island mon," he yells as he nears the bus. Thirsty sticks his head out the window and takes a deep sniff of the proffered bud, a healthy looking stick about 12 inches long.

"How much?" he asks loudly.

"Two hundred!" the salesman yells, the bus moving away from him. Thirsty pulls his head back in the bus as we cross the bridge, leaving the salesman in our dust, still waving the bud.

"Probably could'a got it for half that," Thirsty says. Probably could'a got it for around $75, I'm thinking.

Marijuana although ubiquitous, is illegal in Jamaica. However, it is the biggest cash crop on the island and probably its biggest export. The plant is not indigenous to the island, it was brought to Jamaica from India by the indentured servants of the British. The servants revered marijuana as a holy plant just as many Rastafarians do today.

The Ganja Bridge is located on the eastern side of Lucea Harbour (pronounced 'Lucy'). Beyond the bridge is a large flat plain where fields of sugar cane grow. The plants are topping off at ten feet, it will soon be time to harvest them.

Next we pass through Johnson Town, where a long strung-out collection of fishing huts line the south shore of the harbor.

We round the bay of Lucea Harbor and enter the town from the south. Lucea is the bustling capital of Hanover parish and the biggest town between MoBay and Negril. The town has a lot of character and, as Ricky Ricardo used to say, I love Lucea.

Saturday is market day in Jamaica. The narrow main street of Lucea is completely clogged with people and vehicles. Some of the market goers pause to look into our bus as we creep past. I wonder how many hundreds of busses and vans pass by this way each week. Lassive slows the bus down to a crawl, weaving slowly through the crowd. The smells of fresh-cooked patties, curry and jerk chicken intermingle and swirl deliciously through the open windows of the bus.

A pushcart filled with fresh-cut sugar cane bearing a hand-painted sign promising 'Cool Drinks' is partially blocking the road. Lassive leans on the horn, the pushcart pusher moves it slightly, yielding just enough space for us to squeeze by. Tinny music screeches from the roadside booth of a cassette tape vendor, competing with the booming dancehall vibes coming from the bar across the street. We finally emerge from the happy chaos of the market and veer to the left up the hill that overlooks Lucea.

The City Hall, an old building that used to be the Lucea Courthouse, dates back to the 1800's. It's built on the side of the hill and is crowned with a magnificent, four-sided clock tower. The clock has been running since 1817 and to this day it keeps perfect time. The clock was built by European craftsman and was intended for delivery to the island of St. Lucia but was mistakenly delivered to Lucea. The townspeople, who were quite taken by its beauty and exquisite craftsmanship, refused to exchange the clock for the one they had commissioned. So they kept St. Lucia's clock and took up a collection to make up the difference in cost. The clock tower itself was the gift of a wealthy German landowner. He immortalized his ancestry by having the roof of the tower built in the shape of an old Prussian army helmet, resembling those worn by the Royal Guards of Germany.

At the top of the hill there's a small sign that points to Negril and we make a right turn, heading back to seaward. But this road is clogged with cars and soon we see the reason why, there is a funeral in progress at the graveyard at the top of the hill. We pass slowly by the crowd that has gathered to pay their last respects, all dressed in their 'Sunday-go-to-meetin' duds.

I'm surprised to see another Jockey manufacturing plant to the west of Lucea. Do Jamaicans go through an inordinate amount of underwear? And are the underwear that are manufactured here tailored specifically to the Jamaican physique? Perhaps, but in fact, most of the products manufactured here are destined for export to the U.S. and the plant is located here only to take advantage of cheap Jamaican labor.

Once past Lucea, it's all downhill to Negril, figuratively speaking. Some sections of the new road are completed here and we are borne on stretches of new asphalt, literally whisking along. I see segments of the old road snaking off along the coast, reaching for memories that I can't quite recall. Someday most of the old road will be bypassed and this trip will become routine, I rue that day.

We're passing through the little village of Lances Bay when Thirsty yells out that he has to *'take a piss'*.

"Yeah mon," Lassive says, "we're going to stop just ahead."

Minutes later we pull into a rest stop at Cousins Cove, so named because the land was once part of the dowry of an heiress who married her fortunate cousin. There's a cave nearby that several years ago was the site of a bat guano mining operation.

A few Jamaicans are sitting at a table near the outdoor bar, drinking beer and playing a loud, table slapping game of dominoes. Jamaicans are passionate about their sports and although dominoes, played normally, is a clam table game, in the hands of Jamaicans it becomes an aerobic sport.

I pick up a cool Red Stripe and take a long pull at it. It slides down my throat like golden nectar. I can get Red Stripe back home in Canada but for some reason it just doesn't taste the same in northern latitudes. Besides, I don't feel right drinking Red Stripe unless I'm standing under a hot sun wearing a pair of shorts.

Soon we are back on the road. Davis' Cove is the next waypoint, it is my favorite spot along the road to Negril. Rounding the curve above the little cove I feel as if I am transported back in time, what an incredibly picturesque little place it is! It's so perfect that it looks like an overly contrived movie set. The road hugs a placid tree lined cove with crystalline water lapping on its shores. In the distance beyond the tranquility of the cove, the deep blue Caribbean crashes in a white spray on the reef. A small collection of fishing huts is nestled on a beach in the sheltered end of the cove. Multi colored fishing boats are pulled up on the sand. Beside them are stacked numerous hand made fish traps constructed of sturdy branches and chicken wire, each a different shape and size. It's mid afternoon and as we pass through Davis' Cove there isn't a soul in sight. The only sign of life is a goat sleeping in a patch of shade at the end of a long tether in the front yard of a modest house. This little cove will be bypassed by the new road, which is probably a good thing. Someday I plan to come here and spend an afternoon checking it out.

Beyond Davis' Cove is Blenheim, the birthplace of the avuncular Sir Alexander Bustamante, Jamaica's charismatic first Prime Minister.

I'm still daydreaming about Davis' Cove when we're stopped by a lady in work boots and a hardhat waving a red flag. Could it be road construction? There's a big bulldozer working up on a high ridge of light colored marl beside the road. Marl is a type of limestone, consisting of sedimentary layers of crushed seashells and coral built up over millions of years. It's the primary road bed material in Jamaica.

The bulldozer is pushing the marl around and some of it has come down onto the road where a front-end loader is busy clearing it. A burst of black diesel smoke rises from the bulldozer and a big boulder crests the ridge and tumbles down the slope. I note with more than a little consternation that its present path will bring it right on top of our bus! Somebody in the back yells "Holy shit!' This gets Lassive's attention, up until this point he was quite bored with the whole operation. Eyes glued to the approaching boulder, he jams the bus into reverse but as he does, the boulder topples off in another direction, rolls a bit further and then settles in the middle of the road. We all look around at each other, shake our heads and then start to laugh. The front-end loader goes to work clearing the boulder and other debris off the road. The process takes some time, but after a few minutes the flag lady waves us back on our way.

About a mile after the construction stop a shiny black Cadillac swooshes past us. It looks way out of place on this road and I do a double take. A 'Sandals' flag is flapping from the radio antenna. Lassive sees me looking, "VIPs," he says.

We press on through Green Island, a busy, industrious looking hamlet that is blessed with a splendid little bay. We are getting really close now and I'm starting to get restless, eager to stick my bare feet into the sands of Negril. Lassive is eager too, he has to get back to MoBay and do another trip today, and he has his foot in it again. Soon the neat cinderblock houses of the government project in Orange Bay, perched up on the hill overlooking the sea, come into view.

Then suddenly we are into the home stretch, the terrain flattens out and we hurtle past a big billboard sign welcoming us to Negril. Thirsty sees it and lets out a rebel whoop. We roar past the big, recently completed Spanish Riu hotel on the shores of Bloody Bay. Then we see the sign for the Couples resort and then the gas station with the Negril airstrip tucked in behind it. Next is the colorful sign for Hedonism, otherwise known as the zoo. Finally we are on the long straight Negril Beach road zooming past dozens of hotel and restaurant signs. There are quite a few people walking along the roadside.

Mine is the first hotel stop, we pull into the Legends parking lot. I say goodbye to my bus mates and jump out, excited to be here. I can see a little part of the beach from the parking lot. Lassive retrieves my luggage and I thank him with a tip.

The young lady in the front office seems distracted and she spends several minutes talking on the phone before giving any sign whatsoever that she has even seen me standing there. The check-in is predictably slow. It has been my experience that the term 'quick check-in' when applied to small hotels in the Caribbean is an oxymoron.

Finally I get the key to my room. For me, opening the door to a room in an unfamiliar hotel is akin to the anticipation that I feel when opening a box of chocolates -- high hopes. When I open the door to room #306 at Legends, high hopes give way to stark reality.

A Likkle Slice of Paradise

'In Jamaica, if it's nice you do it twice.'
Jamaican Proverb

The little seaside village of Negril is located in the parish of Westmoreland in the county of Cornwall on the western tip of Jamaica. The map coordinates are latitude 18 degrees, 16 seconds north, longitude 78 degrees, 20 seconds west. It's nestled in the elbow of land between a spectacular outcropping of cliffs to the south and seven miles of white sand beaches to the north.

The South Negril River runs along the northern edge of the village proper. Within the village there's a police station, a couple small shopping malls and a bank. A roundabout sits at the intersection of Negril's three main roads, one that runs along the beach, another that follows the cliffs and a third that snakes inland to the east. The village is equipped with twin cement piers that can handle large cruisers. There's a small residential area and a few restaurants, and that's about all you would notice if you were just passing through. The larger region of Negril encompasses the area starting in the south at the Negril Lighthouse at West Point and extending north to North Negril Point at the extreme northern tip of Bloody Bay. As the buzzard flies (called John Crow by Jamaicans), the distance between these two points is a little over nine miles. This area, with a resident population of just over 4,000 people, is what most people are referring to when they talk of Negril.

The southern part of the beach, the village and the cliffs are in the Parish of Westmoreland. The cliffs are home to dozens of hotels, clubs, restaurants and residences. The view of the Caribbean Sea from the cliff tops, some up to fifty feet high, is magnificent and unencumbered. Sunsets viewed from the cliffs are inspiring. People call the cliff area 'The West End', even though it makes up the southernmost part of Negril. However, the cliff area does jut out into the sea, making it the most westerly part of the island of Jamaica, which is why it is quite rightly called the West End.

North of the village lies seven miles of the world's most beautiful beach. Along the beach there are many, many more hotels and establishments. At high time, the beach is a hubbub of activity. Walking north along the beach, at about the halfway point, one crosses an invisible line that delineates the southern boundary of the parish of Hanover. There's a rocky break at Rutland Point and then the beach continues around the rim of Bloody Bay, which, in spite of its name, is a refuge of tranquility. The north end of the beach and a portion of Bloody Bay are dominated by the high-end super all-inclusive resorts.

From the roadside, if it weren't for the resorts' large and colorful signs, it would be easy to drive by most of them without even knowing that they are there. The local building code does not allow construction of any structures that are higher than the tallest palm tree.

Negril is narrow, bounded on the west by the Caribbean Sea and on the east by a large deserted tract of wetlands called the Great Morass that stretches for miles to the Fish River Hills further to the east. 'Great Morass' is a colorful euphemism for 'large swampy, mosquito infested area'. Mosquitoes aside, the Great Morass is a beautiful and tranquil spot. Some people report having problems with mosquitoes when staying on the beach, but other than the occasional bite on my ankles and in the tender area at the back of the knees, mosquitoes have never been a problem for me. I'm sure that's because there are a lot of people around whose bodies are filled with blood that is much sweeter than mine.

Negril residents refer to the high ground to the east of the Great Morass as 'the hills', as in, "Yeah mon, I 'ave a big ganja farm up in de hills." If there are half as many ganja farms up in the hills as have been claimed by the ganja peddlers on the beach, the smoke generated by a fire up there would keep the whole Caribbean high for months.

Negril has an uncontrolled and unlighted airstrip that's hidden behind the gas station at Rutland Point. The runway is large enough to handle small turboprop commuter aircraft. Many years ago, during my first trip to Negril, I was walking along the north end of the beach when I came upon the hulk of a crashed airplane. It was a Cessna 337, a small twin with a peculiar push-pull design. The 337 has one engine mounted aft on the fuselage between twin tail booms that pushes and the other mounted conventionally on the front that pulls. It was lying on its back in the surf, sunken almost completely into the sand. Most of its parts had been removed, only the airframe remained. It looked as if it had been there for quite a while. I'm an air traffic controller by trade and an aviation buff by inclination, so I examined the wreck carefully and finished my inspection by climbing up onto its upturned belly. Standing there I realized that I was under the approach path to Negril's small airstrip. Curious, I walked a little further along the beach to a watersports shack.

There were a couple of guys out front working on a Jet Ski. They had removed several parts and their arms were covered in grease up to their elbows. "What happened to the plane back there on the beach?" I asked.

"Dats de ganja plane mon," one of them answered. "It crashed trying to land 'ere at night."

I'm a beachcomber by nature, and I've found many interesting objects over the years, but, to this day, that airplane half buried in the sand remains the biggest thing that I have ever come across. The fact that it had crashed on a ganja run came as no surprise to me. Ganja weighs significant influence on the local culture, constantly swirling just below the surface of daily life.

So much for the topographical layout of Negril, which is pretty nice, but not unique. There are many places in the Caribbean that are endowed with breathtaking natural beauty. But Negril is much, much more than gorgeous beaches, spectacular cliffs and awe-inspiring sunsets. There is a special vibe that reverberates in the streets and clubs and along the beach strip. Negril is the 'capital of cool'. I can feel it as soon as I set foot here, it resonates in my very bones. There is a friendliness here too, a culture that is unique. People are easy to talk to, they approach you with a smile on their face. The Negril attitude is relaxed, carefree and uninhibited. There is something else too, Negril exudes an unmistakable undercurrent of eroticism, maybe even a whiff of sinfulness. This I haven't quite figured out yet, but people feel extraordinarily sensual when in Negril. I know that it sounds odd, but as you shall see, it's true.

When seen from the air, Negril doesn't look like much, merely a thin sliver of land fringed by a white beach clinging to the western shores of Jamaica. It's hard to believe that such a tiny and inconsequential looking piece of real estate could be so important and mean so much to so many people.

But don't be deceived my friend, that thin sliver of land is actually a little slice of paradise.

Barnacles and a Blaze of Glory

Old pirates yes they rob I, sold I to the merchant ships,
Minutes after they took I from de bottomless pit.
Bob Marley – 'Redemption Song'

I dump my luggage in the dark stuffy room and rush down to the water. Legend's is located about one-third of the way up the beach from the village, smack in the middle of the busiest section between Bourbon Beach and Risky Business, two night time music spots that are popular with the party crowd, which accounts for a high percentage of the people in Negril. The beach is just as I remember it. A long stretch of white sand to the right with Booby Cay off in the distance and a shorter stretch to the left leading into town with the cliffs of the West End beyond. I kick off my sandals and walk into the surf, digging my toes into the cool wet sand. The sounds of the waves lapping at the shore and the smell of the sea seep into me like a soothing balm. A wave of contentment washes over me, I feel as if I've returned home after a long and arduous journey.

It's getting late in the afternoon, the sun is already sinking low and will set in about an hour. There is just enough time to take a short tour to see what has changed.

I head north along the beach and soon come across a pair of men who are working on a large overturned fishing boat. There are three broad stripes that run the length of the hull beneath the gunwale, yellow, red and green. The hull is covered with small barnacles and sea growths. The men are scraping the bottom with big rusty machetes, leaving windrows of debris on the sand beneath the boat. By the sweat dripping off their faces and the wet stains on their shirts, it looks like heavy work. A section where the transom joins the hull has been scraped clear and a fresh fiberglass patch has been applied there, the acrid odor of raw resin drifts on the air. One of the men sees me watching and straightens up from his working crouch.

"Looks like you've got a big job there," I said, stating the obvious.

"Yu can scrape some if yu want," he replies smiling, his voice rich with thick Jamaican country accent. He offers me his machete. I take it, the curved blade is about twenty inches long, three inches deep at its widest point. It's rusty and nicked in many places but the cutting edge is honed keen all the way along the blade to the sharp point at the end. The handle is unfinished wood, worn smooth and stained with honest sweat. It has a healthy heft to it. I grasp the back of the blade in both hands and draw it along a section of hull that's thick with barnacles. They cling tenaciously to the wood, my effort barely leaves a mark. I continue scraping, pulling harder, and after several strokes I make a minor breakthrough to the hull. It's backbreaking work, the barnacle encrusted hull stretches vastly before me, like an un-mown football field. I hand the machete back to the fisherman, grateful that this is not my job to complete.

"How often do you have to do this?" I ask him.

"When de boat push t'ru de water, den we have to take it out an' scrape it," he replied, taking the machete and running its point along a seam in the hull.

"How often would that be?" I pressed, hoping for their sake that it wouldn't be too often.

"Oh. . . about ev'ry six months, yah know, it depends."

I watch them work for a few more minutes, then head back to the hotel to settle in for the first Negril sunset of the trip. The sky is mostly clear with only a few high clouds halfway to the horizon. It looks promising.

All along the beach people are positioning themselves for the main event, cameras ready, clutched in their hands and mounted on tripods. Next to Key West, Negril sunsets are probably the most photographed in the world.

I grab a chair in front of the hotel and point it to seaward. Nearby there are two guys and a young blonde woman sitting on lounges and sipping on island cocktails, apparently waiting for the sunset. I say hello and introduce myself. I probably wouldn't be so gregarious if I were in a similar situation, say, in a park back home. But Negril is different, people are relaxed and friendly and amicable encounters with strangers are the norm. They invite me to join them. They tell me that this is to be their last sunset and tomorrow they'll be returning home to Chicago and the snow-belt. They say this with hurt puppy-dog look expressions on their faces. I empathize with them, I've been in their place many times before. At the best of times, leaving Negril is difficult, at the worst of times, it can be gut wrenching. I watch the big orange orb of the sun sinking slowly to the horizon, and even though my final Negril sunset is still weeks away, I can literally feel the earth rotating inexorably toward it.

As we're talking an old Jamaican gentleman with a battered guitar slung across his back approaches us, limping badly. He looks to be about 70 years old, but I've found that my attempts at judging the ages of Jamaicans invariably results in gross errors, especially for anyone who is over the age of forty. He's walking with the aid of a cane fashioned from a stout branch. One of his knees is jutting out an angle that is definitely not normal. When he smiles to greet us he reveals a mouth filled with more gaps than there are teeth and the few that do remain are crooked and broken; survivors, each and every one of them.

"How 'bout I sing you a likkle song?" he asks in a gravely old voice, un-slinging his guitar and settling awkwardly to the sand.

We hesitate, not wanting to spurn him, none of us responding one way or the other. Sensing an opportunity, he launches into a ditty, which I assume to be Jamaican in origin, about how women truly are powerful and how they always eventually get their way. So true, so true. The young lady, whose name is Kim, enjoys the serenade immensely, clapping along and laughing while us guys roll our eyes and nod in agreement with the lyrics.

The old guy's guitar is toneless, twangy and hopelessly out of tune, but his cracking, aged voice and toothless grin bring a sweet innocence to his performance. He finishes the ditty and we applaud.

"Could you sing *'Redemption Song'*?" I ask him. It's my favorite Bob Marley tune. I've been listening to Bob Marley since my introduction to reggae music during my first visit to Negril, decades back. The beat of Bob's music, the lyrics, the island, and the people had a profound and immediate impact on me.

The old minstrel strums a few licks and then sings one of the most moving renditions of the Redemption Song that I have ever had the privilege of listening to. There, on the beach in Jamaica, with the blazing globe of the sun kissing the sea on the horizon, the crippled old black man dressed in tattered clothing sang of enslavement, hope, emancipation and redemption. I tried to sing along, the words that I know so well, but I was so utterly moved that I couldn't do it, the words lodged in my throat. And then the veil lifted and the symbolism became clear to me. In the words of Bob's song and in the hobbled old minstrel scratching out a living as best he knew how, I saw the tiny country of Jamaica, struggling as a nation against seemingly insurmountable odds, but looking to the future with hope and a strong sense of self-determination.

Behind the minstrel, as the last strains of his sweet song yielded to the sounds of the surf, the sun slowly slipped into the sea and an inexplicable surge of euphoria rushed through me.

It was a glorious sunset with hot pinks dashed across the base of the clouds. I thanked the old minstrel, paid him and helped him get to his feet.

The Chicagoans said goodnight and headed up to the bar. The beach was suddenly quiet.

I sat for a while, dug my feet into the sand and watched the colors fade from the sky. In the distance the minstrel continued his arduous trek along the beach, searching for more customers.

Da Beach

'Nuff Respect'
Jamaican Proverb

I got up early this morning and went for a jog down the beach. The tide was in, so I had to sidestep the waves that were washing up over the sand in many places. Just before my turn around point, which is a large old bare tree trunk stuck into the sand near the Foote Prints resort, I misjudged a wave, stepped in it, and totally soaked my right running shoe. The return half of my run commenced to the accompaniment of a catchy running shoe duet, *'Plop – Squish – Plop – Squish'.*

I enjoy watching the beach wake up. Because Negril faces west and shade trees line the beach, the sun doesn't touch the sand until well after it rises, so it's deliciously cool to the bare foot. The motorboats and jet skis that ply the waters don't get active until later, so early in the morning the sea is quiet and flat, slowly undulating like a great blob of golden honey under the pristine blue sky. In the early hours the beach vendors set up their displays. The beach lounges in front of the hotels remain neatly stacked, patiently waiting for the sun worshippers to claim them. Workers rake the seaweed that has washed up overnight into neat piles to be carted away, burned or buried. Only a few people are out early on the beach; mostly joggers, walkers and the parents of young children sitting on lounges sipping their Blue Mountain coffee as they watch their kids build sandcastles.

There's a tremendous amount of competition for the tourist dollar in Negril, this includes the beach as well as in town, so it's no surprise to see a lot of advertising. The beach is a jumble of colorful signs, large and small, hand-painted and commercially prepared, mounted on posts, nailed to coconut trees, hung and propped on every available surface, each one hawking a particular service or product or event. The signs advertise resorts, restaurants, jet ski rentals, scuba diving, Appleton rum, bars, night clubs, tours and excursions, shows, craft shops, rooms for rent and so on. It comes as no surprise that the *'Hot Diggity Dog'* sign claims the best hot dogs on the beach. Another brags, *'Red Stripe – Every Day 50 J',* you can't beat that price.

The signage isn't limited to those that are posted. There are people who walk the beach with sandwich boards and others who carry signs on poles, waving them about and calling out accompanying advertisements. At dinnertime, tables set with the evening's fare are placed in the sand in front of many of the beachside restaurants. Waiters stand by the candle-lit tables pointing out the entrees to passers-by and inviting them to come up to dine in their establishments.

On the streets in town it's not unusual to see cars with speakers mounted on the roofs cruising around advertising one thing or another. However, it has been my experience that these efforts are usually wasted on tourists, as the audio components used are universally bad and the volume is turned up so loud that the message comes out as a garbled blast of distorted sound. On the few occasions when the audio is good, the announcer inside the vehicle is usually speaking rapidly and in patois such that the message is lost on most.

There's one fellow who occasionally walks the beach wearing a sandwich board advertising, *'2-for-1 Lobster'* at a beachside club called Margaritaville. Waving his arms and turning around so all can get a good look at his neon colored signs, he calls out loudly in a drawling carny voice,

"Negril . . Negril . . Negril! Come on down to Mar-gar-ita-ville! . . . Don't you miss it! Tonite – COLADARAMA!!. . . BE THERE – There – there . . ."

He makes his voice diminish in volume on the three *'theres'* as if it was being piped through a reverberator.

Buy one lobster . . . get another one for free! . . .
Yessirreee! . . Two-for-one lobster . . at Mar-gar-ita-ville tonight! . . ADMISSION!. . . FREE – Free – free'

Again he does the reverberation thing, it's really quite effective.

The most ingenious form of advertising that I've seen was during a particularly frenetic spring break, which is a crazy time of year and a good time to stay away from Negril if I had to choose one. It's an everyday occurrence to see para-sails being towed behind powerful boats, but one day an entrepreneur, upping the advertising ante, hired a para-sail and floated by the beach with a sign advertising his establishment dangling below. This was pretty effective, because a lot of people on the beach noticed it and were pointing at it. The next day he did the same thing except he was equipped with a bullhorn. That time, everybody except the deaf noticed him.

On the last part of my run a flash of pink catches my eye. A large bougainvillea in full bloom, its vines draped in brilliant pink and white blossoms, covers the side of a building in a sandy enclave.

The sand has a pristine look to it in the morning, cleansed by the night seas and mostly free of footprints. The unfortunate exception to this is the stretch of beach in front of my hotel and the neighboring establishments of Risky Business and Bourbon Beach. Here the beach is made up of equal parts of sand, plastic drink cups and straws, cigarette butts, empty beer bottles and bonfire ashes. There are several workers out grooming the sand and picking up trash, attempting to bring the beach back to its pre-party condition.

I finish my jog, sweating profusely in the unaccustomed humidity, and sit on a beach lounge in front of the hotel stripping off my wet shoes and socks. The nicest part of the morning beach jog is when it's over. I'm not a morning exercise person but I force myself to jog in the morning while in Negril only because the rest of the day is so hot. I motivate myself to do it by thinking about the cool, refreshing plunge in the ocean that awaits me at the completion of each run. This morning was particularly tough, so much so that I started to think about a dunk in the ocean when I was only a few steps away from the hotel on the outbound leg.

I'm entering the water, relishing my well-deserved reward, when I spot something sloshing in the surf. It's a big starfish, ochre in color. I pick it up to examine it. Tip to tip it measures about ten inches across. The top of it is covered in light-colored nodules arranged in rows radiating from the center and out along its five stubby arms. I flip it over to examine its underside. The small fleshy parts that line the interior crevices of the stiff outer shell are moving. It's alive. As I'm examining it, a young Jamaican man who is walking by stops to look at it.

"De starfish get confused an' 'im get lost," he said.

"If I put it in the water here will it be able to get back out to where he belongs?" I ask, doubting it, but asking anyhow.

"No mon, go for a swim, an' take 'im out to de marker buoy an' drop 'im dere," he answers.

I look out to the line of buoys about fifty yards offshore that marks the swimming area all along the beach. The buoy line provides a very necessary delineation, protecting all within its bounds from the numerous boats and jet skis that swoosh by at breakneck speed just beyond. The buoy line is a bit further than I had intended to go on my dip, but I'm feeling altruistic today so I decide to do the starfish a favor. I sidestroke out to the closest buoy, clumsily carrying the wayward starfish. The buoy is anchored to the sandy bottom in about twelve feet of crystal clear water. Holding the starfish right side up, I let it go and tread water, watching it slowly sink. About two feet below the surface it flips over onto its back and spirals saucer-like the rest of the way to the bottom, settling on its back. I know that starfish are perfectly capable of righting themselves, but I feel beholding to this one, so I do a surface dive, kick my way to the bottom and put him on the sand right side up. Job done, I turn to swim back and see that the fellow who had suggested I take the starfish out to the buoy is still standing at the water's edge watching me. I wave to him and gave him the thumbs up. He waves back, turns and continues on his way.

I swim slowly shoreward, doing a leisurely backstroke, stopping periodically to float and admire the light blue of the morning sky. It strikes me that the Jamaican people have an innate knowledge of nature and a kinship and sense of responsibility for the plants and animals with which they share their island.

After a freshwater dunk in the pool and a light breakfast at the hotel's disappointingly meager buffet, I head out for my first leisurely beach walk. Well lathered with sunscreen (I remember when it used to be called sun tan lotion) and wearing my 'Jamaica' baseball cap to protect my pasty forehead, I turn north along the beach from Legends.

What better way to spend a few hours than walking the beach? I can't think of any. In fact, walking the beach is my favorite Negril pastime. I can spend a whole afternoon just churning up the sand, talking to people, soaking up the sun and looking at things.

I took my first walk along the Negril beach in the 70's. At that time there were only two hotels at the north end, The Negril Beach Village, which later became the notorious Hedonism II and The Sundowner right next door, which was later torn down to make way for Sandals. Except for a few guesthouses and vendor shacks, the rest of the seven-mile stretch was virgin beach all the way into town. The T-Water hotel, situated near the village and still in business today, was the only other establishment of significance on the beach at that time.

Today the beach is almost completely developed except for a lengthy stretch north of the Beaches resort. It was nice back in those early days, I loved the serenity and the newness of it. But I'm enamored with it just as much today with all of its activity and buzz.

I duck into the shade of the sea grape trees in front of the Coco La Palm resort and sit on the low curved rock and cement wall that fronts the property. This is a very fine vantage point for people watching and gazing out to sea, it's one of my favorite beach spots in Negril.

After a few minutes a tall thin Rastaman carrying a gunnysack approaches me. He's dressed in ragged full-length pants and a tattered long sleeve shirt; the heat of the day obviously not affecting him like it is I. On his head is a white tightly wound, turban-like head wrap, his dreads are contained within. The turban juts in an angle up and behind his head. As he nears me he raises his right fist slightly above the horizontal, I put mine out slightly below the horizontal. He brings his down while I bring mine up, we meet in the middle, the base of his fist tapping the top of mine . . . *peace*. Then we reverse, I bring my fist down on top of his . . . *love*. Next is the straight-on tap, our fists meet between us . . . *respect*. "Respect," intones the Rastaman and I respond in kind. Finally, he holds his thumb upright, I follow suit and we press them together momentarily . . . *unity*. I'm a little surprised at the full sequence, since the normal practice is just the straight-on 'respect' tap, or less frequent but still common, the peace-love-respect combination. The 'unity' thumb press is very rare, somehow it makes me feel special. Whether the long or short form, the fist bumping sequence serves as a greeting 'handshake' for Jamaicans.

Respect for oneself and others is an extremely important principle on the island, perhaps engendered by the following excerpt from the Jamaican national anthem;

> *'Teach us true respect for all*
> *Stir response to duty's call.'*

Jamaicans regularly pay respect to one another by intoning the word when they meet. In this poor country, respect and pride is literally all that some Jamaicans have. If one loses respect, one could lose everything.

"How are you this fine day my good man?" I ask the Rasta.

"I an' I am fine an' give t'anks an' praises to de most high for dis day," he replies holding his arms up to the sky. It's the first time on this trip that I've heard the Rasta term *"I an' I"*.

Rastas have had an influence on the evolution of Jamaican patois by introducing the pre-fix 'I' to many words. For example, Rastafarians do not use the pronouns 'I', 'they' or 'me' as they are considered to be divisive. The Rasta's "I an' I" pronoun is all embracing and communal, and also unifies oneself with the indwelling God. Similarly, 'I-dren' means children or brethren and 'Ital' is Rasta for 'vital', which can be used to refer to a lifestyle or a vegetarian food cooked without salt.

The Rastafarian religion is indigenous to Jamaica. It emerged in the 1930s as a grass roots movement in response to worsening social conditions on the island and what were regarded as irrelevant white-oriented religions.

The basic tenet of Rastafarianism is belief in the divinity of the late Emperor Halie Selassie of Ethiopia, whose given name was Ras Tafari.

Rastafarians believe that Halie Selassie was the Second Coming of Christ and they point to several Biblical scriptures to support their claim. Thus Halie Selassie is the God figure, referred to as Jah, which is believed to be a contraction of Jehovah. In context, Jah may be replaced by HIM, which is an abbreviation for His Imperial Majesty. The term 'Selassie -I' is also employed, again reinforcing the concept of the unification of oneself with an indwelling supreme being.

Rastas will not do business with the government or the commercial world, which they refer to as Babylon, as they regard both as wicked. Nor will they work for anyone as an employee. They will however, work for pay as a skilled craftsman, such as a carpenter, but will never succumb to the role of a subservient employee.

Rastas also believe in re-incarnation and hold to a taboo against males cutting or combing their hair or beards. This has led to the uninformed but common belief that dreadlocks are unkempt and unclean. Such is not the case. Rastafarians are extremely proud of their dreadlocks and they wash and care for them in a regular fashion. However, dreadlocks do not a Rasta make. Rastafarianism has been used as a cover by criminals and as a publicity gimmick by some pop musicians. In Negril there are many dreadlocked men, decorated with Babylon trinkets, who are selling drugs. They are not Rastas. Some Rastas refer to such people as dreadheads or reggae-farians, neither of which are endearing terms.

Rastas are vegetarians, they do not eat fish, fowl or mammal, as it is considered sacrilegious to eat the flesh of another living being. Pure Rastafarians do not drink alcohol, however many regard the use of marijuana as a sacrament and as an aid to meditation, but it is interesting to note that its use was not counseled by Selassie-I.

Among the Rastas that do smoke ganja, some will not use rolling papers without first removing the glue strip along the edge, as they believe that the glue may include animal ingredients. Nor will they smoke ganja that has been grown with animal manure as fertilizer or eat vegetables that have been sprayed with insecticide. A true Rasta will not smoke cigarettes because they contain additives and thus are not natural. There are even some who will not smoke the Sensemilla species of marijuana, as it is seedless and requires human intervention to propagate.

In its pure form, Rastafarianism is a valid faith that respects individualism and human dignity and emphasizes the indwelling God

Spirit in every human being. Essentially, Rastas believe in living a simple, clean and natural life.

All that being said, Rastafarianism is an evolving and subjective religion and depending on the individual, the basic tenets are adhered to with varying degrees of fidelity.

"You from de States?" the Rasta asks me. I notice that he has several buttons pinned to the front of his ragged shirt, each one displaying a photograph of Halie Selassie.

"No, I'm from Canada," I answer, "the land of freezing cold and crippling taxes."

"I an' I no pay no tax to fockin' Babylon," he says.

"Where you from?" I ask.

"De hills mon," he says, waving his arm to the east, "way back up in de hills."

He pulls a Smirnoff vodka bottle out of his gunnysack, but it's not filled with vodka. There's an orange-ish, sludge-like brown liquid in the bottle. He hands it to me.

"Root juice mon. Good fo' de back an make de blood strong," he says, his heavy accent emphasizing syllables with the distinctive island lilt that is music to my ears.

I look into the bottle, streamers of fine bubbles rise slowly to the top. "How do you make this stuff?" I ask him.

"It made from roots from de trees up in de hills, I an' I dig dem up from de groun' and chop dem and clean dem and den bwoil dem down to make de juice."

"No thanks man," I said, "my blood is already strong enough." I had tried mountain root juice on a previous trip and, to put it mildly, hadn't found it to my liking.

"It make you into a man, you know what I an' I sayin'? You drink dis an' your wife will be happy lady tonight." With this he grins, clenches his fist and holds his forearm up at a 45-degree angle.

"Well, I won't be married until next week and my fiancée isn't here yet, but I've tried root juice and I don't like the taste of it," I said.

"Ahhh! You don' like de sas-a-par-illa," he says and fishes another bottle out of his sack. "Some people don' like de sas-a-par-illa 'cause it taste slimy." He twists the top off, pours a cap full and downs it. "Mmmm," he says, "Try dis one, it don' have no sas-a-par-illa in it."

I take it and pour it onto my tongue. The human gag reflex is very strong, but with a supreme effort motivated by the desire not to show disrespect for the man, I swallow the cap full of the sas-a-par-illa free root juice.

"Can you mix this stuff with rum?" I ask him.

"No, mon!" he says, wide eyed and shocked, "you jus drink it ev'ry day, it clean de blood an make it strong."

We sit quietly for a while. The Rasta realizes that I'm not a buying customer. He gets up, slings his gunnysack over his shoulder, nods at me, says "Rastafari!" and moves on.

I gaze out across the sparkling waters of Long Bay. Three happy couples walk by, laughing and conversing as they pass. They're speaking Russian. In all my trips to Negril I don't recall ever having heard Russian. I take this as a sure sign that democracy and capitalism have firmly rooted in the former Soviet Union.

Negril is a veritable Babylon of languages. The two most common, of course, are English and Jamaican patois, that spicy mix of English and derivatives of several West African languages that's delivered in a rapid sing-song patter. English is the official language of Jamaica, but most Jamaicans communicate to one another in patois. After many visits to Jamaica I have developed an ear for patois, but on a good day I can only understand half of it. I find the language so intriguing that I often sit and listen to Jamaicans talking just for the pure joy of it.

This morning, lying in my bead, I dreamed of birds calling to each other in long melodious songs. When I awoke I realized that it was the voices of the hotel chambermaids, calling to each other in patois, that had infiltrated my dreams.

If French is the language of love, then Jamaican patois is the language of argument. I mean no disrespect, because I truly love the language. But take my word on this; you haven't truly heard two people quarreling until you've been in the presence of an argument conducted in patois. There isn't a language on earth that is more suited to loud disagreement. Listening to two angry men arguing in patois is a fascinating and strangely delightful experience. The combatant's bodies become fully engaged in the enunciation of words, arms flail to punctuate phrases, eyes bulge, heads bob and the delivery is non-stop machine-gun rapid. It is *so* island. Once one becomes familiar with a few patois 'cuss-cuss' words, these exchanges are even more interesting.

Most of the tourists who visit Negril are Canadians, Americans and British, but it is also a favorite destination for Germans and Italians, as well as some Spaniards and South Americans. People who live in Negril tell me that in July and August the foreign language most frequently heard on the beach is Italian. How can they stand the heat?

Occasionally I also hear French. To my ear it's of the French Canadian variety. The European French probably don't come to Jamaica. After all, Jamaica was a British colony, so what possible good could have come of it? Isn't it inhabited by heathens and frequented by colonials? Why would any self-respecting Frenchman go to Jamaica when the perfectly civilized French islands of Guadeloupe and Martinique are nearby? I admire the French attitude, they dismiss most of the globe with an insouciant flick of their arrogant wrists, but do it with such aplomb and class that they can get away with it. If they only knew what they were missing.

The British have been coming to Negril for hundreds of years. In 1814, fifty British warships gathered in the waters of Long Bay. They were loaded with 6600 fighting troops. They sailed to engage the American rebels at the famous Battle of New Orleans. Unfortunately for the Brits, they were soundly trounced by armed forces commanded by Colonel Andrew Jackson (a slaver who later became president) and over 2000 of them were killed, the rest were sent packing back into the Gulf of Mexico. The battle was immortalized in the 1960's tune 'The Battle Of New Orleans', by the American singer Johnny Horton.

I leave my roost at Coco La Palm and head back toward the hotel. I don't go far before I notice a small crowd gathered around a dugout canoe that's pulled up on the sand in front of the Whistling Bird cabins. In the bottom of the canoe there's a stringer of small colorful fish and a half dozen conch. A few conch have been removed from their shells and laid out on a piece of plywood, glistening as they writhe in the heat of the sun. The shells are lined up in a neat row on the sand. The fisherman is hunched over a plastic pail filled with seawater, deftly cleaning the mollusks with an old knife. Occasionally, between the cuts, clips and slices, he dunks the meat into the pail to rinse it. A young lady standing near the plywood points to the squirming conch on the plywood, scrunches up her face and says, "Eeewwww!"

The fisherman stops cleaning and looks up from his work, "Please don' scorn de conch Miss," he says. He returns to his work and soon plucks what looks like a short strand of clear spaghetti from the conch. This he holds up and then drops into his mouth, noisily slurping it down. The young lady turns around and beats a hasty retreat. I ask the fisherman about the 'spaghetti' strand.

Without looking up or pausing, he replies, "Dats de nerves of de conch, make you like a bull, good for de ladies. I save some of dem for de beach boys." He tilts his head in the direction of the plywood where a few other clear strands lay.

What gives?   First the mountain root juice, now the conch spaghetti.   I'm beginning to have suspicions about the virility of Jamaican men.   Do they really need extra stimulants to get it up? Somehow I don't think so.

Mon, it's hot today, and not a cloud in the sky. I need another break and some shade so I turn into the number two stop on my walk, Dr. Bill's.   It's one of dozens of bars and restaurants that serve the beach.   Dr. Bill's has an eating area with several tables arrayed on the sand under a corrugated metal roof.   There is also a bar with benches made from rough planks nailed atop sections of tree trunks that are sunk into the sand.   A big old sea grape tree has been integrated into the design of the bar.   Shelves loaded with liquor bottles have been nailed to branches and across the forks in the trunk.   Its bark has been painted a lively orange.   The tree fits the décor perfectly; its upper trunk and branches disappear through the metal ceiling.

During my last visit to Negril I stopped in at Dr. Bill's for a plate of curried conch with rice.   I made the mistake of just walking up and ordering it, without checking the menu or asking the price.   The conch was good, but at $500 Jamaican dollars, I felt I had been ripped off. From that time on I've always thought of the place as Dollar Bill's and I don't eat there any more.   But I do stop in on my beach walks.   I usually order a Ting, a locally bottled carbonated grapefruit drink, with ice and a glass of water, or sometimes I get a Red Stripe.   Dollar Bill's only charges $50J for a Ting, well worth the price when you include a shady bar seat with a million-dollar view.

The young lady behind the bar gives me a friendly smile and delivers my Ting.   Her black hair is coiled in dozens of tight ringlets that are held off of her forehead by a colorful headband.   She looks like a young Tracy Chapman, the African-American pop singer.   She bends over to chip some ice off a big block and I can't help but notice how well she fills her designer jeans.   I must be chillin' out, Negril has a way of gently bringing the fundamental pleasures of life back into focus.

I pivot on the bench, lean back on the bar and gaze out to sea. The sun is spangling off the water creating mesmerizing patterns of bright shifting light.   A parasail floats by, the drone from the towboat like that of a somnolent bumblebee on a summer afternoon.   The air is hot, a small trickle of sweat runs down the back of my neck.   I close my eyes and run the ice filled glass slowly across my forehead.   My shins and feet are poking out of the shade of the bar into the hot sun. They're burning but I like the feeling, it's erotic, like a hot-bodied lover leaning against my legs. I'm lulled into a demi-trance. Last week I was bundled up, shoveling snow in minus 20 weather with the wind tearing at my scarf. Today, wearing only my shorts, I sit under a clear blue sky and the temperature is in the 90's. I find the transition surreal and I ask myself the same question that I often do several times a day for the first few days that I'm in Negril;

'Is this place for real?'

I'm roused from my reverie, realizing that my eyes have settled on, and are tracking, a most lovely pair of naked breasts. It's not that naked breasts are unusual on the beach in Negril, quite the contrary. Topless is very fashionable here. Although I do wish some of the guys would leave their shirts on. My woman, being of German descent, is genetically programmed to strip off her top as soon as she feels warm sand between her toes, so Negril suits her well. Spend a couple of hours on this beach on a hot day and the novelty of bare bouncing boobs rapidly fades. Except for those special cases, and a particularly special case was jiggling in my direction.

She's young, beautiful and toned with olive skin and dark hair and all she's wearing is a pair of sunglasses and a black T-back. I realize I'm quietly whistling the 'Girl From Ipanema' tune. Her boyfriend, a lucky Latino looking guy, is following several paces behind her. He calls her name, "Aylin!" and when she turns he flips her a Frisbee. It sails out over the water and she dashes after it, splashing in the surf. She reaches high above her head and snags the Frisbee with a superb jump-catch. For reasons that are not clear to me, I've observed this whole scene in slow motion. As for the jump, I give her a 10 for artistic impression and another 10 for technical merit. Her tanned torso now beaded with seawater, she bends forward and flicks the Frisbee back at Lucky. My whistle has dried up so I go to take a pull on the Ting, but to my surprise, it's empty. I decide I'm not in that much of a hurry to continue my walk so I order another one, it's so hot today. The Frisbee goes back and forth. I sit enjoying the scenery as the game moves slowly past Dollar Bill's and down the beach. The Girl From Ipanema splashes in the sea and cuts up the sand. It's times like this that I give thanks and praises to the most high that I was born male.

After the second Ting, I wave goodbye to Tracy Chapman and continue my slow trek back to the hotel. I pass a clump of shade trees under which there is a small vegetable stand and a massage table. The lady sitting beside the table calls out to me, "Come up for a nice massage honey!" I smile and wave to her but continue walking. Hers is one of several massage tables that are set up along the beach.

Big Joe runs a beer stand on the public beach. That's the section of beach, toward the town end, that is used by Jamaicans when they come to Negril for a swim, which surprisingly is not that often. Standing about 6' 6" and weighing around 280lbs, it's obvious how Big Joe got his name. He is wearing a tight T-shirt (the better to show off his bulging muscles), and he has decorated himself with numerous thick gold chains and rings. Big Joe speaks in a deep, booming voice, but for such a mountain of a man he has a kind, calm and gentle demeanor.

When I first saw Big Joe several years ago he was waving me over to his beer stand, which is really just a picnic table with a large blue cooler on top of it and an awning mounted above. I was thirsty for a Red Stripe, so I cut over to his stand.

As I approached he stood up and offered his hand, "Hi, I'm Big Joe, you look like you could use a cold beer."

"You are very perceptive," I said. I bought one, it was cool and frosty, and I sucked back half of it in one big gulp.

"I'm thirsty too my friend, how about buying one for Big Joe?" he asked. I nodded my head and 'bought' one for Big Joe. There were a couple of young Jamaican guys hanging around the beer stand.

"Could you buy one for my friends here? They're thirsty too." Big Joe's voice was soothing, deep and mellow. I bought two more Red Stripes.

Then came the usual litany of offerings; mushrooms, ganja, coke, ecstasy, Quaaludes plus other things that I didn't recognize. I shook my head to all of them.

"How about one of Big Joe's special brownies?" he offered. I declined.

I've been stopping in to see Big Joe on every beach walk I've made for about three years now. Today he spots me and raises his ham-sized hand, waving me over. I approach his stand, putting my fist out for the tap, and ask him as I always do "How's business Big Joe?"

To this he sighs deeply, as he always does, shakes his head and says, "It slow today mon, hawd to make a dollar, yah know what I mean?"

And I respond, as I always do, "Well, it will probably pick up later today, it's hot and people will want beer."

I don't know how he does it, but Big Joe remembers me from year to year, even though he must meet hundreds if not thousands of people on the beach in a season. The first couple of times that he smiled and greeted me as an old friend, I thought he was faking recognition because it was good for business. But I now believe that he actually does recognize me, and here's why. One year I was in Negril with my Amy. Eventually we got around to Big Joe's stand and I introduced him to her. We had a beer and sat and talked for a while ("Oh, business is slow, slow today, mon"). The next year, the first time that I saw Big Joe I was by myself. Again, he greeted me as someone whom he recognized. Then he asked about my 'woman', why she wasn't with me. I decided to test him.

"Do you remember my woman?" I asked him.

"Yes mon! De pretty slim blonde woman," he replied, "about dis tall," he held his hand to about Amy's height. "Big Joe remembers his customers."

I believe him. He's one of Negril's iconic beach vendors. For the price of a beer I get a half-hour of updates on the latest Negril news. Big Joe is a character.

I see the big yellow awning of Legends up ahead. In front of the hotel four Jamaican guys are engaged in an impromptu game of football. They're standing in a circle and taking turns at keeping a soccer ball in the air using only their feet, heads and chests. These guys are all in excellent physical shape with muscular upper bodies and matching taut six packs. One of them taps the ball up four or five times and then kicks it over to another one across the circle. He receives it, attempting to keep it aloft at all times, and so it goes. The receiver of the pass often has to make scrambling, gymnastic moves and dives into the sand to keep the ball in the air. Their athletic bodies are covered with sand-caked sweat. I watch them for a while but their exertions tire me, so I 'an I go to my room for a nap.

Booby Cay and Bloody Bay

'If yuh cyann fight Bushman, tek way im bush.'
Jamaican Proverb

Booby Cay is a small island that sits about 300 yards off the beach at the north end of Long Bay. It lies near the promontory called Rutland Point, which marks the end of Negril's seven-mile beach. The resorts closest to Booby Cay are the notorious Hedonism II and the tranquil Point Village, both of which we will visit later on.

When I spotted Booby Cay during my first visit to Negril, it stopped me dead in my tracks. I stood on the beach awestruck, staring at the little island. It was perfect. A small, green, deserted tropical island fringed with a surf washed, white sand beach plunked down in an emerald sea. And within swimming distance of the shore! Booby Cay was the Treasure Island of my boyhood dreams.

I gazed at the island, daydreaming of the pirates that, given Negril's buccaneering history, doubtless trod its shores. *'Harr mateys!! Thar be Treasure Island off the starboard bow! Heave to lads!'* I had to go out and explore it right away. I walked up the beach a little and came across a fisherman who was cleaning his catch. I asked him if it was possible to go out to the island. He assured me that it was and then offered to take me over.

"But der's nothin' out der," he warned me.

"Perfect," I said, not wanting it any other way.

He rowed me across the straight in his narrow, wobbly dug-out canoe and dropped me on a long sandy spit that spiked out into the sea at the south end of the island. I paid him a couple of dollars and he offered to hang around until I was ready to go back. But I wanted to be on that island by myself, so I asked him to come back in about two hours. He shrugged his shoulders and said, "No problem mon."

I stood on the sand spit, ankle deep in warm water, and surveyed my island. As far as I could see, it was deserted. I imagined this is how Christopher Columbus must have felt when he first stepped on a newly discovered island (this in spite of the low drone of an outboard motor in the background). The island looked to be about 1/8 of a mile long. Coconut palms fringed the shore and the hump of the island was covered with bush and trees. The sandy spit gave way to a rocky beach that embraced the eastern shore of the island. Further to the north an outcropping of rock jutted into the water. I walked up the spit to a flat grassy area that sat between the shore and the higher ground of the island.   There were a couple of big bar'b'ques there.   They were made of 45-gallon drums that had been cut lengthwise and mounted on angle-iron stands.   They looked well used. I found out later that some resorts brought people out to Booby Cay for 'all you can eat and drink' island parties with bonfires, music and beach dancing.   Sounded good to me, but for now, unless someone was hiding in the thick underbrush, I was the only person on Booby Cay. Several trails branched out from the grassy area into the bush. I spent the next hour exploring the island walking the paths that crisscrossed it.

The north and west shores of Booby Cay are rocky and pretty well inaccessible, unless you are equipped with good hiking boots and are feeling adventurous.   There the shore is made up of coral that has eroded into very sharp interleaving ledges known as 'dog's tooth', which is impossible to walk on if wearing sandals as I was. The sea is rougher on the west shore, breaking on the coral, not a good place to bathe, but for strong swimmers the snorkeling there is fantastic. One of the paths ended at a high point on the north west shore that provided a sweeping vista of the sea and, way off in the distance, the West End of Negril.

The whole time that I was exploring Booby Cay I kept having visions of pirates stashing their loot in hidden cavities. I hoped that maybe I would stumble across a sign, a half-buried skull perhaps, that marked the spot where fabulous riches lay buried.

Finding no buried treasure, I worked my way back toward the sand spit and explored the tidal pools along the shore. I spent another hour there splashing around and poking at the little sea creatures that inhabited the pools. There were urchins, starfish, anemones, crabs, fish, and other living things that I couldn't identify. The sand spit was literally covered with seashells. I picked a few and put them in my pockets. Finally, I just sat back on my elbows facing out to sea in the warm shallow water and let the surf wash up over my legs. I closed my eyes and tilted my face up into the sun, soaking up its heat and drinking in the magnificent solitude of Booby Cay.

As the eastern religions attest, quiet contemplation nourishes the karma and draws one back to the one's center, (I an' I find that a little bit of ganja aids the process). I was lolling in the surf, tending to my karma and contemplating how I was going to spend the rest of this day in paradise, when out of the corner of my eye I saw a silver twinkle in the sky above the West End.   An airplane, I thought, moving in my direction. Yes, it was an airplane but moving very fast given its low altitude. I watched it approach and in less than a minute it was almost over me. I recognized it as a fighter plane, streaking along at about 100 feet above the beach. It went into a steep banking turn as it flashed over me, the scream of its engine brutalizing the silence of the morning. On the underside of one wing was painted a large red star. It was a Russian MiG fighter! It leveled off, climbed a few hundred feet and streaked northward, the roar of its engine slowly fading as it went. In those days, for a Soviet pilot flying out of a military base in Cuba, a glimpse of paradise was only a short 15-minute joyride away.

Several minutes later the fisherman came and picked me up and my first visit to Booby Cay was over. I've visited it several times since then and it remains very much the same as it was. At one point, some hustlers moved onto the island and they'd approach visitors as they walked onto the grassy area. Someone, probably one of the all-inclusives, built a thatched picnic shelter near the sand spit. All in all the island looks a little more 'inhabited' that it did back in mid '70s, but the north and west shores are still magnificently deserted and unspoiled.

Many people mistakenly believe that Booby Cay got its name from the fact that a lot of nude sunbathing goes on there. It is true that over the years the little island has seen its fair share of bare boobs, but alas, that is not how it got its name. While no one is absolutely sure, it is generally accepted that Booby Cay was named after the blue-footed booby bird, a tern that spends most of its time out over the ocean but returns yearly to the smaller cays off the coast to breed. But alas, there's ne're a blue-footed booby bird to be seen on the cay these days. The unfortunate bird was named booby, as in 'dumb', due to the fact that it could be captured with relative ease. As if that wasn't bad enough, its eggs were once prized as a delicacy and its nests were plundered with relish. Doubtless these two factors led to the demise of the hapless boobies on Booby Cay.

Anyone who has seen Walt Disney's 1954 film *'Twenty Thousand Leagues Under the Sea'* staring Kirk Douglas and Peter Lorre, has seen parts of Booby Cay. The little cay was used as a double in scenes as a South Seas island.

In recent years some tourists took up the practice of camping out on Booby Cay and some locals also squatted there. These fine people neglected to remove their trash, and apparently also left a pair of mating cats behind, which inevitably resulted in a large colony of feral cats that roamed the island.

The trash and the cat problem caused the authorities to close Booby Cay to public access due to sanitation concerns. This is purported to be a temporary measure that will be in effect only until things are cleaned up. However, I've recently heard rumors that Mr. Butch Stewart, who holds significant interest in the Sandals hotel chain and Air Jamaica, has purchased Booby Cay from the parish and is planning on leasing it to the Couples and Grand Lido resorts as a nude sunbathing venue.

Nevertheless, some of the local boat operators, who are willing to run the risk to earn a few bucks, will take people out to Booby Cay if asked. It is also common to see small sailboats from resorts beached up on the sand spit.

In spite of the thousands that have visited Booby Cay over the years, the buried treasure that I'm certain is there has never been found. Next time I get over to the island, I'm going to take a sturdy pair of boots and a pickaxe.

Around the corner from Booby Cay is Bloody Bay, the northern-most segment of the area commonly referred to as Negril. Bloody Bay is separated from Long Bay and its seven-mile beach by Rutland Point. The bay is shaped like a big letter 'C', with the opening, which measures a little more than one mile across, facing to the west.

Although bloodthirsty pirates frequented the area, Bloody Bay is said to be named not for the pirates' exploits, but for the whalers who butchered their catches in the waters, causing them to run red with blood.

Because of the rocky shore at Rutland point and the private resorts of Hedo II, Point Village and Grand Lido, it's not possible to walk from the seven-mile beach to the Bloody Bay beach. But Bloody Bay is easily accessible via the beach road (Norman Manley Boulevard).

Before the Grand Lido was built at the extreme south end of the bay, the tranquil white beaches and tree-lined shores of Bloody Bay were free of resorts. Then Couples was constructed next to the Lido and in recent years a large resort called the Riu Tropical was added. These three luxury, all-inclusive resorts form the first three invasive links in what will probably be an unbroken chain that will someday completely rim the bay. However, as for the present, once past the Riu, the beach is almost entirely undeveloped. Just north of the Riu, a short dusty road leads from the beach road to the public swimming beach on Bloody Bay, located at about the midway point on the crescent beach. There are a few concession stands located there where one can rent lounges, buy food and trinkets and freshen up the herb stock.

A walk along the beach north of the public swimming area is like taking a walk along the Negril seven-mile beach in the '70's. That stretch is a favored nude sunning area. Bloody Bay is very shallow and the undeveloped part of the beach is in its natural state. There are many big pieces of driftwood to sit on and one has to dodge the occasional windrow of decomposing seaweed. Patches of eelgrass still grow in areas. Eelgrass used to grow in the shallows of the Negril beach in days past but it is almost entirely gone now.

A seldom visited but spectacular cove called Little Bloody Bay is situated a short distance north of Bloody Bay. It's separated from its big brother by a rocky point that prevents ground access from the south. The easiest way to visit the pristine 100-yard stretch of secluded beach that's located in Little Bloody Bay's sheltered cove is by boat. The local boat operators are happy to go there. When the seas are calm, the snorkeling in Little Bloody Bay is phenomenal.

Although I've never seen it personally, I've been assured by a couple of boat captains that the wreck of a twin-engine 'ganja plane' lies at the bottom of Bloody Bay. I'm sure there's a story there but I haven't been able to root it out.

People who frequent Bloody Bay beach know that it is not wise to leave personal items on the beach unattended while swimming. Apparently some unlucky travelers have been the victims of thieves who hide in the bushes and come out to steal bags, backpacks and articles of clothing while the unsuspecting are in the water.

For the beachcomber, a visit to Bloody Bay and Little Bloody Bay provides a quiet respite from the hubbub of the beach on Long Bay.

Diving for Dollars and The Sundowner Goddess

'Man noh dead, noh call 'im duppy.'
Jamaican Proverb

 Although I won't be scuba diving in Negril on this trip, it was the exciting prospect of exploring the reefs off shore that was largely responsible for drawing me to Negril on my first Caribbean visit.

And thinking of my first exploration of Booby Cay puts me in mind of a particular dive that I made on that same trip, and the two Jamaican brothers that I met on the beach near the old Sundowner Hotel.

Yes! The following is a *'flashback'*, please indulge me . . .

⏮ ⏮ ⏮

I met Danny and his older brother Keith when I stopped in at their craft stand on the beach. They had commandeered a spot at the edge of the trees about 200 yards south of the Sundowner Hotel. The brothers were pedaling the usual stuff, mostly woodcarvings, a few conch shells, and ganja of course. I walked up to their stand and looked over the things that they had on offer. A little shark carved out of a piece of brown coral caught my eye, so I bought it. We struck up a conversation. Danny and Keith were in their mid-twenties and I was interested in seeing how a couple of Jamaicans my age lived. I suppose the opposite may have been true for them. They were fine looking fellows. Like many young Jamaican men, they were well muscled, strong and not an ounce of fat on them, both natural athletes. Keith had short hair but Danny sported a full head of dreadlocks. They lived in their shack on the beach, eking out a meager living from the sales that they made to the few tourists that ventured their way. Back then, the north part of the beach was virtually deserted.

Their shack was made from an assortment of sun-bleached planks and lengths of bamboo that had been cut lengthwise and nailed together to form the walls. There was a rudimentary 'display counter' erected out front. The floor of the shack was earthen, except in one corner there was no floor and the shack hung precariously over a washed out section of beach. Outside, a length of wood anchored in the sand was propped up against the eave in an apparent effort to prevent the shack from toppling into the washout. The sloped roof of the shack consisted of panels of corrugated metal held down and in place by numerous large chunks of sun-whitened coral. In the back of the hut were a couple of cots constructed of assorted pieces of scrap wood and some sturdy branches. Nailed above the entrance to the shack was a hand-written sign on a rectangular piece of cardboard. It was so faded that it was mostly illegible, except along the bottom the words; 'JAH RASTAFARI', which had been over-written with a heavy black marker, could easily be made out.

I made a habit of stopping in and chatting with Danny and Keith on my daily walks down the beach. Danny and I were kindred spirits and we connected right away. One day while we were talking a very pretty young Jamaican girl walked up. She was wearing a form-fitting white dress with a hibiscus print on it, a floppy red hat and a necklace made of white sea shells. Danny introduced me to her, "Dis is my wife Angela," he said. They marry young in Jamaica.

We eventually got around to talking about scuba diving. Danny dove to augment his income. I dove for the fun of it, I was, and still am to this day, a fair weather diver. I had made a few dives with the Negril Beach Village, but was disappointed. Their dives were on the sand flats in front of the hotel in about twenty-five feet of water. The regular dive boat was on the fritz so we were using the water ski runabout and it was a clunker and very difficult to get in and out of with scuba gear on. I dove with them and looked at sandy bottom and eelgrass until boredom had set in. In fact, I had given up on diving any more that trip. Danny offered to take me further out to sea to the drop-off, for a price of course. He captured my imagination, telling me that it was beautiful out there and that there was a forest of black coral along the wall. Because of its hardness and inherent beauty, black coral was a staple material for the craftsmen along the beach. That was before harvesting black coral became illegal in Jamaica. I was keen to get in a good dive and see black coral in its natural state, so we made a deal.

Looking around their shack, I wondered how we were going to get out to the wall. "Where's your boat?" I asked.

"Don't worry mon, jus' be heah tomorrow mornin' at seven," Danny assured me.

"You're bringing a tank for me, right?" I asked.

"Yeah mon! Me bring you a tank, don't worry." *'Don't worry, be happy'*, I thought.

The next morning I slipped from between the sheets and dragged my sorry butt out of bed as quietly as I could. I didn't want to wake Keri. I stood still for a moment as a wave of dizziness washed over me. Oh boy, I was hung over! I tiptoed over to the window to check the weather. It looked like it would be nice for diving.

Who's Keri? Keri was from Miami. She was beautiful... and Jewish. She laughingly told me that her mother wouldn't approve of me, being a 'gentile' and all. She had long, curly auburn hair and brown eyes, a one-two knockout combination. To be honest though, it wasn't her hair or her eyes that attracted me to her at first.

One morning I was returning from a walk along the beach, kicking along in the surf and wondering, as single males do, if I was going to get lucky this trip. Looking ahead I saw a tall, slender young woman coming out of the water. She walked up the beach and sat down on a towel on the sand in front of the Sundowner Hotel. Oh! I should mention that she was topless, a small point perhaps, but an important one, especially to a twenty-something, testosterone-doped, single male. Come to think of it, the 'twenty-something' and the 'single' qualifiers don't really modify the significance of the appearance of a young, beautiful, topless woman. Nevertheless, not being one to pass up on an opportunity for a closer look at a beautiful young woman, I altered my course so as to cross just in front of her. As I approached, she looked up at me and flashed a dazzling, heart-thumping smile. That was all the encouragement I needed, I dropped down onto the sand beside her and introduced myself.

"Hi, I'm Thomas," I said, offering my hand.

"Keri," she smiled, raising hers. We shook. Her firm little boobs jiggled, my blood pressure dropped and I almost fainted. Her hair, tied up in a bob atop her head, was wet. Beaded droplets of water glistened as they slid smoothly down her tanned skin. Her nipples stood erect. I looked into those deep brown eyes and even though I was sitting on terra firma, I felt myself falling. It took no more that half a heartbeat for me to fall helplessly and totally in lust with Keri.

We talked away the morning. The beach bar was close and we visited it frequently. We swam in the ocean together. I thought I was in paradise, laying on the beach, the hot sun beating down, not a care in the world, drinking in the beauty of this stunning creature who had simply walked into my life. Thinking back on it, I truly was in paradise.

From that first chance meeting, Keri and I became a pair. We hung around and partied with a loosely associated group of other travelers. Keri was sharing a room with a girlfriend. They were both primary school teachers. I couldn't figure where they had learned to party so hard. In the mornings we breakfasted together and Keri accompanied me on my beach walks. One morning we wandered way down that deserted stretch of sand. She took off her bikini top and then surprised me by removing her bottoms. She ran splashing into the water, challenging me to catch her. I did of course. We embraced and fell, her screaming and me laughing, into the water. It was there, in the warm waters fronting the present day location of Swept Away resort, that I made the amazing discovery that it was possible to make love in the ocean, which, until that time, I hadn't even considered was a possibility.

We spent our last night in Jamaica together. What had started out as 'The Manager's Rum Punch Cocktail Party' had evolved into a long, loud drinking and dancing session. Keri and I both overindulged on pina coladas. Later, we broke away from the party and walked around Rutland Point until we came to a deserted little cove decorated by a big old piece of driftwood. We sat down and Keri pulled a monster spliff out of her bag. She licked it down, teasing me with her tongue movements. We smoked it and got pleasantly wasted. We sat there on the beach and held each other and looked at the ocean and time stood still. We laughed a lot. I buried my nose in her hair and breathed her in. Sitting there it struck me that this wasn't reality. My real world was waiting for me and tomorrow I had to go back. So did Keri. The moment was ethereal, a dream.

That night is indelibly burned into my memory. I visit it when I'm in need of a little pick-me-up. Over the years I've called it up so often that I'm worried I might wear it out and someday when I go there, it will be faded and scratched like an old black and white film. But for now it still works, and it plays in the most vibrant of colors. The water was perfectly flat. The moon was incredibly bright; almost full, it hung three-dimensional in the heavens, flinging a silver mat across the sea. Our bodies cast deep moon-shadows on the sand. And the sky, in spite of the bright moon, was spangled with a quilt of twinkling stars. The air was warm. Keri was warmer. It was achingly romantic.

It's like that in the Caribbean, everything, including emotions, are supercharged.

We stayed out on the beach until very late. Then we went back to my room and tumbled into bed, our bodies entwined. We made desperate, young, energetic love, each knowing that we had only a few hours left together. After, she lay on top of me, her chest coated in a sheen of perspiration, some mine, some hers.

"Thomas, will you call me when you get back home?" she whispered.

"You can count on it," I said. Then sleep came.

Keri rolled over in the bed. A soft shoulder poked out above the sheet. I reached down and slowly dragged the sheet toward the foot of the bed, pausing as it slid over her chest, then down past her belly button, (she had an inny), then down to her knees, revealing her long tanned thighs. I stood there drinking her in. She took my breath away. For a long moment I debated, *'Should I go diving? Should I get back into bed with Keri? Diving? Keri?'*

In the end the dive won out, but just barely. Keri stirred, reached down and pulled the sheet back up to her neck. She brushed back her curly main and peeked at me through one pretty, half-opened eye.

"I'm going diving," I whispered.

"Hmmmm?" Her eye slid shut.

It was a beauty of a morning; in Jamaica most of them are. The only sign of life was a rooster crowing somewhere back beyond the trees that lined the beach.

I trudged along the sand to the brothers' shack. Two scuba tanks were standing in the sand next to the... *'Boat'*? I stood there, mouth agape, looking at what I assumed was our dive boat. In fact it was more like a punt, and a small one at that. It was made of flaking plywood, about twelve feet long with a flat bottom and a wide, blunt bow. Faded yellow paint covered the hull and there were two thin, jaunty blue racing stripes painted down the sides. It had a short fore deck, painted the same blue as the racing stripes. Affixed to the middle of the fore deck was a chrome handle that looked like it had been salvaged from a kitchen cabinet door. There was no engine. Two oars made from sturdy branches with flat boards nailed to the ends were attached by oarlocks fashioned from several strands of twine looped around a hole gouged into the gunwale.

Christ! I thought, are we going out on the ocean in *THAT*! I was beginning to have second thoughts about my Keri - dive decision.

Keith came out of the shack, rubbing his eyes. I pointed, "That's the boat?"

"Yeah, mon," he replied, "help me drag it to de sea". What the hell, I thought, I'll wear my vest. If I have to, I can swim for it.

The surface of the water at beachside was calm, but out to sea I glimpsed the occasional spray of white water breaking on the reef.

Danny joined us, still fastening his shorts. We loaded the diving gear into the boat and pushed off. I put my vest on, trying to be nonchalant about it. We sat quietly as Keith rowed us out to the drop-off. Once we got beyond the protection of Rutland Point and Booby Cay, the surface began to roll with two-foot swells. I sat there dealing with my hangover, my mind continually turning to Keri, warm in bed back at the hotel.

I noticed that the boat was leaking, in spite of the thick bead of silicone that occupied the seam between the gunwale and the flat bottom. The water wasn't pouring in, but we would probably have to bail a little before we were back on shore.

I checked out Danny's diving kit. He was armed with a rusty, twelve-inch knife and a homemade spear gun, the sling of which appeared to have been made from a bicycle tire inner tube. His mask and fins were old and sun bleached, made of cheap blue rubber that had gone stiff and was badly cracked. I doubted the mask would keep the water out. He didn't have a snorkel or weights, but he didn't need weights, his lean body would sink without them. He attached his single regulator, which looked like a relic from the sixties, to the scuba tank. He had no depth gauge or tank pressure gauge. Danny was a minimalist diver. I had brought all of my own gear, except for the tank.

Keith's well-muscled back was beginning to shine from the effort that he was putting in at the oars. The color of the sea around us changed from light to dark blue. I checked the distance to shore, about a mile I estimated -- still within swimming distance. Inexplicably, I envision a byline from the 'Jamaica Gleaner' newspaper *'Foolhardy Tourist Lost at Sea, Presumed Drowned. Remains Probably Consumed by Sharks'*.

Keith had stopped rowing. "Okay, lets go," said Danny.

I looked around for the anchor, there wasn't one. I mentioned it to Keith.

"Don't worry mon," he assured me, "Me follow de bubbles an' pick you up when you surface."

The wind was freshening and the surface of the water was beginning to break. *'Bubbles?'* Oh well, like grandma used to say, *'In for a pence, in for a pound'*.

Danny disappeared over the side in a big splash. I bit down on my regulator, put my palm on my mask and rolled backward into the deep blue Caribbean. My vision was obscured by a swirl of bubbles. I took a deep breath. The regulator hissed and the metallic taste of cool, dry compressed air filled my mouth. Ahhhh! That first hit is always the best. The greatest cure for a rum hangover is a few lungfuls of compressed air and a cool ocean dip. I felt better immediately.

The bubbles cleared and I looked down, searching for Danny. I spotted him, already twenty feet below me and sinking like a homesick devil. I have no problems equalizing pressure, so when diving with a group, I'm usually among the first to hit bottom. But try as I might, I could not catch Danny, the human fish. I looked beyond him, searching for the bottom, but I couldn't see it. I expected the visibility to be about eighty feet, so not being able to see the bottom wasn't a big deal, since we were planning on a dive of about one hundred and ten feet. Still, when diving in deep water, not being able to see the bottom is a little eerie, especially when there is no anchor line. Normally, shafts of sunlit water provide a vertical reference frame, but as it was early in the morning the sun wasn't yet high enough for that. Looking down, I saw Danny's fins and the column of bubbles that trailed above him. We were enveloped in an azure blue void, gradually darkening as we descended.

I checked my depth gauge, 60 feet... 80 feet, I still couldn't find the bottom. Danny was head down, energetically kicking his way deeper. Passing through 100 feet I finally saw the bottom, still far below and too indistinct to estimate its depth. At 130 feet, my self-imposed personal limit, I leveled off. The visibility was about 70 to 80 feet. At this depth it begins to get gloomy and the colors are muted. Danny was getting to the bottom, which was the edge of the drop-off. I estimated that he was about 30 feet below me. He looked up at me and waved me down. I shook my head 'No' and pointed at my depth gauge. I checked my tank pressure gauge, the needle was pointing at the 1700lbs mark. We were using steel 72 cubic foot tanks that take a 2200lb charge. *'Holy shit,'* I thought, *'I've already breathed off 500 pounds!'* I did a quick mental calculation, at that depth there was no more than 10 to 15 minutes of air left in the tank.

From my vantage point the bottom sloped upward to the left. Danny turned and started to swim up-slope, I followed above him, level at 130 feet. Clumps of rock and coral lined the ledge of the drop-off with narrow runnels of sand separating them. Soft coral fronds were rooted along the edge, slowly waving in the surge. Beyond the ledge was the blue abyss of the deep ocean.

I noticed a movement to my right. A big barracuda was suspended motionless, hovering at the edge of visibility. He was about six feet long and as thick as a big man's thigh. His skin was silver with diamond shaped black markings along the dorsal ridge. He slowly fanned his tail to keep his body horizontal to me, but he moved deliberately closer. His long, tooth-filled mouth was permanently twisted into a malevolent grin. We watched each other for a while, he drifted close enough that I started to get uncomfortable. Barracudas are not normally a threat to divers, but they have an innate strike reflex that I sincerely did not want to trigger. He moved close enough that I could see that his pupil, steadily fixed on me, was rimmed with green. Suddenly he lost interest, gave one mighty flick of his powerful tail and disappeared into the blue gloom. I took a big gulp of air, realizing that I hadn't taken a breath for a while. The 'cuda left no doubt in my mind that he was master of his domain.

I turned my attention back to the bottom. I looked up and down the slope as far as I could see, searching for Danny or his bubbles, but found neither. I started to feel a little spooked. I pictured myself from an extreme long-view perspective; a vast rolling ocean, a flimsy boat bobbing somewhere above, a tiny, solitary diver figure suspended 130 feet down in the void. I finned around a little, wondering what to do next, when an urgent thought asserted itself; *'Surface!'* I realized that I was already ascending.

I took my time going up and hovered to decompress at 20 feet for a couple of minutes. When I broke the surface I found myself in the middle of a four-foot trough. My inflated vest buoyed me and I crested the swell, scanning the surface for Keith. I spotted the boat a couple of hundred yards away. Keith was looking the other way searching the surface, so much for the *'bubbles'* plan. I shouted and waved and rode the swells. Keith didn't see me. I checked the distance to the shore. It would be a long swim, but with no current, I could have made it. I recalled chuckling at divers who wear whistles, knives, strobe lights, compasses, writing palettes and myriad other odd and ends. I didn't find it funny then; at that moment I wished I had a whistle. After more shouting and waving Keith finally spotted me and paddled over.

He stooped over the side to help me with my gear, "Where Danny?" he asked, looking around, big brother concern written across his face.

"I don't know man, he disappeared." I heave myself into the boat.

"What you mean he disappear? Me no see 'im bubbles, where you see 'im las'?" Keith was worried.

"He went way deep on me and I lost him and came up 'cause I was getting low on air," I said, starting to worry myself.

We both searched the surface, no bubbles, no Danny.

"How deep he go?"

"I think he went to about 150."

"Rassclaat! You should'a stayed wid him mon, dat was de plan!" Keith was starting to freak out.

There was a splash behind the boat. Danny. He spat his regulator out and took off his mask. He pointed at me and started to laugh. "White mon no know how fe dive!"

His spear gun clattered into the bottom of the boat. It was followed by a five foot brown coral tree. Then he pulled a good-sized triggerfish out of his shorts and heaved that aboard. All the while he was laughing and berating me on my poor diving skills. He clambered into the boat and gave his head a shake; ribbons of water streamed off his locks in all directions. Standing, he pressed one nostril shut with his index finger and did a farmer blow over the side of the boat.

"Why you no follow me mon?" he asked.

"You went too deep," I said.

"Too deep? Me no go too deep mon! You want to see de wall, you 'ave to go deep."

Keith pulled on the oars and we headed into shore, the sea had a good roll to it.

"You should be careful about how deep you dive. You could get bent," I said.

Danny puffed out his muscular chest and thumped it, "Ha! Me no get no blood claat, mon! I a fish! Me in de sea since me was born!"

I shrug my shoulders and let it go, thinking he's probably right anyway.

We went a little further and they both suddenly became silent, looking solemnly to port. "What's up?" I ask.

"Duppy," Keith said quietly, slowing at the oars a little.

"What's that . . . some kind of fish?"

"No mon, one of our friends, Anton, he drown out 'ere las' week," Danny said.

I was dumbfounded. "He drowned?"

"Yeah mon."

"What happened?" I asked, looking in the direction that they were.

"Don't know," Danny shrugged, looking at a spot on the sea, "Maybe big fish get him. 'im go divin' for coral an' nevah come back. A fisherman find his boat on de sea, empty. He wait a while dere, but Anton, him nevah come up."

"What's a duppy?"

"We seen Anton walkin' de road near our house in town las' night," Danny said.

I was confused. "Walking on the road? But you said he drowned."

"Yeah mon, but we seen 'im duppy," Keith offered by way of explanation.

"You mean . . . like his ghost?" I asked, still confused.

"Yeah mon, but not a ghost, we seen 'im duppy," Danny said.

"How do you know it wasn't someone who looked like him?"

"No mon! It was Anton, de way he walk, it 'im for sure. Yah know, people walk a certain way, yah know it them before yah see dere face. Yah know what I'm sayin'?"

"Yeah...yeah, I know what you're sayin'."

"An' when people die, sometime dere duppy come back, 'til t'ings are right for dem to go, yah onnerstan'?"

I nodded my head, thinking that 'duppy' must be some kind of a ghost, Jamaican voodoo style, and decided not to press the issue. I was feeling creepy enough as it was.

On later trips I was to learn more about duppies, the Bush Doctor, the Obeah man and other Jamaican superstitions.

We rode the rest of the way back to the beach shack in silence.

Back on shore Keith pan-fried the triggerfish on an open fire behind their shack. He added some ackee, a local fruit that looks like scrambled eggs and some hand-squeezed spicy dumplings that he called 'Johnny Cakes'. It was delicious, the best breakfast I had while in Jamaica.

After the dive I caught up with Keri at poolside. She admonished me for 'sneaking' away from the bed in the morning. Later we said goodbye. She had to catch an early flight back to Miami. We embraced and kissed. She cried a little, I swallowed the lump in my throat. We traded addresses and phone numbers, promising to stay in touch. We did too. In the summer of that year she came and visited me for a week and we had a great time riding around town on my motorcycle. One day we cruised up to a secluded waterfall in the country that not many people know about. We had it to ourselves and it was a hot day, so we went skinny dipping in the stream. She pressed her wet naked body against mine and I thought of Jamaica. As we were drying off, she suddenly yelped and grabbed her behind. She had stepped on a ground hornet's nest and a squadron of them had flown out and retaliated, scoring several direct hits on her butt. She swelled up a bit and the ride back was uncomfortable for her, but in the end, literally and figuratively speaking, no great harm was done.

We passed the time together talking, playing backgammon and making love, which we did until we were sore and had to take a break, even though we didn't want to stop. And we tried to figure how we could get our lives together.

Keri's family ties kept her in Miami and my career kept me in front of a radar screen, moving little green blips in and out of airports. Inevitably, the time apart and the distance worked against us and gradually we lost contact.

But I still have that night on the beach.

For a couple of years after that I wondered what became of Keri. It would hit me at the weirdest moments, like when I was riding my bike or looking at a cloudless sky, then BANG… there she was, sitting on her beach towel in front of the Sundowner Hotel that morning we first met…. a glistening bronzed goddess. I have an idea that Keri and I might have had an interesting future together. But then again, maybe not, I'm a strong believer in karma and fate has its way of arranging things. I hope things worked out for Keri. I wonder if she ever went back to Negril.

Later that day, after seeing Keri away and before heading off myself for the MoBay airport and the real world, I went down the beach for one last visit with the brothers. They were both there, Keith sanding down a mahogany bust of a dread-head and Danny hack-sawing the brown coral tree that he picked on the dive into workable sections. Keith tried to sell me a conch shell to take home as a souvenir. We talked for a while and had a photo taken of the three of us standing in front of their shack. That picture hangs in my studio at home in a small frame adorned with seashells that I collected on the beach. We all have big grins on our faces, arms over each other's shoulders. Keith's 'tool kit', a ragged plastic 'Sun Tours' beach bag, is on the sand beside us. Danny's wearing a tattered T-shirt with a print of 'Jaws' on it. His pearly white teeth stand out against his sun-darkened skin. The tips of his dreadlocks are bleached to a brownish shade of orange.

I gave them my Jamaican cash and handed Danny my swim fins. We did guy-hugs, thumping each other on the back, avoiding eye contact. I wished them both well and we said our good-byes. Halfway back to the hotel, I turned around to look at them. Keith waved and Danny held up a clenched fist.

That was the last time I ever saw them.

"Cigarrrreeeeeettts!"

Sun is shining, weather is sweet,
Make you want to move, your dancing feet.
Bob Marley – 'Sun is Shining'

 Although 'Norman Manley Boulevard' is the proper
name of the road along the beach section of Negril,
locally people call it 'the beach road'. Recently the
roadbed was rebuilt, proper drainage and
shoulders were added and a fresh coat of
pavement was put down. The Negril beach road
project is a small part of a huge undertaking to
widen, improve and pave the road all the way to MoBay. The new
pristine surface of the beach road seems oddly out of place in
Jamaica where poor roads are part of the local landscape. I liked the
old beach road, it had character, like the weathered face of an old
man. Now there isn't a pothole, wrinkle or a washout to be found
from the flats beside Bloody Bay to the roundabout in town. But time
will deal with that.

Until it does, the new highway provides a seamless ribbon of fresh
asphalt for the resident corps of testosteronies. They now have a fine
new racetrack, the 'Norman Manley Memorial Autobahn'. Vehicles
and motorcycles zoom down the new road flat-out in top gear. Even
the goats won't venture near the road any more.

I was up early today. I can't say for sure what time it was,
probably around 6:00 o'clock; the sun had just risen. The roosters
were heralding the new day and I was watching the morning colors fill
the sky. I had wandered down to the beach, which was totally
deserted, and then back through the hotel parking lot to the road. At
that hour of the morning there is virtually no traffic. I was standing in
the hotel driveway beside the road when I heard the rising scream of
a kamikaze bike approaching at full throttle. I looked in the direction
of town and saw it coming, a rapidly growing blue and white blob of
color. Within moments the apparition was upon me,

"*EEEEEOOOOOOWWWWWWWWW*", it blasted by creating a
sharp gust of wind in the still morning air. It was moving FAST, how
fast, I cannot say, but the Doppler effect on the shriek of the engine
was very pronounced, and I swear the color of the bike as it flashed
by me seemed to shift from blue to red.

I caught a blurred glimpse of the helmet-less driver as he streaked by; bent over the gas tank, teeth bared in a wide grin, his shorts and T-shirt slapping in the slipstream. A moment later the bike was out of sight around a slight bend in the road, the sound of its engine rapidly fading. Soon all traces of its passage were gone and the tranquility of the early morning reclaimed its rightful place. It's odd, but standing in that cool calmness, I began to question if the bike really had gone by, or if the whole thing was a fanciful flight of my imagination, or perhaps a lingering dream. Or maybe I had just seen a ghost? As I knew from my experience with Danny and Keith, some Jamaicans believe in phantoms. Had I seen the duppy of a young man who had met an early demise on his fast motorcycle, condemned to ride the Jamaican roads in the chill of the early mornings to atone for his sins?

I know not, but I do know that in Negril, the line that divides reality and fantasy is narrow, fuzzy and meandering.

Later in the morning, after my obligatory jaunt, I trek up to a quiet section of beach a little beyond The Negril Tree House resort. I walk along in the surf, kicking my bare feet in the warm, clear water, squinting into the bursts of reflected sunlight dancing off its surface. At this precise moment, I don't have a care in the world. I'm slowly making my way toward the north end of the beach. Ahead, at the far end of the long crescent of surf and sand that stretch enticingly before me, I see Booby Cay, my Treasure Island, sitting just off shore.

I walk for what feels to be about twenty minutes, not that I care, as time has become fluid and I've totally lost track of the hours and minutes. I know that it's mid-morning, and that's good enough. The sun is pounding on my back and right side. I'm plastered with sunscreen and I have a T-shirt draped over my shoulders, but there is no shade on this stretch and I feel the sun slowly gaining the upper hand.

On a previous visit, I was caught out here in the middle of a blistering afternoon without a T-shirt on a cloudless day and it was brutal. That day, I made my way back to the hotel in hundred-yard bursts across the parched sand from one shady refuge to the next. Only mad dogs and sun-starved Canadians go out in the noonday sun, and there are plenty of both in Negril. I have no idea how far I'm going to go this morning, but since my agenda is clear today (like every other day), I'll go until I turn around, wherever and whenever that may be.

I'm walking on the last undeveloped section of beach in Negril (excluding Bloody Bay) and although I dearly hope it stays undeveloped, it probably will not. Along this five hundred-yard stretch the beach is wide and the sand is white and clean and has a fresh look to it. It massages the bottom of my feet as I walk. The fact that this portion of the beach is undeveloped hasn't stopped vendors from setting up here, because there is still a lot of walking traffic that passes by. All along the edge of the beach, where the sand gives way to the grass and trees, vendors have set up shop. There are no permanent stands or stores, everything on display is set up early in the morning and torn down just before sunset. For a couple of hundred yards along the beach, lines have been strung from tree branches to poles stuck into the sand and hung from them are sarongs, wraps, towels and T-shirts in a dazzling array of colors and prints. They flap and wave in the breeze, creating a phantasmagoric, ever changing kaleidoscope that summons passers by, *'Come on over! . . . Look at me!'* they beckon. On the sand, laid out on tarps and planks in and amongst the flapping fabrics, are rows of seashells and woodcarvings, and liberally interspersed throughout are makeshift display stands with the inevitable collection of bracelets, necklaces and earrings.

I'd visited these stands before and had no particular interest in looking at them again, but as I pass a bright flash of color teases the edge of my vision. I make the fatal mistake of glancing, just for a microsecond, in its direction. This brings the sharp-eyed vendor, who until this moment was hidden in the shade of a tree, abruptly to her feet. Any passerby with white skin will draw the attention of the vendors, and newcomers whose skin is still pallid or is showing tones of pink or red are especially attention grabbing, akin to waving a red flag in front of a bull.

"Suh! come heah. . . over heah suh!" she calls out, walking out a bit toward me, raising her arm high above her head and making the 'come over here' motion with her fingers.

I shake my head, wave and keep on moving. "Suh! Come an' see what I have, you can jus' look, no problem." The 'come over here' motion now involves her whole hand and lower arm. I do a mental shrug, remind myself that I'm in no hurry and walk over to her, reasoning that it's the courteous thing to do.

"Hello, suh, how are you today?" she says, smiling and holding the magazine that she was reading up to her brow, shading the strong sun.

"Oh, I'm great today!" I reply. "What more could one ask for? The sun is shining, the weather is sweet . . ."

I examine what she has on display. Hanging from a line strung between the curved trunk of a coconut tree and a length of weathered 4 x 4 lumber stuck deep into the sand, are several large multi-colored beach towels. One of them is decorated with the Jamaican flag, a large yellow 'X' with green triangular patches above and below and black triangles to the sides. The yellow is emblematic of the sunshine that blesses the island, the green represents the verdant vegetation, agriculture and hope for the future and the black is symbolic for past hard times, oppression and burdens borne by the people. I've also heard some say that the black is representative of the skin color of the majority of the Jamaican people. The flag, adopted on Jamaican Independence Day, August 6, 1962, also has a motto;

'Burdens and hardships there may be, but the land is green and the sun shineth.'

I grasp the edge of the flag-towel and stroke it, considering its symbolism.

"Dat's our national flag," the vendor says.

"Oh yes! I know, and a very beautiful flag it is," I say. And I mean it. I don't know why, but whenever I see the Jamaican flag, I get a warm, comfy feeling, more so than when I see my own Canadian flag. I'm somewhat baffled by this. My wife says it's because I think I'm Jamaican. She jokingly calls me 'white Rasta'. When we have company and they see my collection of Jamaican memorabilia and note that reggae is my music of choice, Amy says, by way of explanation, "Oh, he thinks he's Jamaican." Maybe there is something to it. Some day I'll visit a hypnotist and get regressed, I have a suspicion that I may have lived a past life in Jamaica.

I briefly check the other beach towels, one is decorated with large multi-colored parrots perching in green foliage, there are several with varying hibiscus flower patterns and one is adorned with starfishes and sea horses on an aqua background.

"Do you like dat one?" the vendor asks, pointing to the starfish-patterned towel. "I give you special price today."

"I don't' think so," I reply, "I'm all fixed up for towels." I move over to her little display stand. Among the trinkets I spot an interesting looking pipe in the shape of a horn. I pick it up.

"Dat's made from de cow's horn," the vendor says.

The pipe is polished to a high sheen. It has a bowl mounted in it for smoking material, a mouthpiece and there's a plug that can be removed, I pull it out.

"You put water in dere, dat's a water pipe," she explains.

"Oh, very nice," I say, admiring the workmanship.

"You can have it for twenty dollars," the vendor offers.

I put it down, "No thanks," I say, "it's very nice but I don't need a pipe."

"I'll let you have it for fifteen dollars," she counters.

"Naw, I really don't need it . . . thanks anyhow," I turn to leave.

"Ten dollars," she says.

Aha! That's it, the 'walk away' price, always the lowest! Some vendors refer to it as the 'Italian' price.

I move a short distance down the beach and spread my mat on the sand, settling in to catch a few rays on my still pale body. I'm flat on my stomach, eyes level with the beach, when I notice a quick movement directly ahead of me. A tiny sand crab is busy working on his burrow. With mighty little heaves he flings divots of sand from the opening of his lair. He disappears back down the hole and re-emerges about ten seconds later with another clump, which he adds to the growing fan shaped drift of darker colored sand at his doorstep. Occasionally, he exits the burrow completely and goes on a jerky, sideways scuttling expedition across the sand. The purpose of these outings is not apparent to me. The coloring of his carapace is so effective that when he stops moving he blends completely into the beach and I'm not able to detect him until he moves again. His movements are swift and darting. With remarkable navigation skills he unerringly finds the portal of his home, hidden in the tumbled landscape of the beach, after each excursion. Each trip ends with a final frantic diving dash into the shaft. Shortly thereafter he pokes his pivoting stalk eyes above the rim of the entry and carefully examines the environs. Satisfied that it's safe, even with my gargantuan body beached nearby, he hurls a lump of sand and then continues with his excavations.

Thus I peacefully passed the time, watching the little sand crab carry out his business, periodically flipping from my stomach to my back, and dozing. During one of my naps I dreamt that legions of sand crabs had tied me down with hundreds of tiny ropes fashioned from strands of seaweed. Then, with great difficulty, they carted me away to their capital city to be interrogated. Their leader, a huge blue crab with dreadlocks, crawled up on my face and stared at me with his beady eyes. To my great relief, when I awoke, I was unencumbered and my industrious little friend was the only crab in sight.

"Cigarrrreeeeeettts!"

A loud, gravely, rasping voice calls out. *"Cigarrrreeeeeettts!"*

Closer this time. I look up from my prone position on the mat, squinting into the brilliant sun. I see the silhouette of a tall, skinny, gawky looking figure wearing a tall wide brimmed hat striding toward me. "Oh my God!" I think, "It's The Cat In The Hat!" Am I having another beach-mare? I sit up to get a better look at the apparition. Now clear of the sun's glare I'm relieved to see that it's only a beach vendor, not the grinning, creepy character from the Dr. Suess book. To make sure I check his shoes. Pheww! He's wearing a tattered pair of sneakers, not the bell tipped slippers that The Cat wears. I enjoyed reading most of the Dr. Suess books to my girls when they were little, but I never did like that Cat In The Hat dude. He gave me the creeps, like the clown in Stephen King's 'It'.

But the more I look at this guy the more he does look like The Cat, he's even got the grin. That and the tall, wide brimmed, color banded top hat. If he had a big tail and the red bow tie, he would be a dead ringer for his namesake. Into the brim of his hat are tucked numerous packages of cigarettes, matches and other smoking paraphernalia. In addition to the wares stuffed in his hat, he's carrying a large, clear plastic bag that's filled with stuff. In it I can make out several brands of smokes, rolling papers (for your ganja, mon) along with matches and lighters. Under his arm are a couple of boxes of different types of cigars and God only knows what else. The Cat in The Hat is a fully equipped, ambulatory smoke shop.

"Do you need cigarettes mi frien'?" he asks.

"No, but what kind if cigars do you have?"

"Cubans – Monte Criscos, Cohibas..."

"Do you have any Romeo Y Julliettas?" I ask, thinking I might want an after-dinner cigar.

"Yeah mon."

"Number ones?"

"Yeah mon."

We complete the transaction and The Cat saunters on down the beach. "Cigarreeetttttsss!" he calls out as he passes a woman walking the other way. She shakes her head.

I can imagine the Pavlovian effect that his unusual trademark call must have on the nicotine addicted. You can hear him coming long before you can see him and there is no doubt as to what he is selling. One loud raspy - "Cigarreeettttttsss!" – and any needy smoker within hearing distance will begin to pant and foam at the mouth. There are numerous tobacco hustlers on the beach, but The Cat in The Hat is surely the most fascinating of the bunch.

Many visitors to Negril, and other Caribbean islands in general for that matter, complain about the hustlers on the beach. Some hustlers refer to themselves as 'Beach Boys', another common term is 'higglers', but this mostly applies to the women. Call them what you may, but as far as I'm concerned, the hustlers are one of the most interesting characteristics of the beach.

In Negril there are all manner of hustlers. There are placard carrying people, a guy that rides a bicycle on the hard packed strip of beach between the surf and the loose sand selling ice cream from an dry ice packed cardboard box. Younger boys rush around with plastic bags filled with chunks of pineapple and coconut. In the early morning, vendors move quickly up and down the beach, offering rum bottles filled with fresh-squeezed orange juice. Later in the morning, fishermen carrying stringers of fish and lobster ply the beach in front of the resorts that are equipped with kitchen facilities. When you get right down to it, the beach hustlers are simply entrepreneurs, trying to make a few bucks. In Jamaica, unemployment is high and wages are very low, and a good hustler can make a better-than-average wage working the beach.

Each of the roving hustlers has his own 'beat', a two to three hundred yard stretch of beach that he sticks to. Within his domain, he has an agreed-to quasi-monopoly on the particular product that he's selling.

I'm not sure what the legal status of the hustler is, but they do keep an eye out for Babylon, and sharply curtail their activities when the police beach patrol is around. Yesterday, in front of the hotel, I was in the process of buying a little bag of cut-up pineapple from a beach boy. I was reaching for some cash when he suddenly thrust the baggie into my hand, said, "I gotta go, pay me later," and split. I looked up and saw a pair of beach patrol police approaching. When I looked back to see where the beach boy was, he had disappeared. Later, after the police had gone, he re-appeared and I paid him for the pineapple. I asked him if selling on the beach was illegal. He said it wasn't but sometimes the cops demanded money from the beach vendors and he preferred to keep his business expenses down by avoiding them as much as possible.

I think one's opinion of hustlers is directly related to how one deals with them. I personally see them as a form of entertainment. These guys and girls, aside from adding a lot of character to the beach, are bountiful founts of information. I've visited Cuba, once when vendors were allowed on the beach and once again after Castro had decreed 'no contact' between tourists and Cuban citizens. The second time was much less interesting, the beaches seemed dead, sterile and boring. I can't image what the Negril beach would be like without hustlers. Just a bunch of tourists milling aimlessly about. No, in my opinion, the hustlers are the lifeblood of the beach.

For male tourists, it's not unusual to be offered the services of a woman, either directly from the young lady or by her 'promotional agent'. However, this year a new and interesting marketing angle is being exploited. Yesterday, after visiting with Big Joe, a hustler dressed in a shinny red football jersey and wearing a cell phone headset over his kerchief approached me as I walked onto his beat. I'd never seen him before.

"Hey mon," he said, approaching me with his fist up for the tap, "how t'ings today?"

"Just fine," I said. I brought my fist up and tapped his. He looked around, checking for the beach patrol.

"Yu want a black woman?" he asked, lowering his voice a little. "Me can get yu a 'small panty woman', 'cause me know dat yu white guys like women wid small ass." With that, a broad knowing smile spread across his face.

"No thanks," I said, "I have enough women in my life right now."

"Yu sure mon? Me can give yu some Viagra wid dat," he added.

"Viagra?" I repeated, louder than I had intended. A couple of tourist guys standing nearby, who had probably been offered the same package deal, heard me and started to laugh.

"Yeah mon, no problem," the hustler replied, glancing around.

"Well, that's very thoughtful of you," I said, "but I think I'll pass. Thanks anyway." I walked away shaking my head, amazed once again at the entrepreneurial spirit.

My SPF 30 seems to be losing its sun-blocking efficiency so I seek the refuge of a shady spot, a bar perhaps. My stomach lets out a small growl to remind me that breakfast was a long time ago. As if on cue, approaching me I see a man pushing a bicycle with a big cooler placed in a basket at the front of the bike. A hand painted sign, - "Patties" is affixed to the front of the cooler. Occasionally he squeezes an 'Aaooggaaahh!' horn mounted on the handlebars. I recognize the vendor as a Negril regular, it's Neville, The Patty Man.

"Hello Neville, what do you have today?" I ask him.

"Veggie patties and cocobread, is all dat's left." he says. With that he opens the cooler and my nostrils fill with the delicious aroma of the cooked pastries.

"Mmmmmm, that's blackmail Neville." He grins at me.

"Is the cocobread still warm?" I ask, reverently hoping that it would be.

"Yea mon, it still hot."

"Neville, you are the Most High," I say, meaning it. He hands me a small brown paper bag, its outside blotched with stains from the butter leaching out of the cocobread. I open the top of the bag and look inside, the cocobread, a squat wedge shape about 5 inches to the side and 1½ inches thick, is nestled inside. I plunge my nose deep in the bag and take a big hit of the heavenly aroma.

Warm cocobread is doubtless the most delicious bread on the planet, bar none. It is so delectable that I'm surprised it isn't a banned substance. Cocobread has no cocoa or coconut in it. It gets its name from the turnip-like root of the plant that is ground into the flour that's used to make it. Yeast is added to the dough, it's then shaped into a big flat pancake. Butter is then slathered on, it's folded in half, slathered again, folded once more and then baked. Eaten, it has a light fluffy texture and the taste is divine. Of course, cocobread is fattening, but it's a well-known fact that calories consumed while on vacation don't really count.

The Perfect Conch Shell

'De olda de moon, de bryta it shine.'
Jamaican Proverb

Roots Bamboo is a large live reggae showcase near the town end of the beach. It's easy to see when a major show is coming up at Roots Bamboo because, for a week before the event, there's a huge hand painted sign, and by huge I mean eight by ten feet, declaring in large neon colored letters who will be headlining.

NIKKI!...SWALLOW!...
THE HURRICANE BAND!

Then, on the day of the show, a tall-corrugated metal fence is erected all around the property, blocking off a chunk of the beach. The fence in itself is an enticement to attend the show because it's impossible to miss it when walking by, and it gets one to thinking, "If they're putting up a fence for the show, it must be worth going to." Besides, if you're staying at a place that's anywhere near Roots on the night of the show, you should plan on attending, because you won't get any sleep until the show ends in the early hours of the morning anyhow.

During my visits over the last several years I've been stopping in next to Roots Bamboo to see an old friend who peddles his wares on the beach there. I'm sorry to say that I don't even know his name, he told me once, but I lost it right away. Not knowing his name, I think of him as 'the old fisherman'. His 'shop' is a small stand consisting of some weathered planks nailed together and balanced on a rickety sawhorse. Mostly, he sells shells, but he also has the odd bracelet and trinket. Selling things has become his main source of income since, at the age of 75, he doesn't get out to sea much anymore. His canoe, a Cottonwood Dug-Out-by-Hand Mark I model, lies on the beach, overturned, resting on a couple of logs behind his stand. He asked me to help him move it once. I was astounded at how heavy it was. It would take an extreme effort from two very strong men to move it any more than just a few feet. A little further back from the stand, hanging on a pole suspended between two braces stuck into the ground, are his ropes and blue fishing nets. On the sand beside his display stand are stacked several inflated swimming pool rafts that he rents out. One of them is pulled into the shade under the stand.

The old fisherman rests on it between customer visits, which, with all of the competition on the beach, are few and far between.

I look forward to my talks with the old fisherman and I stop by several times on each trip. He's withered and bent from years of hard work under the hot Jamaican sun. His hands are cracked and heavily callused and he has problems with one of his hips. But his eyes are happy. His clothes are worn and threadbare and his shoes are tattered. But his smile is easy and sincere and he exudes the dignity of a life well lived. The first time I saw him he reminded me of Hemingway's Santiago character from 'The Old Man and The Sea'.

Each time I talk to him I realize how very fortunate I am. His life, no doubt, has been one of struggle and hardship. Mine, by comparison, an easy walk in the park. That realization is probably what compels me to always buy something from him, even when I'm not looking for anything in particular.

Last year while I was chatting with the old fisherman, another old-timer came to join us from the next stand over. He was an old Rastaman, wearing a sun-bleached leather cap that was creased and cracked all over. It had a puffy top (stuffed full of dreadlocks) and was dyed in segments of black, yellow, green and red, the red sections having long ago faded to orange. His gray dreads cascaded down from under his cap and merged with his beard, which had also grown into long gray dreadlocks, some of them dangling halfway down his chest like ropes spilling out of a barrel. He was wearing a red and black golf shirt, two of the Rasta colors, which represent blood and hard times. We talked for a while and then I asked him, "How's business?"

"Mon, it all focked up since de all-inclusives," he replied.

"Fe true, fe true," the old fisherman nodded in agreement.

"Why's that?" I asked.

"People doan wanna come out from de fockin' all-inclusives, dey eat dere an' dere's crafts dere an' entertainment and dey doan come down de beach any more. Many years ago, business was good, evr'y day many tourists come by, a man could make a livin', but now, it all focked up and times is hawd. . . times is hawd."

For many years now, I've been a collector of shells and other things from the sea. A couple of years back, when Amy and I were visiting the Dominican Republic, she spotted a metal sphere, about the size of a ten-pin bowling ball, that had washed up on the shore. It was half sunk in the sand and covered with seaweed. How she saw it, I don't know. She plucked it out of the sand and brushed it off. "You want this?" she asked casually, knowing full well how excited I get about finding stuff on the beach. I took it from her and examined it. The metal reflected a dull sheen, it looked as if it was made from pewter. There was a weld around its equator where two halves had been joined to make the sphere. Four raised ribs ran around it at evenly spaced latitudes. Spanning the top of the sphere there was an arched tubular piece, about two inches long, attached to the sphere. On the surface of the sphere, written in raised letters, was the following:

FLOTADORES HERCULES PATENTADO

And in smaller letters:

MADE IN SPAIN

It was a fishing net float! I still have it, it's one of my prized beach finds.

I used to have a beautiful conch shell that I got in the Florida Keys back in the '70's. I would pick up that conch shell, run my fingers along its exquisite form and put to my ear to 'listen to the sea', just as I did with other shells when I was a kid. I would bury my nose deep in its chamber and breath deeply of the vestigial smells of the sea and of the animal that once inhabited it. I loved that shell, but when my ex and I separated, she kept it. Funny thing, I didn't think she even liked it.

During my previous visit to Negril I was still in the market for a replacement conch shell. I had been casually looking for a really good one for years. My perfect conch shell would be large, unblemished and its insides would be filled with ravenous pink. Most of the shells that I had inspected were either dull in color or, if they had good color, were chipped along the delicate leading edge or had nodes broken off the spirals on their backs. And every one of them had a machete-chop hole near the apex that is made to break the suction so that the beast can be extracted from his home.

In Jamaica, the conch season is closed from July 1 to October 31, but since virtually all of my visits to the island have been during the winter, there is always a large selection of shells on offer.

I checked the half dozen conch shells that the old fisherman had on display. No single one of them met the stringent requirements that I had set for replacing the perfect one that I had lost, although each one was beautiful in its own way. He pulled a couple of unfinished shells out from under the stand. These still bore the mossy coating that they have when they are taken from the sea. They needed to be scraped down before they could be put on display. Still, I didn't see anything that I liked enough to buy.

I pointed to the chop-holes in the shells that he was holding, "I would like one without a hole in it," I said.

"Dey all have de hole in dem, dats how we get de meat out," he replied.

"Yeah, I know, but I want one without the hole in it." I insisted. "And I want it pink like this one," I said, pointing to a beautifully colored shell on his stand, "and with no breaks along the lip," I said, running my finger along the edge of the one he was holding, "and with no damage to these bumps on the back. And if you do find one like that, leave the moss on it, I want to scrape it down myself," I added. "If you get one like that, I'll buy it from you. I promise."

Two days later I was walking past the old fisherman's stand. He was lying in the shade of his stand on the inflated raft. I thought he was sleeping but he spotted me, struggled to his feet and waved me over. When I got there he reached under the stand and pulled out a package and handed it to me. Wrapped in coarse paper was the perfect conch shell! It was a good size and the leading edge was beautifully flared, and except for a couple of small notches on its most delicate edge, it was chip-free. The cavity was adorned with a rich creamy shade of pink. I thanked him and paid him immediately.

I went back to the room and started on the job of scraping the moss and small deposits off of the shell. That process took more time and quite a few more Red Stripes that I had anticipated. But I enjoyed it immensely and a couple of days and several scraping sessions later, I had my perfect conch shell. I put it on the dresser in the room and admired it for the rest of my stay, although I must say that it stank up the place a little.

When it came time for the trip home, I packed it carefully in my tote bag and coddled it like a baby all the way back.

I detest going through customs on arrival back in Canada. You'd think it would be the other way around, getting back to one's homeland should probably fill one with a warm and comfy feeling. It doesn't work that way for me. To make it worse, I'm usually entering the first stages of Post Negril Syndrome (PNS) when I get there.

I'm sure that the basic qualification to become a customs officer is a surly, cold disposition. I always get the feeling that I am supposed guilty and it's up to me to proclaim and prove my innocence. A dozen rapid-fire questions are fired at me just to get back into my home country. When I crossed the border from Mexico to the States at Tijuana, I merely held my passport up high and the US Customs officer waved me through. It's different coming back into Canada. But I understand why they are there, after all, someone might try to bring in an extra bottle of rum, and if several people did that it, the tax base could collapse and the entire socialist Canadian economy would crumble.

It was with such trepidation that I presented myself to the customs officer upon landing in Toronto after my successful conch acquisition trip. He waved his hand, prompting me for my passport, all the while scrutinizing me through his grimy, dandruff-flaked glasses.

"Where are you coming from?" he demanded.

"Jamaica." (*Strike one*).

"How long have you been away?" he looks me up and down.

"A couple of weeks."

"Business or pleasure?"

"Vacation." (*Strike two*).

The questions continue; a form of institutionalized harassment. I reply cum gravitas, providing minimal answers reflecting his level of disinterest in my responses. Finally he scribbles something on my card and waves his hand vaguely indicating that I should proceed to the next step of processing somewhere behind him.

I arrive at the next checkpoint and show my card to the guy sitting there. "Go over to the baggage search area sir," he says, pointing to a row of stainless steel tables. (*Stee-rike Three! Yer Out!*) The first line of defense must have spotted something in my demeanor. Maybe a quivering bead of sweat on my upper lip, perhaps my shifty eyes. Whatever it was, he had flagged me for a detailed bag search.

I wheeled my bags into the inspection area, hoping that maybe there would be a rookie female agent waiting there, snapping on the latex gloves, who would inform me that she was going to have to do a strip search. No such luck, just another frumpy, disinterested, middle aged drone. I opened my large suitcase and he bent dutifully to his task, rooting around in my damp, soiled beach wear, looking like an old woman rummaging for bargains at a yard sale. Within moments he had expertly mined out two bottles of Appleton, which I had declared and was my meager legal limit. He lifted one of them, turning it slowly upside down, then back to upright, all the while peering intently at the contents, craning his neck to see up under the screw cap.

"What are you looking for?" I asked, perplexed.

"You just never know," he replied slowly, eyes never leaving the suspect bottle of Appleton. Such intrigue!

In due time he finished with my large suitcase, apparently satisfied that I hadn't hidden any contraband or secret Jamaican government documents within. My tote bag was next. Inspector Clouseau immediately found my perfect conch shell.

"Is this a konsh shell?" he asked, mispronouncing the word, saying 'konsh' instead of 'konk'. The look on his face was that of supreme triumph.

"Ahhh, no….the guy that I got it from told me that it was an African tree snail shell . . . but I'm not really sure," I answered, knowing immediately that I was going to lose a second perfect conch shell.

At this point I'll come clean and admit that I knew that bringing conch shells into Canada is not allowed. The queen conch is on the Canadian endangered species list, placed there by the anxious, hand wringing, left-est do-gooders who dominate Canada's self-righteous, fence sitting, socialist government. The fact that harvesting conch is legal in many free and democratic countries does not deter the intrepid Canadian legislators, who are more than eager to meddle in the affairs of other sovereign nations by exporting their particular form of eco-socialism at every opportunity. I find it maddening that I can buy queen conch meat at La Point's Fish Market in Ottawa, but I'm not allowed to bring in a souvenir conch shell from Jamaica. This is undoubtedly due to the fact that someone has done a favor or is politically connected to someone well placed in the current or previous government. Corruption and rampant patronage is not limited to some governments of Third World nations. It is alive, endemic and thriving in Canada's current parliament.

Inspector Clouseau took the conch shell, handed me a receipt and delivered me a smug mini-lecture on endangered species. I bit my tongue throughout, wanting to tell him to fuck off and mind his own business. Two weeks later I got an official notification in the mail from some obscure government department, 'The Official Office for the Identification of Stuff Confiscated by Customs', or something like that. The form letter confirmed that the confiscated shell was indeed a Strombus Gigas, ('giant spiral shell') and that it would not be returned to me.

It's probably sitting on a shelf in some bureaucrat's office.

Buzzard's Ass

'Wha no good fe breakfas, no good fe dinnah.'
Jamaican Proverb

In addition to the craft stalls that are literally everywhere along the beach, there's a very large craft market near the town that's situated in the triangle formed by the beach, the South Negril River and the beach road. This is where the highest concentration of craft vendors in Negril is found.

The market is a very crowded, ramshackle village of huts arranged on a collection of narrow, interconnected dusty lanes. I've never counted them, but there's probably upwards of a hundred stalls tightly packed into the cramped quarters of the craft village. It's a great place to visit and browse to see what's on offer. Other than some very large woodcarvings, there's really nothing in the market that can't be found along the beach or in town, but it is a unique setting. I go there to soak up the ambiance and to interact with the vendors. For me, it's a mandatory stop, even if I'm not looking for anything in particular.

The vendor's stalls open onto the hot dusty lanes of the village. Vividly colored T-shirts, wraps and other items of clothing are pegged to lines that are strung hither and to and draped on hangers that are hung from every available natural and manmade fixture. Inside the huts are woven baskets, seashells, bracelets, paintings and woodcarvings of every imaginable size and shape. And of course, ganja is readily and widely available, as is the case virtually everywhere in Negril.

With so many vendors in the village, the competition to make a sale is fierce. Visitors who stop by the craft market when the tourist traffic is low should be prepared to experience the full brunt of the vendors' efforts to entice them into the shops. People have told me that they stay away from the craft market because they find the vendors to be overly aggressive. I don't find the vendors threatening in the least, but they are incredibly persistent in their tactics. They will see someone exiting a shack three stalls down from their own and call out to the person waving them over, extolling the virtues of their merchandise and beseeching each passer by to come into their stall. Some will come out into the lane and stop in front of visitors, insisting that they come in, just to look at their displays.

"Come an' see my t'ings . . jus' look at dem, it won't cost you anyt'ing to look mi frien' . . jus' come in an' look around out of respect for me," is a variation of the common plea. "I give you special price today, for you only," is another.

Once inside, beware of the 'push play'. Here's how it works. If a customer shows more than a passing interest in an item, some vendors will pick it up and put it in their hands. Then they ask what the person is willing to pay for it. "Go ahead, jus' make me an offer, what do you t'ink it's worth?"

If the customer answers that they're just browsing and attempts to hand the item back or put it down, the vendor will gently push their hand away or lift it back up from the table, with the item still in it, all the while encouraging the person to make an offer. This is actually quite an effective tactic. I've seen it used and have been subjected to it myself. In many cases, once the item is placed in the person's hands, they will end up holding it until they buy it; the item never leaves their hands. My defense for this and all other tactics is to tell the vendor that I'm here with 'the wife', even when I'm not, and that I can't buy anything without her approval. The male vendors seem to understand this and upon hearing it immediately cease their sales pitch.

The asking price for items in the craft market is generally double what the bottom-line price will be. However I rarely haggle down to the bottom line. If I like an item and it's of good quality and craftsmanship, I'll pay a premium for it. I have a tender spot for Jamaica and Jamaicans and if I pay five or ten dollars more for an item than I could have eventually haggled it down to, it doesn't bother me in the least.

The craft village can be entered via the beach by crossing through an opening in the frost fence that is erected there. This brings one onto the slightly meandering 'main drag' of the village. The two stalls that are located immediately inside the fence are unremarkable in their appearance, however I always stop and talk to the vendors that run them. The shack on the south side is run by an old veteran who, I believe, lives in the back. He's tall, wiry, dreadlocked and has a crusty personality. If browsers don't buy something from him, he takes it personally and gets right pissed off. I think this is a ploy that he plays at the last minute when customers exit his shack empty handed. It probably works sometimes. The fellow directly across from the crusty-man is the antipathy of the other. He's also dreadlocked with a full beard, but younger, heavy set and jovial with happy eyes, an easy laugh and a friendly smile. Almost like a young Jamaican Santa Claus without the red suit.

Today I'm in the craft market looking for a Bob Marley T-shirt, extra large and tie-dyed in reggae colors. Next week is Bob Marley's birthday celebration and I'm in need of a new shirt for the occasion. I'm being picky because I know that if I go into enough shops, I'll eventually find exactly what I'm looking for. I'd thought that I'd found one at the crusty-man's shop, but when I tried it on it was a smidgen too small. I took it off and handed it back to him, he reluctantly took it but harrumphed and told me that it would be okay and that it would stretch a little as I wore it. Then he muttered something about 'I an' I' and 'sufferin' and waved his hands around in the air as I left.

The stalls in the village are roughly arranged in departments based on what they are selling. Most numerous are the mixed selection stalls where there's a cross section of items. Generally, I find these the least interesting to browse. Then there are the specialty stalls. Along the dusty 'avenue' that parallels the beach, most of the stalls are run by ladies who specialize in clothing, sarongs, baskets and small jewelry items.

I make my way down the 'main drag' passing a couple more stalls and then turn left down the clothing avenue. As I pass each stall the ladies greet me with hellos and friendly smiles and invite me to come in and look around. Of all the vendors in the big craft market, the ladies on this avenue are the most pleasant and use the least pressure to sell. I stop in front of one stall that appears to be unattended. I walk a few steps into it, and when I take my sunglasses off I see a large woman who is up on a stool dusting some carvings.

"Oh!" she says, climbing down, "I didn't see you come in." She turns to greet me and stops, frozen in her tracks, looking at me with a sudden smile and bright eyes. "You're goin' to live a long and healt'y life sir!" she announces.

For a moment I'm taken aback, beginning to suspect that I'm being softened for the sales pitch that is about to come.

"Me?" I answer, "why do you say that?"

"Oh yes," she assures me still smiling and nodding her head, "I see t'ings 'bout people. I can see it in your aura, you goin' to live to be a very old man."

I'm not sure how to react because I really don't want to live to be a very old man, but I suddenly comprehend the situation. There are many people in Jamaica, mostly women, who claim to have special powers to 'see' things that others don't. Somewhat similar, but nowhere near as contrived, to a North American fortune teller but spiced up with a mysterious hint of Creole and a dash of voodoo.

Jamaicans also have their witch doctors, although 'witch doctor' and 'voodoo' are terms that they do not ascribe to. Rather, the practice is referred to as 'Obeah'. Obeah is an ancient craft that was brought to Jamaica by African slaves. Obeah was utilized as a means of communication and was used to cast spells on the slave masters. The plantation owners, who didn't understand Obeah but recognized it as a threat, attempted to stamp it out. Obeah also served as a strong slave-culture rallying factor and as a symbol of rebellion against the oppressors. Many of the major slave uprisings in Jamaica were influenced by the practice of Obeah and several were led by or had Obeah men as instigators. In spite of the slave drivers' efforts to snuff it out, the practice of Obeah survived in Jamaica, passed down from father to son, uncle to nephew and grandfather to grandson. And it has persisted to this day, predominantly in the countryside in the eastern tracts of the island where the most powerful of the Obeah men are said to reside.

Although it's officially illegal to practice Obeah in Jamaica, and anyone found practicing it could be arrested, the law is seldom enforced.

Obeah men fall into two categories, good and evil. One visits the 'evil' Obeah man to have a spell cast upon one's enemies. If one finds that things are suddenly and inexplicably going bad, it's possible that an enemy has had an Obeah man cast a spell. Then it's time to visit the 'good' Obeah man and have the spell taken off. Thus, the good and evil Obeah men keep each other in business.

One does not undertake a visit to the Obeah man on a whim. To the believer, the Obeah man is dreadful. He knows that you are coming and what you are coming to ask of him (or what's wrong with you) before you do. As you approach his yard, if he doesn't want to see you, he will come out of his house and chase you away, yelling and flailing his arms as you fearfully retreat.

This situation is doubly bad, not only have you been routed, but neighbors and townspeople keep track of the comings and goings at the Obeah man's house. They may shy away from someone who has visited the Obeah man, lest he be calling down a spell on them, and at the very least, gossip will start, and no good can come of small town gossip.

So, one visits the Obeah man only after all alternate avenues have]been exhausted. The Obeah man is a measure of last resort.

Obeah men are not to be confused with 'bush doctors', who are herbalists. The bush doctor might also practice just a smidgen of 'white magic'. Bush doctors concoct various herbal remedies from plants and roots and whatnot, but certain of them might also be called on to perform other acts.

If an unwanted duppy is hanging around the house and making a nuisance of himself - - - who do you call? Bush Doctor! The bush doctor will bring a live goat into the house, where he will hang it from a handy beam and slaughter it right then and there by slicing its throat. All of the blood that drips from the goat must be caught, not one drop can touch the floor or the effect will be ruined. The bush doctor will dip his finger in the goat's blood and inscribe a cross on the forehead of the master of the house. Presto! The duppy is banished. This procedure can also be used in an attempt to cure an illness that has not responded to the treatment of a physician. In a variation, the bones of the slaughtered goat may be harvested, cleaned and placed in the house for a period of time.

Prior to pouring the foundation or erecting the first pillar on a new construction site, or commencing the laying of the bed for a new road, it is tradition in Jamaica to slaughter a goat or a cow on the grounds. In this case the blood from the animal is allowed to splash on the earth, and the more widely distributed, the better. It is believed that the blood consecrates the site, banishing evil spirits and imbuing it with good fortune. It is especially important to do this if there has been an accident or if someone has died at the site. Bush doctors may be called upon to perform the ceremony. At a recent inauguration of a construction site for a new hotel on the beach, eight goats and two cows were hoisted up and hanged, head down, from the branches of trees and from tripods erected for the purpose on the grounds. Their throats were cut and the blood sprayed and splashed widely upon the earth. The animals were then cut up and the meat was cooked on the premises at the ensuing celebration. A bloody good time was had by all.

Now, what does one do with the entrails and the heads and hoofs of the slaughtered goats? Make up a pot of Mannish Water, of course! Mannish Water is a traditional Jamaican dish, prepared for special events such as Christmas, anniversaries and big family get-togethers. The recipe varies, but if you're interested in cooking up your own pot of Mannish Water, try this;

Ingredients:
- The complete entrails of one goat,
- The head of the goat, intact,
- The legs of the goat, from the knees down,
- Spices and vegetables to taste.

Instructions:
- Cut the stomach free of the entrails, empty it of its contents, clean it, chop it up into little chunks and throw it into a big pot of water.

- Use the handle-end of a wooden spoon to turn the intestines inside out, clean them, cut them up and add to the pot.
- Cut the liver, heart, spleen and remaining entrails into small chunks and throw them into the pot.
- Grab the head, pull on the tongue and cut it out. Chop it up and put it in the pot.
- Crack open the skull and scoop the brains out, throw them to the dogs.
- Pop the eyeballs out of the scull with a butter knife, do not add them to the pot, but put them aside, they make delicious appetizers.
- Hold the head, shins, knuckles and hoofs over a hot open fire until the fur and whiskers are singed off, the carbonization adds to the taste. Add the complete head to the pot, for effect, but chop the legs up with a sturdy cleaver before throwing them in.
- Add chopped yams, scallions, green bananas, squash, onions, breadfruit and whatever else suits your palate.
- Spice to taste (garlic, thyme, scotch bonnet pepper, allspice)
- Bring to a boil and them simmer for a few hours.
  Bon appétit!

It's called Mannish Water because it is believed to contain manly power. For that reason, it is said that the entrails and bits and pieces of a 'ram-goat' makes the very best Mannish Water.

Back to the craft market. I look around in the shop of the soothsayer for my Bob Marley T-shirt, but don't find anything that suits my needs. So I leave, without having been subjected to any sales pitch and feeling strangely uplifted.

Along the northern edge of the craft market are the stalls of the serious wood carvers. A walk through this section treats one to sights of the most exquisite creations, the likes of which exist nowhere else in Negril. Some of the carvings are massive, standing five feet tall and weighing several hundred pounds. There are large renderings of eagles, lions, Rasta heads, and many different styles and types of fish. My favorites are the carvings that depict small schools of fish.

On every visit to this part of the market I sneak a peek into the backs of the shops. There the craftsmen work, bent over pieces that are in various stages of completion, chipping, chiseling sanding and polishing.

Where I live the air gets extremely dry in the winter. Over the many visits that I've made to the Caribbean I've brought many a woodcarving home. It has been my experience that the only wood that is guaranteed not to crack and split during arid winter conditions is cedar.   I've mentioned this to carvers who are pitching pieces carved from other types of wood and they invariably tell me that they use dried wood and that there is no need to worry about cracking and splitting. But in Jamaica's humid climate, it's difficult to completely dry the wood and if the carving has a lot of grain in it, it's probably going to split when placed in very dry conditions. I know, I've had several that have done so, including one named Irie, whom you'll meet later.

The craft market can also be entered from Norman Manley Boulevard (the beach road). When walking northbound toward the beach from the roundabout in town, the entrance is immediately after the bridge over the South Negril River. It's down a steep slope of hard packed dirt interlaced with roots, rocks and crude steps that have been gouged into the embankment. At the bottom of the embankment is a small creek spanned by a makeshift rickety bridge made from old planks that have been thrown over it. If it sounds challenging, it is, a little.   Entering the market via the steep embankment brings one onto the other end of the village's 'main drag' and into the 'produce' area. Here the stands display an assortment of fruits, vegetables and drinks.

The craft market can also be entered via the road that comes in a little further north off of the beach road, but it isn't as interesting as the beach and embankment approaches.

My search for the ultimate Bob Marley T-shirt continues. I circle the outer avenue of the craft market, passing the produce stands, and enter the 'main drag' from that end. A short distance up the lane I'm hailed by an older Jamaican fellow sitting on a stump outside of his small bar. "Come in from de sun an' 'ave a cool drink. You look hot mon," he says.

I am hot; the sun is relentless today and there is no breeze within the dusty confines of the village. A cool drink sounds appealing so I take him up on his offer. I take a seat at the rudimentary bar and try to decide if it's going to be a Red Stripe or a Ting. Finally I decide on a Red Stripe.

When I'm about half done, the barman asks me, "Would you like to try somet'ing stronger?"

"What did you have in mind?" I reply, suspecting that he'll offer me a shot of white 151 over proof rum, affectionately know as OP.

"Have you ever tried jon-crow-batty?" he asks.

"Jon-crow what?"

"Jon-crow-batty! It a strong, strong rum, straight from de bottom of de barrel. It will light you up mon!" he says, pumping a closed fist.

"Stronger than OP?" I ask. Back home we call the uncut and un-aged rum from the bottom of the barrel 'swish'.

"Yesss mon! De strong-est!" he assures me.

"What do you call it again?" I ask, still not sure of the name.

"John . . Crow . . Batty," he repeats slowly. "You know de black buzzard? We call him 'John Crow'."

A light comes on and the meaning of the name suddenly becomes clear to me. John Crow is the Jamaican name for a buzzard. No problem. Except Jamaicans look down on the buzzard because it eats rotting carrion, so I'm a little suspicious. And I'm not too sure about the 'batty' either, which is the Jamaican term for backside or ass. I first heard the term 'batty' used in the patois 'batty-mon', which is a rather derogatory term for gay men. So, if my etymology is correct, 'John Crow Batty' parsed into the Queen's English, is literally 'Buzzard's Ass'. Which doesn't sound too appealing.

I'm not sure, perhaps it's a bit of *when in Rome do as the Romans*' or maybe a touch of sunstroke, but I say, "OK, let's have some of John-crow's-batty, or whatever you call it."

The barman seems delighted and ducks below the counter, coming up with a Finzi coconut rum bottle. But it's not Finzi. I have some personal experience with Finzi, enough to know that it's clear. This bottle is filled with a translucent, somewhat murky, brown liquid. He pours me a little shot in a tumbler-sized glass.

"Pour another one and join me," I say, not wanting to go blind by myself. He does so, we clink glasses and I tip mine back. The second that the rum touches my tongue, I know that I've made a bad mistake, but I force it down. It is the vilest tasting thing that has ever crossed my tongue. It sears its way down my throat leaving a scorched path of raw flesh in its wake. Tears fill my eyes. I gag-choke and have a coughing attack that lasts a full minute.

When I recover somewhat I look at the barman through tear-blurred eyes and try to tell him what I think of his 'buzzard's ass'. All that emerges from my shocked vocal cords is a froggy croak.

"Are you okay mon?" the barman asks, still holding his glass. I can't speak so I nod in response. He tips his glass and drains it. Then he slams the glass down on the bar, snaps his head to one side, blinks once and licks his grinning lips as if he has just downed a shot of a fine, sixty-year old, single malt scotch.

"Ahhhhh, john----crow----batty," he says, pumping his fist three times, once for the 'john', another for the 'crow' and the last for the 'batty'.

Still unable to speak, I give him a little salute and leave the bar, older but wiser.

The Jerks

'Yu dam lagga head bud!'
Jamaican Saying

Negril is a magnet for the atypical. Characters somehow gravitate here and many have taken up permanent residence. This is definitely not the Disney World or Las Vegas crowd.

Take, for example, the characters that are bunking in the room next to mine, Jim and Randy. They're a couple of good ole' boys from the Toronto area. I think of them as 'The Jerks' but in a non-derisive, kind of sympathetic way. They arrived in Negril on the same day as I, but on a later flight. I was in my room writing in my journal. All was quiet. Then Jim and Randy entered the room next door. *'Commandeered'* might be a better word. As soon as the door slammed behind them there commenced a long series of resounding thumps, bangs and knockings interspersed with raucous laughter, singing and snatches of loud conversation. The toilet flushed several times and the shower ran on and on. The boys were getting settled in. Even though there was only the two of them, they raised a commotion that was more befitting a group of sailors just released on liberty.

Eventually, the noises subsided and the boys emerged onto the patio. "Let's get some fuckin' weed man," said one of them, whose voice I later recognized as Jim's.

"Yeah, an' I could use a few more beers too," added Randy.

Jim and Randy are here for a good time, which requires only three ingredients; booze and ganja, these in stupefying quantities, and pussy, anyhow, anywhere and as much as humanly possible. Although indications are that they haven't had much luck on the latter so far.

They both work in the automobile industry. Randy drives an auto parts delivery truck and Jim works on a vehicle assembly line, specializing in doors. Jim's right arm is noticeably more muscular than his left. When I asked him about it he said it was because he used his right arm on the assembly line all day long, wielding a large rubber mallet, pounding widget 'A' into slot 'B' of part 'C', or something like that.

Because their room is right next to mine we cross paths often, but I never see them before noon, when they emerge bleary-eyed and stumbling from their dank, shuttered room, which has become the local den of iniquity. A couple of days ago, I was on their patio, swapping stories, when I peeked into their room through the open door. I was appalled. It was a disaster area! I truly pity the chambermaid who got stuck with cleaning up their mess. The interior of their room resembled a homeless camp, littered with clothes, wet towels, empty beer and rum bottles and food containers. The smell wafting out was a miasma of rancid beer farts and stale cigarette smoke laced with traces of body odor and puke.

Out on the patio, the boom box that they brought down with them constantly screeches out heavy metal, head-banging music. I use the term 'music' in the extreme liberal sense, there is nothing more out of place than heavy metal on a quiet, sunny Jamaican afternoon. The boys are equipped with one of those plastic coolers on wheels that they pull behind them everywhere they go. It has a *'Hooter's'* sticker on the side and it's filled with Red Stripes, rum and coke.

Jim is the leader of the duo, Randy kind of tags along. They remind me of that old cartoon with the two dogs. One a big loud bulldog, I think his name was 'Chopper', and the other a yippy little thing that was always prancing around Chopper's feet and asking him, in an excited squeaky voice, "Where're we goin' now Chopper? Huh, Huh? Hey Chopper? Hey Chopper? What we doin' now, huh Chopper?" Randy always wears the same T-shirt, a white one with a big yellow Corona beer label on the front.

Jim, the older of the two, is on his first trip to the Caribbean. His hair is longish and he has an earring in his left earlobe. He wears a goatee and has several tattoos on his shoulders and back that are too faded to clearly distinguish, although one of them might be a bear or perhaps a naked woman, I'm not sure. Jim is a heavy smoker with a deep, gravelly voice. He always has a lit fag in his hand. Anyone within five feet of him is accosted by the cigarette smell leaching from his pores. He wakes up in the middle of the night with booming volleys of hacking smoker's cough that I hear through the wall. Jim's sole beach wear consists of a pair of blue jean cut-offs that are three sizes too small for him, revealing a large valley of hairy cleavage when he bends over. (Please, say NO! to crack.) Today he is sporting a 3rd degree sunburn because he passed out on the beach yesterday afternoon. Looking at his scarlet back I imagine sticking one of those big meat forks into it and seeing the juice ooze out of his body, running clear. 'I think he's done, Honey!'

"Hey Jim, nice tan you got there ..... a bit red though, does it hurt much?" I asked.

"Aww, it'll be gone by tomorrow," he assured me, poking his finger into his rather substantial gut, making a little island of white floating in a massive sea of red.

When Jim gets up at the crack of noon, appearing on the patio in his natty beach wear, he reaches into the cooler-on-wheels and fishes out at bottle of orange juice (the kind the beach boys sell), opens it and downs the entire contents in four enormous gulps. "AAHHHHHH!" he says, wiping his mouth with the back of his hand and favoring all within earshot with a resonating belch. Then he sits down, lights a smoke, and is set for the day.

That's usually how it works, except today he took a huge gulp from a bottle that had gone off. Cleverly planning ahead, Jim had bought a whole week's supply of O.J. the day after they arrived. They had let their little cooler run out of ice and, in the heat on the patio, it didn't take long for the inevitable to happen. The fermented O.J. got as far as the back of Jim's throat, then was forcefully propelled out of his mouth in a big, coughing spray that arced clear over the front garden and splattered down on the walkway ten feet away.

"Awwww, fuck man, that's gross!" he roared, then quickly opened a Red Stripe and guzzled half of it to clear his palette.

After the ruckus of their moving-in night, I considered requesting a room change. But I'm glad I didn't because, frankly, I couldn't buy the kind of entertainment that they are providing me. I guess I'm living vicariously through them because I look forward to seeing them every day, just to observe their antics and to hear what kind of trouble they've gotten into.

They've hooked up with a Jamaican guy, who tours them around in an old wreck of a car that's pulling up in front of their room at all hours of the night. They've covered a hell of a lot of ground in the time that they've been here and they're having a blast. They know where all the cash machines in town are located, as they have to visit one every day. Randy had some cash flow problems and had to call home to get some more money transferred into his account so he could access it from down here.

Yesterday I was sitting on the patio, enjoying the quiet of the late afternoon, reading a book and sipping on a Stripe. The breeze was rustling through the coconut fronds, the birds were singing to each other. It was comfortably hot and, all considered, it was a typically idyllic Jamaican afternoon. Then I heard the junker that The Jerks ride around in come rumbling down the lane. It lurched to a stop in front of their room and gave out several dying 'FFUUTTT. . . FFUUTTT. . . FFUUTTs' before it finally expired. I closed my book and put it aside, knowing that the calmness of the day was about to be brutally and irrevocably shattered.

Jim opened the front door; ganja smoke roiled forth. "Hey man, you should'a fuckin' come with us, man," he bellowed as he stumbled out of the wreck.

Randy attempted to climb out of the back seat but only got halfway up and then fell flat on his ass. Both of them were totally wasted. Jim helped Randy over to a chair on the patio. Their Jamaican driver nodded to me, flopped down on the patio, and hung his head between his knees.

Jim continued, "We went to this big fuckin' ganja field man, you should'a seen it, ganja trees taller'n me and so thick you couldn't fuckin' walk through them man!"

Jim had made the discovery, as many of his ilk have, that the word 'fuckin'' added that extra *je ne sais quoi* to conversation and could be injected pretty well anywhere in a sentence.

Randy reached into his pocket and pulled out a balled up tissue that he carefully unfolded. "Look at this man, n'tit beautiful!" He passed me a big marijuana leaf that spanned my entire palm and outstretched fingers.

"Yeah, an' we took some pictures to show the guys back home," he said, "just 'n case they don't fuckin' believe us."

Later I found out that they were going to get the pictures developed in Jamaica because they were worried that if they got them done back in Canada they would get busted. I can picture it, Jim walking out of the local Wal-Mart after picking up his photos and being nabbed by two big RCMP officers (they always get their man, you know) as he climbs into his battered old half ton truck. They take him down to the station and book him for illegal trafficking in ganja photographs. *'But they're only fuckin' pictures man!'*

Last night there was a big reggae party at Bourbon Beach, just two properties down the beach from the hotel. I went over there with Jim and Randy, hung around until about midnight and then came back to my room. The closed shutters were no impediment to the extraordinarily loud music from Bourbon Beach, but eventually I did fall asleep. At about 2:00am I was wakened by the sounds of a noisy argument coming from The Jerks' patio. I rolled out of bed and peeked through the shutters. Jim was there, engaged in a heated discussion with a young, good looking and well-dressed Jamaican lady. She was giving him hell, hands on her hips, really leaning into it and yelling at him. Jim 'shushed' her a couple of times, glancing around at the other rooms.

This afternoon I ran into Jim on the beach and asked him, "What was that argument on your patio last night?"

"Oh, you heard that, eh?" he replied taking a big drag on his cigarette.

"Kind of hard not to. What was the problem?"

"Well, I pick this chick up at the bonfire, right?"

"Yeah," I nodded, there were a lot of people hanging around the big bonfire on the beach in front of the Risky Business disco last night.

"Yeah . . . so I take her back to the room," he takes another big drag, "an' when we get to the patio she tells me that she wants a fuckin' hundred bucks . . . . US!"

"So she's a hooker," I said.

"Yeah! But she doesn't say anything until we get back to the fuckin' room!"

"Jim - - - are you telling me that you didn't *know* she was a hooker when you invited her back to the room?" I asked.

"Fuck no man!"

"C'mon, did you think she was going for your dashing good looks?"

"Fuck you man. I didn't know, honest."

"Yeah right. So what happened?"

"Ahh...we argued for a while and then she calmed down and said she would do me for eighty bucks."

Jim and Randy are planning on getting some more cash and renting motor bikes later this afternoon. I must remember to tell them where the Negril Medical Clinic is.

Dutch Treat

'Alligator lay egg, but 'im noh fowl.'
Jamaican Proverb

There's a couple from Holland traveling with their 23 year-old daughter who are staying at the resort. The husband, Derik, is tall and very thin and has a long braided ponytail hanging down his back. His wife, Anik, is a nice, quiet and somewhat introverted woman. Their daughter, Hailey, who is named after Hailey's comet for some reason that was never fully explained, is tall, slim, blonde, blue-eyed and very good looking. She is also extremely intelligent. (I know this because she told me so.) I think of this family as 'The Dutch People'.

The Dutch People stay close to the resort. They have a spot picked out under one of the green canvas gazebos that Legends has erected on the beach and they claim the lounges there early every morning by tying towels to them. This is a strange and annoying practice that many beach goers, especially Europeans, are wont to engage in. They will appoint one of their party as a 'lounge staker'. It is this person's duty to rise with the sun, get down to the beach and claim a number of lounges in a specific location on behalf of the group. Mission completed, the appointee can march blearily back to bed to rise later at a more respectable hour, all the while sleeping contentedly with the knowledge that the claim has been safely staked. However, I am a claim jumper, and a marked but unoccupied lounge is fair game when the need strikes me.

The Dutch People spend pretty well the whole day on their stake. I stop by and talk with them whenever I see them sitting on their claim, which has been every day so far.

This morning while heading back to the room after an ocean dip, I heard Hailey, the daughter, calling my name. She was at their 'camp' arranging towels on the lounges and when I looked in her direction, she waved me over. I saw that she was by herself.

"How are you this morning Thomas?" she asked, her voice lilting with a slight Dutch accent. Her long blonde hair was hanging loose. She was wearing a hibiscus-patterned sundress with billowy skirts and a bodice that was tight to her slender frame from the waist up.

"Fair to middlin'," I said.

"What's 'middlin'?"

"Oh --- it means I'm OK. How're you doing?"

"Middlin' too," she said, flashing an unexpected brilliant smile. The moment drew out and my mental metronome skipped a couple of beats. Then I had one of those, *'Ohhh, if I were twenty years younger'* pangs that I have occasionally since I've been looking at forty from the downhill side.

Consider the plight of the poor male for a moment; he struggles through his life, coping every day with a seemingly endless series of strong primal urgings to mate, through no fault of his own of course. Although well past the age where he should rightly be producing children, his parts are still all present and accounted for and connected and functioning as originally specified. Would that there was a male 'woman-o-pause', the life of the libido beleaguered male would be so much simpler.

"What's up today?" I asked, still feeling a little off balance.

"Well, I think we are just going to stay here and get some sun this morning . . . and then go into town later and get a couple of bottles of rum," she replied.

With that she kicked off her sandals, removed her sunglasses, then clutched her skirts and pulled the sundress up over her head. But it didn't go all the way, it bunched up and stuck just under her ribs. She was wearing red bikini bottoms.

"Oh, damn it!" she said, dropping her skirts and stomping her foot in the sand, "this dress is so tight on me!"

Being a chivalrous fellow, I have never passed up the opportunity to come to the aid of a damsel in distress and I wasn't about to start here in Negril.

"Here, let me help," I offered. I have some experience removing clothing from the female body, having started in earnest when I was sixteen.

I moved close to her and she raised her arms above her head. I reached down, grabbed her skirts, and without too much difficulty and with a little bit of wriggling from Hailey, the dress was up, over her head, and off.

She gave her head a shake and let her hands drop into the thick of her hair, fluffing it, all the while keeping her elbows up. She was topless.

I confess I had previously noted her rather magnificent chest while she was sunning, but let me remind you, this is in accordance with my original programming, so no apologies, excuses or rationalizations are offered or inferred.

However, it was one thing to casually brush her bare chest with my eyes from five feet away, but quite another thing to have it brushing up against my own bare chest. Her nipples stuck up and out like the tips of the barrels of Yosemity Sam's six-shooters. She canted her head back a little, cocked her hips, looked me straight in the eyes with those big blue peepers, smiled sweetly and said, *"Dank je wel."*

This time my mental metronome stalled out completely. The devil perched on my left shoulder, let's call him Beelzebub, who wakens at moments like this, whispered in my ear;

Beelzebub: *'Hey, she's putting the moves on yah mon!'*

The angel who sits on my right shoulder (naturally), let's call her Virtue, who invariably counters any suggestions that Beelzebub offers, chimed in;

Virtue: *'Come on! You are old enough to be her dad, dude! You're imagining it, no way she has any interest in you whatsoever.'*

Beelzebub: *'Then why, pray tell, is she standing there in front of you, showing off her tits and smiling at you like that?'*

Virtue: *'Forget it, act your age, put your eyeballs back in their sockets, get your act together and say "Your welcome" like the gentleman that you aren't.'*

Slowly my synapses began to fire again and I was on the verge of backing away and saying 'You're welcome' when I heard, from behind me, "Ahem!"

It was Hailey's mom.

Hailey immediately stood up straight, dropped her hands to her sides and transformed from a temptress back into the proper young lady who was traveling with her parents. And there I was, holding her dress in my hand, looking like a forty-something lecher who had been caught with his finger in the honey pot, which was pretty close to the truth.

Fortunately, the Dutch are very open minded about such things and Hailey's mom, assuming that whatever it was that she had walked into was all my doing, gave me a stern look and nothing more was ever said or alluded to.

Hailey never 'came on' to me again, so she probably never did in the first place. In fact, she never even looked at me with anything other than a normal 'how you doin' look. So I probably did just imagine the whole thing . . . probably just a middle-aged man's daytime fantasy . . . . probably.

But there's something in the air in Negril, a sub-rosa resonance. Karmic connections tease loose and float free, live ends brush one another . . . sometimes fusing.

Anything is possible.

A couple of hours after the dress incident, I was sitting on the beach, passing some time in the sun talking with Derik. He rolls his own cigarettes, and was in the process of rolling one up when a group of Negril's finest spotted him while on their regular beach patrol.

There are two types of police patrols on the beach, and I've heard that there are also undercover patrols, but I've never spotted them. The most visible are the foot patrols, usually two or three officers in a group, walking slowly down the beach, taking everything in and stopping periodically to talk, mostly with the local beach people. They make entries in their small brown leather notebooks as they go.

A foot patrol is usually three members led by one that is in full uniform. The leader's uniform consists of a black-billed police cap, pulled low over the eyes, encircled by a red band with a shiny silver badge affixed front dead center; a crisp gray-blue short sleeved shirt with regulation creases, open at the neck, and epaulettes bearing rank markings; a pair of long, tapered black pants with wide red stripes running down the sides and a broad red cummerbund. There's a black belt from which are suspended a holstered sidearm, a radio and a pair of handcuffs. And to complete the ensemble, a natty pair of highly polished black shoes.   The effect is a somewhat officious British look with a slightly relaxed Caribbean influence.

Accompanying the leader are one or two 'red caps'. They are dressed less formally, wearing jaunty red berets, blue short sleeved shirts and matching pants with cargo pockets. Hooked to their utility belt is a very functional looking baton. The red caps usually wear a cool pair of shades. Patrols such as these are very common on the beach and there is no doubt that their presence keeps a lid on things. The proper name for the island's police is the Jamaican Constabulary Force.

There is also the beach buggy patrol. They drive up and down the beach, day and night, in an oversized green Kawasaki 4 X 4 mule with 'POLICE – Dial 119' written across the front and back. Yes, 1-1-9, it is not a misprint. There are usually three of them on board, but they don't wear uniforms and don't appear armed, although I am sure they are. The buggy is really easy to spot because it's usually being chased by a pack of barking beach dogs.

Back to Derik and his smokes. The trio that spotted him came over to see what he was up to. Obviously, they figured that he was blatantly rolling a spliff in full public view and I believe they intended to bust him right then and there. The leader of the group leaned over and said, "What you got in the pouch mister?" He put his hand out, pointing at the pouch on the beach lounge and made the 'gimme' gesture with his fingers.

"It's tobacco," Derik said, handing the pouch to the officer.

The police officer opened it and took a sniff. "Pass me the cigarette," he said, doing the 'gimme' thing again at the cigarette that Derik had just rolled. The red caps were standing to the side of the officer, scanning the beach. One of them was playing with the handcuffs dangling from his belt. He was pushing one of the bracelets closed, *'Criiik,* and then pulling it open again, *Criiik'*. He did this over and over again.

"It's just tobacco," Derik said again, passing his cigarette to the officer.

The officer sniffed the cigarette. Satisfied, he passed the pouch and cigarette back to Derik and straightened up. He nodded to the other two and the group turned and departed without saying another word.

The Dreadful Lion

Babylon system is the vampire,
Sucking the blood of the sufferers.
Bob Marley – 'Babylon System'

The days seem to glide by in Negril, each one flowing easily into the next.   Here, time has a slippery, seamless texture. What day is it anyhow? I have to think. I believe it's Wednesday but it could easily be Thursday. And what did I do yesterday? I can't say for sure. Back home the days march by, frame by rigid frame, I always know exactly what time it is, and I know what I'll be doing and when I'll be doing it days in advance, precisely, by the hour. Here, well, things are fluid. Time doesn't tick by in measured lurches, it slides. But it's amazing how quickly it can slide. I can't believe that I've been here for three days already. And I haven't even done anything yet!

My only real assignment this week is to go up to the Point Village resort, where Amy and I will be getting married next week, to meet with the wedding coordinator and ensure that everything is in order. I plan to get that done tomorrow before a couple more days sneak by.

It's mid morning and I'm off to The Pickled Parrot, a cliff-side restaurant and bar located in the West End. It's a very long walk from Legends so I'm planning on taking a taxi.

Nothing could be easier than getting a taxi in Negril. There's no need to phone ahead, simply walk out onto the side of the road and one will be there within thirty seconds. There are two types of cabs for hire, the licensed legal taxis, equipped with red license plates bearing a 'PP' prefix, and the entrepreneurs who are out driving around in the family car hoping to earn a few bucks. Negril taxis are not equipped with roof signs, meters or company paint jobs. Nor do they have two-way radios since there is no central dispatch. One should not expect anything but basic transportation when taking a Negril cab. The cabs are all compact car size and many of them are wrecks.

I walk out to the street in front of the hotel. Immediately across the road is a taxi stand where several 'red plates' are parked. The drivers are out of their cars standing in the shade of a clump of bushes. Dance hall vibes are blasting out from one of the cars. One of the drivers spots me even before I've exited the hotel gate. "TAXI?" he calls out, beckoning with an outstretched arm. I shake my head, I want to walk a bit before catching a ride.

I plan on going as far as the Cheap Bite restaurant, about a five-minute walk, before grabbing a cab.

About halfway there I find what I'm looking for, a pushcart parked in the shade of some tall trees. It's loaded with pineapples, oranges and coconuts. The pineapples are small and the skins on the oranges are green and tinged with brown but, having eaten the local fruit, I know that the pineapples are sweet and the oranges are firm and bursting with juice.

"How much for the coconuts?" I ask the vendor.

"One hundred for de jelly an' one-fifty for de ripe," he answers.

"I'll take one of each."

He hands me a ripe hard-shelled coconut. I hold it to my ear and shake it, the milk inside sloshes heavily from side to side. I place the coconut inside my backpack, it will be cracked open tomorrow morning at breakfast.

The vendor has a big green coconut on the ground and is hacking the top of it off with his machete. He makes the last cut carefully, opening the top of the liquid filled cavity within. He puts a straw in the top and presents the big coconut to me. It's about the size of a five-pin bowling ball. I take a sip, cool, fresh, sweet liquid slips down my throat.

"How do you know when the green coconuts are ready to be cut?" I ask him.

"We look for de brown an' gold color patches on de skin . . . like dis," he says, pointing to a telltale spot on the side of the coconut I'm holding.

I pay him and continue on my way. As soon as I step back onto the road a car slows beside me, the horn beeps and the driver leans out the window, "Taxi?" he shouts. I shake my head and continue down the road, sipping on the jelly coconut.

Twenty seconds pass, another car slows, the horn sounds, "Taxi?" the driver asks, I shake my head. Shortly, I arrive in front of Cheap Bite. I've eaten here several times, the food is good, served in large portions and the prices are reasonable. I dump my now empty coconut into a trash barrel. Now I'm ready for a cab. I cross the road to get on the left side. A car approaching on the opposite side of the road slows. I wave it over and it does a screeching U-turn and comes to a neat stop beside me. It's kind of dilapidated and I note that it doesn't have red plates.

Since there are no meters in the taxis, fares are negotiated prior to stepping into the car. Haggling over price is expected. Pity the poor uninformed tourist who jumps into a Negril cab and gets underway, or worse, all the way to destination, without confirming the fare. I always negotiate the price first and I use a rough rule of thumb of about $50 Jamaican per mile, per person.

I lean in the half opened passenger side window and ask, "How much to the Pickled Parrot?"

"Four hundred J," the driver tells me.

"I'll give you one-fifty," I said, knowing that we would settle on two hundred.

"No mon, I can't make no livin' at one-fifty!" The driver has a pained expression on his face, as if I have insulted his dignity. This is a sure sign that I am at his absolute minimum.

"OK, two hundred," I say.

He lets out an exasperated sign, "Get in mon." I climb in, sit down and promptly hit bottom on the clapped-out passenger seat. We get underway and I reach for the window handle to lower it completely but there is no crank. Instead, a pair of vice grips are clamped to the shaft. I twirl the vice grips and the window reluctantly lurches the rest of the way down.

"You like Buju mon?" the driver asks. Buju Banton is one of Jamaica's premier pop stars. He sings a fusion of reggae, dance hall and island rap, which is intriguing but a bit too far from the roots reggae that I prefer.

"Yeah mon," I answer, just 'cause I like to say it. The driver turns up the volume on the stereo mounted under the dash which appears to be the newest and most functional piece of equipment on the car. We trundle up the cliff road, dodging potholes, pedestrians and dogs as we go, the stereo blasting at one increment below distortion levels, and I love every minute of it.

The main attraction at the Pickled Parrot isn't the food or drinks, it's the location and the water. The restaurant sits atop a cliff overlooking Pirate's Cove. Below the restaurant, fanning down to the sea at different levels are several terraces with tables sitting in the shade of thatched awnings. Steps cut into the cliffs provide access to the water at a couple of locations.

The view from the cliffs across the cove is stunningly beautiful and quintessentially Caribbean. The water is so clear, so glorious, so inviting, it beckons, pulling irresistibly at all who visit.

I pass the time swimming, sunning, splashing into the sea from a rope swing suspended from the cliff and swooshing down the water slide that ends in a twenty-foot drop into the crystal clear water. I retrieve my mask and snorkel from my backpack and explore the cove, thinking that there could be treasure in some forgotten cranny. The water depth varies between fifteen to twenty feet. On one dive I saw an octopus hiding in a crevice in the coral, his skin flashing a kaleidoscope of camouflage colors as I examined him.

The atmosphere at the Pickled Parrot is congenial and relaxed. I meet a couple from Michigan who are on their twenty-fifth trip to Negril.

About mid-afternoon, waterlogged and sun-weary, I slung my backpack over my shoulder and headed down the dusty road into town. It's a mighty long walk, especially in the hot sun, but the stretch of road from the Pickled Parrot to the roundabout in town has so much character that I walk it at least once per visit.

I see a young fellow coming up the road toward me. By the look on his face and his gait, I can tell he's going to offer me something. I'm looking forward to his pitch, curious to see what he has to offer and what his line will be. He stops boldly in front of me, blocking my way.

"Hey mister, today is my birt-day – can yu do somet'ing special for me?"

I've heard this one before, in Mexico. I wonder to myself how many birthdays he's had this week. "How old are you?" I ask.

"Twelve."

"What's the date today?" I ask him. He looks a little perplexed. "It's your birthday right? So what's the date?"

"Ummmmm, it's de fifteenth," he says.

He's off by a long shot. "Wrong, but nice try," I say, "happy birthday." He moves on, casting a look back at me.

A short distance down the road, across from the Pirates Cave bar, I see a craft stand that looks interesting. As I am always on the lookout for something unique to add to my collection, I cut across the road to check it out. A young Jamaican lady is looking after the stand and off to the side, sitting on a log in the parking area, is a Rasta with a long set of dreads and a beard. He's bent over a partially completed carving, working it with a short, wooden-handled knife. The ground around him is littered with wood shavings.

I did a quick check of the shop. Most of the usual stuff was on display, carved Rastaman heads, turtles, fish, brightly painted parrots, some smiling-sun wall plaques and a collection of very nicely carved and painted walking sticks.

There were a couple of 'Ready Freddies' standing on the floor of the shop. A 'Ready Freddie' is a carving depicting a man with a colossal erection. The penis is way out of proportion to the rest of his body, thicker than his arm and standing higher than the top of his head. I'm not really sure what Ready Freddie is supposed to represent, but he could be some kind of Jamaican fertility idol. It comes as no surprise that Ready Freddie always has a big idiotic grin pasted across his woody face. On second thought, that may be a grimace caused by overly stretched skin. Why anyone would buy a Ready Freddie is beyond me, but there must be a market for him because he's available at almost every craft stand. I suspect that some women may take Freddie home as a reminder of a special someone that they've met while in Jamaica.

I worked my way to the display rack at the back of the shop. There, propped up against the wall, was something that I had never seen before, a football-sized carving of a lion's head adorned with a full set of dreadlocks. The lion is a powerful symbol to the Rastafarian and this creation captured all the power and dread that the lion embodies.

I was immediately taken by it and knew right then and there that I had to have it. He was awesome, his mouth was filled with sharp white teeth and was wide open as if he was roaring. His pink pointy tongue was sticking straight out. All around its head, where the mane would normally be, was a twisted mass of curly black dreadlocks. I pictured a wild lion roaming the plains of Africa, his mane naturally matted into proud dreadlocks. I'm sure the carver had a similar image in his mind when he created this work.

I held the carving in my hands and turned it over. It was hewn from a solid block of cedar. The back was unfinished and to my surprise and pleasure, there were two rusty nail points sticking out of the wood. The nails were of the old type, each individually forged with angular sides. They had been in the wood for a long, long time. The Rasta whom I'd seen in the parking lot had come into the shop and saw me examining the nails, "I can take de nails out for you," he said.

"No, no, leave them in," I replied, "they give it character, they give him some real teeth."

I tried to look nonchalant, playing the disinterested browser, figuring that I might get a better deal that way. That lasted about ten seconds. I decided that I really wanted the lion's head and that I wasn't going to leave without it. The Rasta, who introduced himself as Junior knew it too, my body language gave me away. I turned the piece over in my hands, it had heft. I knew it was unique. The craftsmanship was exquisite. Junior had worked hard on it and had produced a masterpiece.

"How much?" I asked.

"Eighty-five dollars," replied Junior.

"How much in Jamaican?" I asked, since I was carrying Jamaican currency. Meanwhile I was mentally calculating how many Canadian 'pesos' it would take to add up to eighty five almighty US bucks, it was way too many.

Junior paused for a second, "Thirty-four hundred," he said. It always amazes me how the vendors know the current exchange rate and can go from US to Jamaican to Canadian to pound Sterling with relative ease.

I considered bartering with him, which would have been the normal thing to do, but after a moment's thought I gave him what he was asking, no argument. It was a very reasonable price for the quality of the work, and besides, I thought that Junior could put the money to more immediate use than I would. He took the lion from me and carved the following inscription in the raw wood on the back:

Junior 2001

Negril JAWI

"What's JAWI," I asked, looking over his shoulder.

"Jamaica, West Indies," Junior replied.

Then he rubbed the lion with an old rag, polishing it to a high shine. It looked magnificent! Just before he handed it over to me he held it in front of him for a moment and then brought it to his lips and gave it a big loud smacking kiss. "Mmmmmmmahhhh!" Then he hoisted it high above his head and, still looking at it, he cried out, "I LOVE YOU!"

For a moment I was stunned. Junior was looking at his lion with the intense pride of a parent in his eyes, he was saying goodbye to one of his children. I quietly took it from him and placed it carefully in my backpack. I walked across the road feeling like I'd bought one of his children from him, and in a way, I had. I walked the road a little and then turned to look back at Junior's stand, he was still standing there with the tattered polishing rag in his hand, watching me.

When I got back to my room I took the Rasta-Lion from the backpack, laid it on the bed and admired it. It was truly a beautiful and powerful sculpture and I felt very fortunate to have it.

The next morning after jogging and showering, I set about preparing my pre-wedding week restricted breakfast. (Diets come and go, wedding photos last a lifetime.) The coconut that I bought on the road yesterday was about to meet its demise. My method of opening coconuts comprises three steps. First I use my trusty corkscrew to drill an opening into the 'mouth' of the coconut. This is the coconut's Achilles heel, the only soft part on its hard exterior. The shell of the coconut has a pointy end and a blunt end, the 'mouth' is located at the blunt end. At the blunt end there are three indentations, two that match, I call these the 'eyes', they even have little ridges above them that look like eyebrows. Below the eyes is my target, the 'mouth'. I twist the corkscrew into the 'mouth' and when it breaks into the cavity there's a pleasant little hiss as the pressure equalizes. I then pull the corkscrew out, creating an opening to the milk cavity. Next, step two; I invert the coconut and set it on a drinking glass to let the milk drain out, this takes a couple of minutes. Step three requires a hard surface, like a concrete patio or a flat stone. Holding the coconut lengthwise in my hand I smash it to the patio. The outer shell cracks open in several places and the firm white meat of the inside is exposed for the picking.

My breakfast this morning consists of a banana, one of the protein bars that I brought to the island with me and a generous portion of coconut meat. I also guzzle the coconut milk and several glasses of fine Jamaican tap water. In my mind's eye I see a little dietician in a white lab coat consulting her clipboard, nodding in approval and ticking off; carbohydrate, protein and fat. That's what I get from living with Amy for eight years, she is very much into healthy eating, except for the occasional chocolate binge.

Gorged on my massive breakfast, I straighten the room a bit before striking off for Point Village to see the wedding coordinator. I place the Rasta-Lion on the pillow at the head of the bed, when an idea hits me. I grab the pillows from both of the beds in the room and pile them on the one that I sleep in. Then I throw a blanket over the pillows and punch and knead them until it looks like there is an enormous body under the covers. I top it off with the Rasta-Lion head, propped on another pillow and turned slightly toward the doorway. I stand back and look at my handiwork. It's perfect! There's a huge dreadlocked monster lying in the bed, his head poking out of the top of the covers. Its mouth and eyes are wide open, its skin has a shiny reddish-brown color, its pointed tongue is sticking out over lips pulled back to show two rows of white teeth. I grab a book, leave the room and go next door to The Jerks' patio, sit down, get comfortable, and wait.

About half an hour later the chambermaid, Leslie, comes down the walkway pushing her cart and singing to herself in a clear, beautiful voice. She parks her cart in front of my room and, seeing me next door, greets me with a cheery, "Good mawnin' sah!"

I almost call the whole thing off at that moment, but I wave and smile, "How are you this lovely morning, Leslie?" I ask.

"Jus' fine, jus' fine," she replies opening the door to my room, humming to herself. A moment later a bloodcurdling scream erupts from the open door. Leslie, a rather large proportioned woman, comes flying out of the room, eyes wide, hands clutching her chest. She's moving like a fullback five yards from the goal line. On her quick trip across the patio she kicks over a cleaning bucket that she had placed there. Her flight continues to the walkway where she stops and turns around, panting and still holding her hands over her heart. I'm laughing so hard that I almost fall out of the chair. Leslie sees me and realizes that she has been had.

"Oh my God, sah! Did you . . ? Oh.... my, you gave me a start," she says, rapidly patting her chest above her heart.

"I'm sorry . . . .I'm so sorry Leslie," I said, still laughing and doubling over, tears in my eyes. I go down to the walkway and put my hand on her shoulder. She appears to be recovering but I feel her still shaking a little.

"I'm sorry, I didn't think it would scare you so badly," I said, starting to feel somewhat chastened. "But you should have seen yourself come flying out of that room," and I start to laugh again.

"I t'ought it was a dead mon!" Leslie said.

A couple of moments later, having calmed down a bit, Leslie chuckled and shook her head, seeing the humor in my little prank, which was lucky for me. I took the lion's head out of the bed and placed him on the dresser and Leslie got back to her chores.

I remind myself to leave her a decent tip when I check out of here on Saturday.

Wild Thing

It's you, it's you, it's you I'm talkin' to . . .
Why do you look so sad and forsaken?
When one door is closed, don't you know, another is open.
Bob Marley – 'Coming in From the Cold'

This morning I hike up to the Hi Lo grocery store (High Quality! Low Prices!) in town to pick up a few provisions. At the top of my list is guava juice to use as mix for my after-five patio rum drink. The excursion also gives me an excuse to go to the bakery and get a couple of fresh cocobreads, I'm hopelessly addicted to the stuff. I had originally planned to take the cocobreads back to the room and have one at lunch and the other one at dinner. But as soon as I get out of the bakery I sit down at a table in the adjoining plaza and devour one of them while it is still hot.

Walking out through the parking lot to the road I run the gauntlet of taxi drivers waiting there. I'm asked forty or fifty times if I need a lift. It reminds me of the time that Amy and I took a walking tour of Havana. We rounded a corner near a park in the downtown area. Sitting on the long window ledge of an office building were about a dozen or so young men, idling away the afternoon. As we walked by the first one, he called out to me, "Hey amigo! You want Habana cigar?" I shook my head negative. We passed by the next fellow, sitting immediately beside the first, he looks up and says, "Mister, you want cigar?" I say no. The third guy also asks me if I need cigars. And so it continued all the way down the row of them, each one piping up as we passed him, asking in his own way if I wanted to buy cigars. By the time we got to the end of the line-up Amy and I were laughing and some of the guys, seeing the absurdity of it, had joined in. These young men were living dangerously as it is illegal for them to sell cigars. Punishment is a Cuban jail, no questions asked.

Clear of the parking lot I strike out for the hotel, backpack laden with provisions and one still-warm cocobread that I can't stop thinking about. I'm walking past the roundabout when I see a motorbike coming toward me at a good clip. There's a Jamaican guy driving it with a woman passenger on the back. The road here hasn't been fixed and is perforated with scores of potholes. I do a double take. The driver is controlling the bike with one hand and in the other he's holding a cell phone to his ear. He's laughing out loud as he beats it down the road, swerving around potholes! His girlfriend is clinging to him with both arms.

'*Is this place for real?*'

I get about 200 yards past the bridge when I hear another motorbike approaching slowly from the rear. The driver, a male, and the passenger, a woman, are speaking loudly to each other in Italian. Or perhaps they're just speaking to each other in Italian, which always seems to be spoken loudly. I look behind me to see what's going on. The driver is leaning to one side and is twisted toward the rear of the bike. They're talking a mile a minute, she's waving her hands in the air as she speaks. She's topless and wearing a thong (some Jamaicans call them 'batty-riders'). Her ample boobs, jutting out proudly and sitting high on her chest, could be used as models in a breast implant advertisement, '*Ladies, you could look like this!*' I watch them cruise slowly by, wishing I understood Italian. They continue making their way slowly down the road, as they proceed they're greeted by a chorus of beeping horns that gradually fade in volume the further that they get from me.

'*Is this place for real?*'

I reach down below my backpack and pinch myself hard on the ass. Seeing as I don't wake up, I assume that I'm not dreaming.

Back at the hotel, I dump the groceries in the room and head down to the beach for a dip and a little stroll along the shoreline. As I'm lolling in the flat clear water I see a young lady, a tourist, walking along the beach dressed in a pair of tight black jeans, black evening sandals, a black sheer top and a lacy black see-through bra, her nipples clearly visible. This is not the first time that I've noticed her. I've seen her up and down the beach for a few days now, wearing the exact same outfit, morning, noon and night. She's always walking by herself and is never carrying anything with her, no beach bag, no purse. Her clothes look a bit bedraggled and her short black hair is tousled. She has a big loopy smile on her face and is stumbling a little as she meanders her way along the sand. She looks as if she might be high on something. It's odd, but somehow she looks lost, almost homeless. She stops and exchanges a few words with a couple of guys sitting in a lounge, giggles and then moves on. I've seen several bizarre sights during my visits to Negril, but this young lady has piqued my curiosity so much that I exit the water and go over to the guys that she was talking to.

"What's the story on the chick in the black?" I ask one of them.

"Oh . . . she's right barmy she is," he replies in a heavy cockney accent.

"Is she alright," I ask, "I mean, she looks kind of lost?"

"Her? No! She came over on the plane with us on Sunday. She's staying at Merrill's. But she is a bit of a nut-bar that one. Don't worry, we're keeping an eye out for her."

I'm not entirely convinced of the story on the dippy British chick, I think there might be more to it, but who knows for sure? This is Negril and anything is possible. I strike out northbound on the beach to see what there is to see. I want to try a Flaming Marley today and I've heard that Alfred's Ocean Palace makes a good one. The Flaming Marley is a world famous Jamaican island cocktail.

I plunk myself on a barstool at Alfred's. "Could you do me a Flaming Marley?" I ask the barman.

"No problem, mon" he says. With the practiced moves of the experienced bartender he snatches up a shot glass, flicks it upright and places it on the highly polished bar with a flourish. Into it he pours a shallow layer of Grenadine. This is followed by another shallow layer of Crème de Menthe poured slowly on top of the Grenadine. Then he gingerly adds about half an ounce of Appleton rum. The shot glass now holds a three layered drink, red on the bottom, green in the middle and gold on top. Red, green and gold are important Rasta colors and, as Bob Marley lived his life as a Rasta, the drink is named in his honor.

"We cap it off with a likkle bit of OP," he says, pouring a smidgen of Wray and Nephew's 151 Over Proof white rum on top of the Appleton. "Do you know how to drink dis?" he asks.

"No, I'm a Flaming Marley virgin," I answer.

"You drink it like a shootah, all at once, but tru' a straw," he says, placing one carefully into the drink. "When you ready, tell me an' I'll light it. Den drink it quick from de bottom wid de straw. You have dat?" He fetches a butane lighter from his pocket.

"Yeah, fire away," I said. He flicks the lighter, turns it up to max and waves the flame over the top of the drink. The OP rum ignites with a happy little blue flame.

"Quick now!" the barman says. I lean to the straw and take a big suck on it. The Grenadine slides down as does the Crème de Menthe and half of the Appleton. I take a little breather and sit up from the straw. That was a mistake.

"No mon! You 'ave to drink it all at once or de straw will melt." Sure enough the straw in my drink has succumbed to the flaming rum and is toppling over in slow motion. A couple across the bar who have been watching me burst out laughing. The barman takes the straw out of the glass and blows out the flame. "You drink de rest an' we're gonna try it again," he tells me.

I toss back the rest of Flaming Marley number one, it's warm and oh-so-good. Over the years I've developed a taste for rum straight up. The barman prepares Flaming Marley number two. I consider dispensing with the straw and drinking it like a normal shooter but drop the idea since I don't feel like scorching the hairs from my nostrils today and I would look odd in wedding pictures with my eyebrows singed off.

"Okay, dis time you suck it all up in one quick shot," says the barman. He fires up the second drink. I do as instructed and Flaming Marley number two, little blue flame and all, disappears in one big slurp. The couple across the bar applauds and I nod a small, humble bow. The drinks leave a pleasant little warm knot in my belly.

With the Flaming Marley's behind me it's time to continue my excursion. I stumble a little getting off the barstool, it seems I've got a bit of a buzz. I wander around a while and find myself a short distance from the CoCo LaPalm hotel. I almost walk into a small mast stuck into the sand there. The sail flapping from the mast bears an advertisement for cruises on the 'Wild Thing', a catamaran party boat that plies the waters around Negril. It's impossible to miss the sail. It's at a narrow point in the beach and virtually blocks all passing traffic. I plot a path around it. If I go to the seaward side I'll get my feet wet, so I detour around the other way up onto the coarse sand under some shade trees.

There's a young woman sitting at a table in the shade of a sea grape tree. A sign hung from the table says;

Wild Thing - Sunset Cruises

It's a hot day, as they all have been since I arrived in Negril, and I need some shade and a break from walking, so I sit down on a natural seat in the crook of the sea grape's trunk.

"You look like you're interested in a sunset cruise," states the young woman.

"Yeah, I was thinking about it," I answered, surprising myself, "tell me more."

"Well, you should come with us. We go out on 'Wild Thing'," she points to the catamaran moored in the sun soaked sparkling waters off shore, "we cruise up to Rick's Café and we dance and have a lot of fun. It's an open bar."

"Yeah mon, you should come, we 'ave a lot a fun." This from a young, good looking Jamaican guy lounging in a chair in the shade. I assume he's one of the crew.

Two older women, successfully diverted by the sail in the sand, walk up to the table. The young lady greets them but they have eyes only for the young guy.

"What's your name?" one of them asks, looking at him, her southern drawl identifies her as American.

He gazes up at them through his ultra-cool shades, "Ahhhh, people jus' call me Trouble," he says slowly, putting his head back and chuckling.

"Ohhhh . . . Trouble are you?" one of the ladies says, reaching over to rub his head, which is covered with tight, scull hugging rows of braids each tipped with four beads, black, green, yellow and red.

He pulls his head away, dodging her hand, "No, no ... don't touch. If you touch my braids I lose all of my powah." We all laugh.

"Maybe you should change your name to Samson," I suggest.

The young saleslady seizes the moment to launch into her sales pitch again. She promises a fun time, unlimited drinks, pizza snacks, music, dancing, a leisurely cruise along the Negril shoreline and a great sunset.

I do a quick mental check of my appointment calendar, and finding it completely blank for this week, I book a cruise. Since arriving in Negril I've had a hankering to get out on the ocean and the 'Wild Thing' sounds like it might be a fun way to pass some time.

Later that afternoon I'm standing on the same patch of beach with a group of people, about twenty-five of us, each clutching our yellow 'Wild Thing' boarding passes in our hands. The group is relaxed and chatty, anticipating a hearty party. There's a good mixture of people, singles, couples, groups, mostly young people and a few older.

'Young people?'

I look around and suddenly realize that I am most likely the oldest of the group. Yikes! It's bizarre how that creeps up on you. I look up the shore toward Rutland Point and think about the first time that I came to Negril. I can see myself standing on the beach, decades ago in front of the old Negril Beach Village, pumped full of testosterone, beer in one hand, spliff in the other, not a care in the world. Where in hell did the time go? I'll be damned if I can figure it out. Jimmy Buffett wrote a song entitled, *'He Went To Paris'*. It's about a guy looking back on his life, and how all the years slipped away. There's a great line in the song; the fellow goes to Paris, lives his life, - *'And twenty more years slipped away'*. It's an old song, from '73, and I liked it back then, but now, standing here in the warm sand looking at the 'Wild Thing' crowd, I know exactly what that line means. I take a sip from a Red Stripe, things haven't changed that much! Negril still lights me up. And in Negril, it doesn't matter who you are, regardless of age, color, shape or religious bent, all are accepted, everybody fits in. In fact, around here, the more eccentric the character, the better the fit.

We get the go-ahead and wade out to the glass-bottom boat tender that will take us out to 'Wild Thing'. The tender is painted bright red and is propelled by a small 15 horsepower outboard, which is much too small for the size and weight of the boat. It's not unusual to see under-powered boats in Jamaica, the excise tax on outboard motors (and everything else) makes them so ridiculously expensive that people have to make do with what they can afford. This tender is a stand-in for the one that is usually used to load Wild Thing. Last week, before I arrived, a big storm blasted the Negril coast and the owner of Wild Thing, Peter McIntosh, lost three boats in one night. I see all three of them on my daily beach walks. His glass-bottom boat is sitting in front The Beachcomber, its roof poking forlornly out of the water with its hull completely embedded in sand. I can't imagine how it could be extracted without wrecking it, it looks like a complete write-off. The tender that was used to load Wild Thing is up on the shore a little further to the south of the Beachcomber, half buried in the beach. With skill and the right equipment, it might be salvageable. Finally, he also lost a small trimaran that was almost ready to go into service. What's left of it is showing the bow portion of one lonely overturned hull bobbing about 100 yards offshore. It, too, looks like a done-deal. I feel for the guy. His experience is proof positive that paradise can rear up and bite you hard on the ass.

Before stepping aboard the catamaran we are instructed to remove our footwear, which we do. Barefoot is good, it goes with the informal, island mood. Besides, there's an open bar and if people drink too much and blow their cookies, my sandals will be safe from the splatter.

The Bob Marley tunes are playing and the bar girl is keeping busy as the second load of passengers clamber aboard. I do a double take. There's this guy getting on board that looks like a young Bob Marley! It's uncanny, I try not to stare. He has the same build, the same color skin and the same dreads. I go over and talk to him, he's an American. I tell him that he reminds me of Bob. He smiles (and in doing so looks even more like Bob) and says that a lot of people tell him that. His girlfriend seems pleased.

Wild Thing is a fair sized catamaran, about 40 feet, it feels good underfoot and looks well maintained. There's a big open deck with an awning mounted above. We all settle in and the engines rumble to life. The captain steps up to center stage, points out the head and gives us our fun briefing. Basically, 'everything goes and have fun'. The mooring is let go and we motor to the west. There's no wind this evening, but the sail is hoisted anyhow, for effect. I look up, a huge 'Rick's Café' logo is emblazoned across the dacron. Capitalism is alive and well in Negril.

Someone has brought out the pizza and before long it's being washed down by gallons of Red Stripe. The blaster is cranked up to the max and Bob Marley urges us to *'stand up for your rights'*. The party has started. I hang on to a mainstay, watching the water swoosh by the hull. It's so nice to be back out on Mother Ocean. I go up front and lie down on the trampoline. Wild Thing lunges happily in the swell, the sinking sun having lost its midday ferocity, now lays warm kisses on my skin. Life *is* good.

The Negril seascape is something to behold! From offshore the whole sweep of the beach from Booby Cay to the cliffs is laid out before us. I see the beach that I've traversed hundreds of times from a new perspective. The hills behind Negril frame the white of the beach with a green wreath. We bounce by the roundabout, the remains of the old Wharf Club are clearly visible. Residential growth is slowly creeping up from the coastline, houses dot the hillsides above the town. The red roof of a church marks the true beginning of the cliff road. We slide by the Negril Yacht Club, people are milling around on the big patio there. Some look out to the Wild Thing and wave. Then there's Cuba's Bar, perched over the last little bit of beach before the cliffs take over. I was in Cuba's one afternoon this week. A couple of brave Jamaican girls decided to take a swim from the beach behind the bar. I felt sorry for them. The boys in the bar put on their best leers and cheers the whole time that the girls were bathing.

There's a picture of a smiling banana painted on a wall below The Happy Banana restaurant. The sunset crowds are starting to gather in spots along the cliffs. The Blue Castle, a hotel fashioned after a medieval castle, looks awesome from the sea! A couple of properties away is Tiny's, a cozy ex-pat bar where I had a few too many rum drinks on Monday night.

There's a cheer from the deck and I look back, one of the girls has decided to liven up the party and has taken her top off. She's holding on to one of the posts that supports the awning and is doing the hip gyration thing. Her friend doesn't need much encouragement, her top comes off too and she joins her friend at the post. They've both got the moves down pat, it wouldn't surprise me if they've had some experience at the brass pole, not that I've ever been in a place like that.

We round a promontory and cruise past Pirate's Cove and The Pickled Parrot. As I look I see someone launch from the rope swing, he lets out a blood curdling scream that echoes off the cliff faces. In the 18th century Negril was a haven for pirates. They used to anchor their ships in this picturesque little cove. I imagine swashbuckling pirates swinging from the yardarms of their ships and splashing into the transparent water.

One of the Caribbean's most notorious pirates was 'three fingered' Jack Rackham, better known as 'Calico Jack'. His nickname was given him because of his preference for wearing calico underwear. Two of his closest sidekicks were the bloodthirsty women pirates, Mary Read and Anne Bonney, who, legend has it, were both pregnant by him. They took a liking to Negril's Long Bay and Bloody Bay area and frequently spent time here, partying and drinking rum. Hence, the tradition of partying, drinking and carousing on Negril's shores was established over 250 years ago; what goes around, comes around. Calico Jack and his women were captured by the British in Negril in 1720. Jack was taken to Spanish Town, the then capital of Jamaica, for trial then summarily executed on a small island near Port Royal that has henceforth been known as Rackham's Cay. As for his two charming shipmates, the mundanely monikered Mary and Anne, at their trials they begged mercy for their unborn children and were allowed to live.

The cliffs, the caves and the water here are hypnotically inviting and stunning in their beauty. I feel a great urge to dive in and swim over to the bar hidden away in the cave. I've spent many a glorious afternoon at the Pickled Parrot, it's a place I think of on cold winter mornings when I'm trudging through the snow. The memory helps me to survive.

Wild Thing rounds another outcropping of cliff and Rick's Café and the old lighthouse slide into view. The lighthouse, a whitewashed 100-foot tall classic that is still functional today, sits atop a high cliff on the western tip of Jamaica. It was built in 1895. In 1985 it was converted to run on solar power, and there is no shortage of sun on this shore.

We motor into the cove in front of Rick's and tie up, the water is rough and Wild Thing bobs at the mooring.

In spite of the chop I can see the bottom at forty feet. Rick's is a mob scene and our boom box is no competition for the big amps above. There are people standing in every available nook and cranny along the cliffs. The bar is crammed three deep. There's a steady stream of people jumping from the high cliff, a thirty-five foot drop.

A tender pulls up to take Wild Thing's passengers ashore. Hey! It's the same tender that boarded us! He's followed us down the coast. Most of the passengers board the tender, which is difficult in the choppy swell of the cove. A couple of people jump in and swim for the dock below Rick's. I opt to stay on board, I like the view from here and I've already done the Rick's scene. The crew of Wild Thing (more fittingly called 'The Cast') get Act Two going; Bob Marley is replaced by dance hall music.

A big motor launch with 'Sandals' painted on the hull cruises slowly by. The people on board appear subdued, they stand quietly at the rail like mannequins, none of them wave like people on boats are supposed to do. They take in the Rick's scene as they pass and continue drifting slowly toward the lighthouse.

Suddenly there's a loud blast of patois from seaward, I look around. A BIG catamaran is pulling into the cove and our crew is yelling and gesturing in its direction. Loud music is thumping from the boat. Five guys on the cat are lined up along the gunwale, they've got their shorts yanked down and are hanging a group-moon at the Rick's crowd. Their bums are tanned deep brown. The cliff side erupts in loud cheers and clattering applause. A Jamaican guy on the big cat is hanging his dick out and waving it around. I sit up in the trampoline and turn around for a better look at the spectacle. Holy wow, the guy's wang looks over a foot long! Man is he hung! I feel hugely inadequate. They drift a little closer and I see that it's just his arm stuck out through the fly of his shorts. Good one! These people, in contrast to the Sandals boat, look like they are having a party. I see an old Rastaman on board the big cat, his dreads and beard are gray. I shout to him, "One love!" and he waves back.

The bar girl on Wild Thing, enjoying the lull in her duties, is sitting on the ledge at the front of the cockpit. "Dats de cruise from Hedo," she tells me. Now it all makes sense, the bare tanned bums and the loud music. The big cat is the sunset party cruise from Hedonism, the human zoo (much more on that, soon come).

The pilot of the big cat maneuvers between Wild Thing and the cliffs. The water is rough and choppy but he does a splendid job. He pulls the cat in close to the cliff face, holds it there for a while, then turns it around and steers back out to sea.

The mob scene at Rick's continues. People continue to dive from the high cliff. After each big splash there's sporadic applause.

I'm getting settled back into the trampoline when there's another loud blast of incomprehensible patois from seaward. I look around, the big cat is returning. More shouting and gestures are exchanged, I don't understand one word of it. The bar girl on Wild Thing quickly ducks into a forward compartment and comes up with a bottle of 151 OP rum. It seems the Hedo boat has run low on party fuel. They maneuver close to stern, the bar girl lobs the bottle of rum into the big cat's forward netting. It's a three pointer! The Hedo people high five each other and shout their appreciation. They leave a little happier and with renewed expectations.

The glass bottom tender is bringing our excursion passengers back to Wild Thing. It bobs and weaves in the swells as it approaches, the driver is standing up in the rear and steering it by turning the small outboard motor. He guides it alongside the starboard hull, the deck of Wild Thing heaves and the tender hammers into our side with a shuddering 'BONK'.

Our captain, who was prone on a cushion snoozing with his cap over his face, is suddenly on his feet, "BLOOD CLOT!" he yells, and runs over to the scene of the incident.

Much arm waving and bursts of accusatory patois ensue, generously punctuated with more 'Blood Clots' and a couple of 'Bumbo Clots'. Both of these are uniquely Jamaican epitaphs, employed universally and liberally. 'Bumbo' meaning 'bum' and 'clot' meaning cloth, both making reference to the days before toilet paper and sanitary napkins.

After several concerned glances at the point of impact it's decided that no damage has been done, nothing that's visible anyhow. The rest of our passengers re-embark, scrambling over the space between the pitching decks. One becomes impatient and jumps off the tender, swims forward between the hulls of Wild Thing and re-boards via the sea stairs there.

The sun is getting low as we depart Rick's for the cruise back home. The party on board is loud and raucous. Everybody is getting into it, up dancing, drinking from the open bar, talking loudly and laughing. From the boom box Shaggy, one of Jamaica's pop artists, insists, "It Wasn't Me", over and over. Some people are getting seriously smashed; they can hardly stand, let alone dance. The bar girl spends more time dancing than she does serving. She comes over to me, puts her arms above her head, pushes her pelvis forward and does that hip circumvolution move that only island girls can do.

The sun has reached the sea, and Wild Thing heaves to, facing the sunset. Old Sol dives into the sea and the cameras click, I give him a six out of ten. In the waning twilight a string of lights around Wild Thing's awning are turned on, adding a gay touch to the party atmosphere. The festivities continue until we reach our home mooring in the dark. Reluctantly we leave Wild Thing. I stay on board until the tender returns for its second load. When I get aboard, it's no surprise to see it's our old friend 'Hammerhead'. Apparently the little collision at Rick's hasn't affected its seaworthiness.

www.LookAtMe.mon

'When yu go a Jackass yard, yu noh fi chat 'bout big iyaz'
Jamaican Proverb

Today I awake to my last full day of 'batching' it. Tomorrow Amy and my girls, Erin and Hannah and the rest of the wedding crew will arrive and the tenor of the days will change significantly. As much as I've enjoyed my time alone here this week, I'm very much looking forward to seeing everyone and spending some time in the sun with them. I'm especially eager to see how Erin and Hannah will react to Negril, it being their first visit to the Caribbean. Will it connect as deeply with them as it did with me on my first trip?

Today I've broken with tradition. I'm carrying my wristwatch, which I had difficulty locating after doffing, in the right leg compartment of my cargo shorts. I have an important appointment to keep later on this morning that I can't be late for. I'm also carrying a rolled up piece of Bristol board that I need for my appointment, but that isn't until 10:00, which is still a couple of hours away, so I have time for a quick stroll along the beach.

I'm sloshing absentmindedly through the water in front of the Beachcomber Hotel when I spot a worn conch shell washing in the surf. I rinse it in the sea and hold it up to examine. It's a little bit bigger than the fist of a large man. The apex has been broken off, exposing the smooth walled, cone shaped home of the beast that once lived within. All of the lip and part of the first whorl are missing. Its surface has been scrubbed clean and worn smooth by the action of the sand and water. The sun has bleached it to an alabaster white, only small streaks of light brown remain in the furrows of the striations that curve gracefully along its exterior. The shell looks and feels like a piece of fine porcelain. It rings when I run my fingers over its surface. I find it extraordinarily beautiful. I bring it to my nose and breathe in its unique scent, which is oddly somewhere between that of wet clay and soap.

Holding the worn-down conch shell in my hands, I wonder why the sea has chosen me to be the recipient of this little treasure. Whatever the reason, I take it as a sign of good fortune.

I have an hour before my appointment, which I cannot miss. I take the opportunity to find a cyber-café so that I can send a couple of E-mails back home.

The Internet, and E-mail especially, is a wonderful thing for travelers. There are many, many cyber cafes along the beach in Negril that make keeping in touch with home, or anywhere else, a simple task.

I walk up to the Charela Inn beach bar and ask the barmaid if she knows where I can find an Internet café. She points down the beach and says that the restaurant next door has a computer.

I walk up to the café and spot an old clunker of a computer sitting on a table at the back of a patio where meals for the attached hotel are served.

"How much to use the computer?" I ask the young lady who is setting up tables.

"Twenty minutes for a hundred J," she answers.

I tell her that sounds good and sit down in front of the computer. It's running but when I start the web browser it doesn't connect. We look at the back of the computer and see that there's no phone line attached to it. There's a cord coiled up beside the machine so the young lady plugs it into the wall jack but it's too short to reach the back of the computer. I pick the box up and put it on a ledge above the table. Now the cord just barely reaches the modem. Finally I get connected. The keyboard is very sticky and the mouse movement is jerky, probably from being outside in the constant heat and humidity. The on-screen mouse pointer has been set up as one of those annoying animated icons, this one is a fire-breathing dragon. I spend the next twenty minutes sending e-mails back home. I've been talking to Amy each night on the phone but I want to send her a note telling here that I miss her and assuring her that all is in readiness for our wedding next week at Point Village. I also sent e-mails to my girls, making sure that I typed Hannah's arcane Hotmail address correctly, how she came up with 'Al_my-99em' as an address, I have never understood.

On my way back down the beach I walk past the bar where I had asked for directions. The barmaid waves me over. A security guard, another woman, is also standing at the bar.

"What do you do when you use the computer?" the barmaid asks me, both her and the security guard have looks of keen interest on their faces. Computers are a relatively new thing on the beach in Negril and it's nice to see more and more people there using them and taking an interest in them.

"Well, it's really quite simple you see," I said. "You write a note on the computer and then you tell the computer to send it to another person's computer over the telephone line. Every once and a while you check you computer's mailbox for notes from other computers.

It's called e-mail."

The barmaid said, "Ahhhh," and they both nodded their heads and thanked me for the explanation.

"No problem," I said. I checked my watch, fifteen minutes until my appointment. "Could you get me a cold Red Stripe please."

Before coming down to Negril on this trip I searched the web for Jamaica sites and read various Jamaica message boards. One day I stumbled across a web-cam showing a live picture from the beach in Negril. I immediately bookmarked the site and thereafter checked the camera several times a day to see what the weather was like and to get myself hyped for the upcoming trip.

The web camera was the type that allowed users to move it via remote control. It always started out at a default view, looking down at a patch of beach to the north, with coconut palm fronds artistically decorating the top of the frame. The browser panel provided controls that allowed the user to grab control of the camera, and once I had it I could point it at anything I wanted, tilting, panning and zooming around to my heart's content. Before I got the hang of it I got some great close-up views of the base of the platform that the camera sits on and a screw-head that I assumed to be part of the mounting hardware. But soon I caught on and had a wonderful time zooming in on boats moored offshore and panning up and down the beach.

One day, about a week before I left, I was gazing out the window in the middle of the cold windswept Canadian tundra, watching an Eskimo as he put the finishing touches on an igloo, when I felt the strong need for a dose of Negril. I called up the web cam, took control of it and soon spotted a couple of unsuspecting fair maidens sunbathing on the beach. I dialed the zoom control up to the maximum and the camera settled in on one of the girl's thighs. Being an amateur dermatologist, I took the opportunity to closely examine my subject's derma. The young lady that was lying closest to the water had one of the nicest belly buttons that I have ever seen and her navel ring, a jumping dolphin, was very nice too. After a time, I finished my inspection and was happy to conclude that they both checked out clean, although one of them did have an interesting mole on her left breast that I wished I could have examined more thoroughly.

While I was scanning the girls, an idea came to me. I put together the following e-mail for my friends and work colleagues who, along with me, were living through another insufferable and endless gray Canadian winter:

Dear people . . . as some of you already know, I will soon be departing this Godforsaken snowbound land for a long vacation and honeymoon in beautiful, tropical Negril, Jamaica. I know you will miss me terribly, but please do not despair. On Friday, precisely one week from today, at 10:00am crank up your computers and tune into the following web cam:

http://www.eye-on-the-world.com/negrilcam
There you will see me...LIVE...on the beach in Negril. Please note the clear warm waters of the Caribbean lapping the shore behind me and see the deep shadows cast by the hot tropical sun. Yes my feet are bare. How do you like my new tank top and shorts? I bought them special for this trip. Observe the red tinge to my skin, I got a little too much sun on my first few days here in paradise, but don't worry, I'll brown up nicely over the next few weeks. The sky is so clear and the sun is so bright that I have to wear my shades all the time! Oh, you're wondering about the small brown bottle in my hand? Yes, I realize that it's past 10:00am, but beer isn't just for breakfast anymore.

Eat your hearts out and keep shoveling!
Kahuna3@I_Don't_Give_a_Shit.mon

My last act before turning off my computer and leaving the office for my vacation was to call up the e-mail and hit the send button.

Earlier this week, anticipating my video appointment, I trekked up to the beach bar in front of a complex of small Jamaican style cottages called Country, Country. This is where the web cam was purportedly installed.

Arriving there, I set about to finding the camera. The bar is covered with a thatched roof, which I had observed on the web cam. I walked all around the bar, checking on and around the roof, but couldn't locate the camera. I stood back a little and imagined the pictures that I had seen from the web cam and did a little mental geometry. I placed myself in the 'picture' and looked to where the camera should be. There was a coconut tree standing there. But who would mount a web cam on a coconut tree?

I moved closer to the tree and saw that there was a platform mounted about three-quarters of the way up the trunk, precisely under a big batch of ripening coconuts, which didn't seem like good planning to me. Sitting under a coconut tree is not a good idea, I learned that on my first trip to the island when one plopped, with considerable force, onto the ground beside me, narrowly missing my shoulder. It is a little known fact that, statistically, a person is more likely to die from being conked on the head by falling coconut than from a shark attack. Although, being as I live in a landlocked city in Canada, death from falling coconuts and voracious sharks is not something that I worry about on a daily basis.

I move around to the other side of the coconut tree for a better vantage point. That had to be it. The platform was made from a couple of old pieces of plywood and had a curved piece of Plexiglas attached to the front of it. I could just make out the little camera inside.

I maneuvered myself into the default view of the camera and stood there looking up, examining it, planning the stage position for my debut on the world wide web. I wondered if I was being watched at that moment. Perhaps some insomniac in India was idling away the late night hours watching me looking up at him.

O'Neil, one of the beach boys whose beat covers my hotel and whom I'd talked to on a couple of occasions, saw me standing there and came over to see what I was gawking at. He stood beside me and looked up at the platform.

"That's a web cam," I said.

O'Neil looked at me as if I had said, *'Bluts nog miffid klimbfrot.'*

"Wha?" he said, with a pained expression.

I pointed at the platform, the web cam just discernable behind the Plexiglas shield. "Up on that platform, there's a web cam in there, you know, for the Internet."

"No mon," he said, shaking his head, surprised that I should be so naïve, "dat a light."

"No mon, dat a camera," I insisted.

Another beach boy, Clive, who calls me Bob Marley, walked up to us. "Bob Marley!" he said, bringing his clenched fist up for the greeting tap. I brought mine up and we did the straight-on knuckle tap, both saying 'Respect' as our knuckles met.

When I met Clive the first day that I was here he tried to sell me some pot. I sat with him and we talked for quite a while and eventually the conversation worked its way around to Bob Marley. I told Clive that I knew all the lyrics to all the songs that Bob Marley had ever recorded. I don't, of course, but I do know a lot of them and certainly all of the most popular ones.

"All eighty-four of dem?" Clive asked, eyebrows arched.

"Yup," I said confidently, bluffing, not sure if eighty-four was even in the ballpark, "try me, go ahead, sing a lyric and I'll sing the one that comes right after it."

Clive put his head back for a moment, then sang, "Until, the philosophy...."

"...that hold one race superior and another....inferior," I returned.

He paused for a moment, then, "When the cat's away, the mice will play...." he intoned.

"Political violence fill your city.... Yeah," I got lucky on that one.

Clive smiled and put his fist up for the tap, we tapped. "Respect," he said. A guy could get calluses on his knuckles around here.

The next day I saw Clive walking toward me on the beach, as he approached he raised his hand in the air and sang, "Man to man, is so unjust..."

I put my hand up, slapped his as we passed and sang, "Children, you don't know who to trust."

We both laughed, but kept on walking on our own separate ways, he pointed back at me and said in a loud voice, "Bob Marley!" This occurred in front of a stand where a lady was selling pineapples and bananas and some other vegetables that I don't recognize. She witnessed the whole thing and couldn't figure out what the hell had just happened, she shook her head and went back to arranging her odd looking collection of vegetables.

Since then Clive has called me Bob Marley.

Back at the coconut tree, I pointed up at the web cam. "That's a web cam up there," I said to Clive.

"Yeah mon, a web camera," he agreed matter-of-factly.

O'Neil, now with a perplexed expression, peered up at the platform. He stood there for a moment, shrugged his shoulders, said, "Check you later," then turned and left.

I look at my watch again, it's 9:55am. I'm standing in front of the web cam in my shorts and tank top with a Red Stripe in one hand and the rolled up Bristol board in the other. Inexplicably, I'm a bit nervous and I have a touch of the butterflies in my stomach. I feel as if I'm about to be interviewed for an important job that I want very badly.

Back home, some of my work colleagues have excused themselves from meetings between 10:00 and 10:30. One fellow has been reminded by his desktop assistant that he has an appointment to tune in to see me. Amy is sitting patiently in front of her work computer. My brother, a teacher in western Canada has grabbed a workstation in the staff resources room and is in the process of logging into the Negril web cam. A couple of guys that I work with on the west coast have come into work a little early to catch my performance. A group of my closest co-workers have gathered in front of a monitor in a colleague's cubicle and several other people in different locales are getting set to see my debut.

In total, about 30 people are looking forward to a little slice of the warm Caribbean in the middle of a cold, friggin' Canadian winter. Many of them successfully log into the Negril web cam. At my place of work, everybody hits it at about the same time. Somewhere, deep in the bowels of one of the company's Internet servers, a little piece of software, whose duty it is to monitor bandwidth usage, wakes up and examines the big spike in traffic that just occurred.

"What's this?" it mutters to itself. In the next quarter second it decides what to do. The Negril cam web address is added to the no-no list in the Internet content security server and, for my work colleagues, the curtain comes down on my show before it even gets started. Instead of the inviting waters lapping on the sandy shores of Negril, they see the following message:

- *Error* -

http://www.eyesontheworld.com/negrilcam
Access Denied
Contact Information Management Help Desk for
Assistance

But down in Negril, as far as I was concerned, the show is on! I unfurl the Bristol board and hold it up to the web cam.

Eat Your
Hearts Out!

I stood in front of the camera for the next five minutes, waving, holding up the sign, taking big swigs of Red Stripe, making muscles and grinning like a demented man. Some passers by stop and watch me for a while, curious as to what was going on. Other just walk by, casting sidelong, disdainful looks. But I carry on with the show, I don't care, I'm a video star!

Night Falls on Negril

'The gal come wine up on me.'
Jamaican Proverb

I fold some clothes and throw them into my suitcase. Tomorrow morning I'll finish packing before heading out to MoBay to pick up Amy, the girls and the rest of the group. Tonight will be my last 'bachelor's' night out in Negril. I'm planning on going up to Tiny's bar to join in his birthday celebrations, then to Cuba's for a bite and a brew then I'll catch the Ark Band on stage at the Negril Yacht Club.

Negril is serene just after sunset. The roads are quiet. The beach is all but deserted except for the few stragglers walking purposefully back to their hotels. All of the vendors have packed up and are gone for the day. Most people are up in their rooms, resting, dressing for the evening, boinking, showering, or possibly boinking in the shower. It's as if Negril is taking a big breather, gathering its energy in preparation for the evening's festivities.

As soon as darkness falls, the little tree frogs start singing for their mates. I hear them in the shrubbery outside the room. Their whistles fill the evening air, 'gleeep! . . . gleeep! In spite of my many attempts to do so, I've never seen one of the shy little critters but people tell me that they are about the size of a thumbnail. Listening to the volume of their musical calls it's hard to conceive that such tiny beasts could raise such a symphony. I am aware of their calls the first night of a visit, but after that their whistles become part of the background noise and I have to consciously tune in to hear them.

The little frogs have some big cousins that also come out at night. During the day these big boys, who are actually toads, live under the buildings along the beach. I've never seen a big toad either but I talked to a couple of women who almost walked into one that was sitting in the middle of a sidewalk beside their room. One of them was quite shaken by the experience. The other thought it was funny. They didn't see the big fella until he moved and when he did at first they thought it was a large cat. But cats don't hop and generally don't make a heavy slapping sound when they land on the sidewalk. When they realized that it was a massive toad one of the women screamed and ran for her life. The other, a spunky lass, picked the big guy up. The toad promptly pissed all over her dress. I asked her if she had that effect on all of the guys that she picked up.

I leave the room, locking the door behind me. Jim calls out from the patio next door, "Where you goin' man?" he says in a high, withheld voice. He's just taken a toke and is holding the smoke in. There are several empty Guinness bottles on the table beside him.

"I'm going up to Tiny's for a few beers. What are you guys doing tonight?"

Jim lets the smoke out, "Awww, we're just hangin' out around here, probably go to Alfred's later. They told us that our fuckin' flight has been changed so we have to leave here at seven in the fuckin' morning!"

Randy, wearing a towel around his waist, appears in the doorway to the room. "Yeah, an' we've still got the bikes and the bike place is closed now and doesn't open until eight tomorrow so we can't bring them back. We're fucked," he says.

"We're gonna to see our travel agent when we get back we're gonna kick some serious ass," Jim says.

"Why don't you leave the bikes with the front desk in the morning and let them look after it?" I suggest.

"Yeah, we'll probably do that," says Randy, "but we're gonna kick some serious ass when we get back, right Jim?"

"Fuckin' 'A' we are!"

I leave 'The Jerks' stewing on their patio and walk down to the beach. Several bats are swooping through the night sky feasting on Negril's ever-abundant mosquito crop. Jamaicans call bats 'rat bats', for obvious reasons. What isn't so obvious is why they call moths 'bats'.

Arriving on the beach I see that Legends has turned on their back-lit sign, it casts a pasty electric light across the sand. Although I've spent minimal time in the room, I'll be happy to check out tomorrow morning. Legends hasn't clicked with me and I've once again proved the maxim, 'You get what you pay for'.

Beyond the bluish pall of Legends' electric sign, the beach is brightly lit by the rising moon.

I see a guy angling toward me from the shadows of a building near Traveler's Beach Resort. I recognize him, he's one of the many 'Pharm Boyz' who work the beach, selling from their cornucopia of stupefiers. He's heavy-set, wearing designer jeans, a branded T-shirt and new expensive looking sneakers. His head is shaved clean and there's a narrow vertical strip of whiskers that run down the center of his chin. This is the same guy that approached me up a couple of nights earlier, offering the usual menu, starting with ganja, which he claimed was the best of course, then working his way down the list, ecstasy, mushrooms, coke, etc. He spoke with a pronounced stutter. It was the standard drill, nothing unusual. I declined his offers. Then, near the end of his spiel, he did this big double take at me and his eyes popped wide open. He stepped back and said, "You dah fa—fa—fa—fockin' FBI!" I laughed, shook my head and kept on moving.

Tonight he starts into the same sales pitch, but he stops abruptly in mid sentence, looks me straight in the face and mumbles, "CIA".

"I'm not the CIA . . . or the FBI." I say, "I'm not even an American."

The Pharm Boy gets agitated, he points his finger at me, shaking it, "In Ja—Ja—Jamaica we n'no fock aroun' wit da FBI."

"I'm not the fucking FBI," I insist, "I'm a fucking tourist."

"We slit d-d-dey fockin' troats an t—t—trow dem into da sea!" he says, pointing at the waves behind me. "Me no j—jokin', mon, now get de fock outah heah!" To illustrate his point he pulls a switchblade knife out of his pocket and flicks the blade open. He's very agitated, his eyes are afire.

My brain finally clicks out of vacation mode and into reality. I back away slowly, hands spread at my side, realizing that this could get real bad, real quick. "Sorry man, but I am not the FBI," I said, as calmly and as reassuringly as I could.

He quickly turns and dissolves into the shadows beside the buildings. My testicles slowly descend back down to their normal resting position.

Deciding that I don't want to repeat such an encounter in the near future, I cut up to the road and grab the first taxi that comes by. We agree on a fare of $250J to Tiny's, maybe a bit high, but what the hay. On the way up the cliff road we experience 'The Negril Rush Hour', which actually only lasts about 10 minutes. A steady stream of cars and vans and tour buses flow past us in the opposite direction. I know from experience that this occurs every night at about twenty minutes after sunset. It's the sunset crowd returning to their hotels from their perches along the cliffs at Rick's, The Pickled Parrot and the other popular sunset venues.

We pull up in front of Tiny's and I hand the driver a $500J note. He rummages through his bills, "Me caan't change five hundred," he says.

He asks an older Jamaican standing nearby if he can change the bill. By the looks of the clothes the guy is wearing I give it a slim chance. A quick check confirms that he doesn't have the change either, but in his collection of rumpled, small denomination bills he does have a little more than $250J.

"Me pay de driver an' den me make change at de store dere," he says, pointing at a small convenience store across the road. The driver nods and grabs his two-fifty. I get out of the taxi feeling like I'm being swept into a scam. The guy with my $500J bill walks across the road and disappears into the store. A few moments later he emerges smiling, clutching the change. As he walks toward me I notice that he is favoring one leg and limping badly. He extracts two-fifty from the pile and puts it in the pocket of his grungy trousers.

"Please suh, can I keep de rest, me have to go'a hospital tomorrow for an operation on my knee and I need de money," he pleads, pointing to his right knee. I try to remember if that was the one he was favoring.

"You need an operation on your knee?" I ask.

"Yes, an' de fuckin' doctor wants forty-five hundred for it," he says, his eyes wide. A couple of his buddies are standing around watching the scam go down.

I look at my money in his hand. How did I get myself into this situation? I shake my head and smile. "OK my friend, you can keep a hundred, give me one fifty."

Not happy with his take, he presses for more, "Please suh, I need it for my operation."

"No, you keep one-hundred and give me back the rest, otherwise there could be trouble," I say looking around as if to locate a cop. He reluctantly hands me the one-fifty then turns and walks away. His limp seems better.

Even though tonight is Tiny's birthday, Tiny won't be here to join in the festivities. No one is entirely sure, but the speculation is that Tiny went for a swim from the cliffs below his bar one morning several years back and never returned. At the time of his disappearance Tiny's health was ailing and some say that he took his fate into his own hands, but we will never know for sure. Tiny's family continues to run the business. He lived his life as a kind and gentle man who was well loved by all who knew him. Like many other big men named Tiny, the Negril Tiny was given his nickname because of his enormous size.

The bar is a thatched hut affair perched on a patio atop the cliffs overlooking the sea. A set of steeply inclined stairs lead from the patio down to the water's edge. It was on the rocks below that Tiny's shirt was found, leading to the speculation that his last swim in the ocean that he loved so much started there. Next to the bar is a dining room open to the outside through large white-washed archways. Atop the dining room is an open deck.

I walk into the bar area. Tiny's is the local hangout for ex-pats and long-timers and there are several of them sitting around the bar engaged in loud boisterous conversation. They stand out from the tourist crowd. It's not just the permanent sun tanned look, they also dress differently and have a certain air about them. I find an empty stool at the bar and park myself there. From the far side of the bar the bar girl holds up a Red Stripe, I nod. I must look like the beer type, which, all things considered, is preferable to being mistaken for the FBI.

There are a few Jamaicans hanging out around the bar. One of them comes over to me and asks if I need any ganja. I decline. He sits beside me and commences to roll a big spliff on the bar top. Tiny's is not on the normal tourist circuit. Some know about the place and a few, like me, stumble in from the road, but it is definitely off the beaten path. We are not talking Risky Business or Bourbon Beach here. 'Laid back' would be a good start at describing the atmosphere at Tiny's. Congenial is another that might apply, but they're both understatements. Tiny's reminds me of the early days of Negril, before the all-inclusive resorts arrived.

A Mento band has set up and is banging out tunes from the corner of the dining room. Some Jamaican kids are stomping to the beat. I sit back and drink in the scene.

The crowd and the ganja smoke around the bar thicken in equal proportions. Everyone seems to be toking. A big, half-smoked spliff is making the rounds.

There has been some talk about legalizing ganja in selected parishes, Negril being in one of them. Politically, this will not happen until American authorities come to their senses about marijuana. I believe that legalizing weed would drastically change the dynamics of Negril, and probably not for the better. Right now a working balance seems to be in effect, anyone who wants to smoke, smokes, and as long as they're not stupid about it, 'ev'ry'ting is cool'. Flaunt it and your ass is grass, figuratively speaking. There are places in Negril, Tiny's being one of them, that are de-facto 'free ganja zones' where Babylon won't bother you, ever. So, in effect, ganja consumption is already 'legal' in some places.

If I don't leave soon I'll end up staying at Tiny's all night . . . which wouldn't necessarily be a bad thing. I get up and walk around to the front of the bar where Tiny's picture is mounted above the bottles. He looks down approvingly with a serene smile. Several patrons are there, holding up their glasses to toast him. I join in wishing Tiny a happy birthday. He is a man well remembered.

Back out on the road I look around to see if Limpy is still there. There's no sign of him. The night air is warm and humid. Cuba's is my next destination, but I stop at the store across the road for a 'walkin' beer. Every available inch of display space in the store is utilized, there is easily twice as much stuff packed into the store as there should be. I have to walk carefully sideways down the aisle to the drink cooler to avoid knocking items off the shelves.

A short walk down the road from Tiny's is the Blue Cave Castle. It's surrounded by a high stone wall with sturdy looking gates. At night from the road it looks dark and forebodingly medieval. I walk by a taxi parked on the side of the road. Expecting to be asked if I need a ride, I'm surprised when the driver says in a low voice, "Sensei? . . . Lambs Breath? . . . Purple Skunk? . . . Callie?" naming different variants of the locally grown marijuana. I must have a ganja aficionado look to me tonight.

The stores, hotels, clubs and houses on the cliff road are liberally interspersed with beer and jerk stands. Smoke from the jerk bar-b-que barrels swirl, mixing with the reggae and dance hall music that thumps from everywhere. Unlike the relatively wide and straight and smoothly paved beach road, the cliff road is a narrow, pot-holed lane replete with sharp, blind corners. There are no sidewalks or shoulders to walk on. Cars rumble by, beeping horns at every bend. Walking the cliff road is an adventure in itself. It's packed with more character per mile than any road in Jamaica.

I approach a roadside 'bar' which is really just a small shack with a corrugated roof. There are several people standing around in front so I stop. There's a hand painted sign over the service counter, listing what's on offer, beer, rum, and orange juice. An old Jamaican man comes up to me carrying a package wrapped in dark plastic. He introduces himself as 'de Bush Doctor'. He unwraps the package to show me several short lengths of reddish colored wood.

"What's that?" I ask.

"It special wood from de mountains. Yu put it in water an' bwoil it to make strong tea. Do you want some?"

"No thanks," I answer. In Jamaica, all things good come from the mountains; water, root juice, ganja, and wood for tea and carvings.

I continue down the road and soon pass the Happy Banana. I empathize. My own banana will be much happier starting tomorrow. A little further and the roadside businesses become thicker. I'm getting the hungry-munchies and the smells drifting from the pizza ovens at Mr. Slice make my stomach scrunch up and take notice. I almost turn in for a wedge, but the thought of what awaits me at Cuba's spurns me on.

Ahead, a consumer electronics repair shop is housed in a simple, small ramshackle storefront. The repairman is out front fixing a big TV on a table beside the road. Its innards are spewed on the table and he's concentrating on a meter that he has connected to a couple of wires. The bare bulb of a work light hangs above his head.

Cuba's bar sits on the seaward side of the road overlooking the last strand of beach before the cliffs get down to serious business. It's designed making full use of the open concept, which is perfect for the local climate. The building is a raw concrete block structure with lots of big openings, the largest of which face the sea and the small beach.

Tonight there are two large banks of speakers erected on the roadside in front of the bar. Huge speaker set-ups are typical in Jamaica. It's not unusual to see a pickup truck loaded with monster speakers heading off to set up for a 'bashment' somewhere. Each of the banks in this particular set-up measures about eight by eight feet. They bracket the frontage of the bar. A jumble of tweeters are mounted on top. A couple of Rasta deejays are at a console busy connecting wires and sorting CDs.

Cuba's also has a kitchen and a small eating area opposite the bar. Jerk chicken and conch soup are on the menu. Cuba serves quite possibly the best conch soup in the world and it's the conch soup that I have come for. I order a Red Stripe and a bowl of conch soup.

Across from the bar is MXIII, pronounced 'Em X Three'. MXIII is Negril's largest open-air reggae and dance-hall emporium. The concrete wall that fronts the road is emblazoned with this week's offerings. Tonight Beres Hammond headlines, Rebel T backs up with a supporting cast of lesser known artists. Tomorrow's lead act is Buju Banton with Anthony B leading off. MXIII definitely draws the big names.

The conch soup arrives and I almost pass out from the heavenly vapors that rise from its surface. I compose myself enough to sip a spoonful. Ahhh...this is truly the nectar of the Gods. Surely Zeus on his Olympus mountaintop was never served anything so divine! My world narrows down to the bowl of steaming conch soup on the bar in front of me, my surroundings shimmer in and out of focus. I scoop a dumpling that has bobbed sacrificially to the surface. The finger and palm prints on it attest to its fresh, hand-squeezed authenticity. After a period of time I rejoin reality with an empty bowl in front of me and a warm spoon clutched in my hand.

I notice a refined looking young Jamaican guy sitting at a table, also enjoying a bowl of conch soup. He's very well dressed but in a casual way. He's wearing a set of neat dreads and he looks bright and alert. There's something about him that stands out, he looks vaguely familiar to me. He finishes his soup, pays the waiter and leaves.

The waiter comes over to me and says, "Dat was Anthony B, yu know him?"

"Yeah, I've heard some of his stuff," I replied. Anthony B is an up-and-coming Jamaican star whose music gets back to the roots of reggae.

Like Tiny's, Cuba's is a 'free-ganja' zone. The two Rasta Dee-Jays have come down to the bar and are rolling up some of Jamaica's finest in plain view of all who pass on the road. No worry of Babylon here, Cuba's is cool, some sort of an agreement is apparently in place. They roll a couple of big spliffs, lick them down and light them up.

"Dis is da purple skunk mon, good for de hed," one of the Rastas says. The spliff makes the rounds. Ganja smoking is a communal thing. The world slows down, the big speakers are cranked up, sending music through my belly and into my bones . . . my perception warps into a shallow sine wave . . . the sea licks at the shore throwing phosphorescent ripples along the sand . . . the throbbing reggae beat envelopes my head, Red Stripe slides deliciously down my parched throat . . . people moving by on the road pick up the rhythms of the music as they pass . . . we are all one with the world.

I find myself walking down the road toward town and the Yacht Club, the beat of the big sound from Cuba's still reverberating in my core. There are several jerk barrels and patty stands along the road here. The smell of curry fills the air intermingling with the scent from the sea. I enter a zone where the music from Cuba's blends with the music from the live band at the Yacht Club. I stand there for a minute, looking up and down the road trying to capture this moment in my memory.

The Negril Yacht Club is my last stop of the night. Curiously, there are never any yachts here and there's no place to tie up if one did come, but the name beckons. Walking in from the parking lot I see a huge island style bar that's three deep with people. The barmen are hopping trying to keep everybody happy, but they're falling behind, way behind. The Red Stripes, rum and pina coladas are disappearing as soon as they're put down. The club has a large open-air bandstand and patio that overlooks the sea. There's a good-sized crowd out on the patio too, grooving to the band. Many are up dancing. The island girls are up there rolling their hips like only they can, it must be genetic, because I've never seen any white girl make moves like that.

Beyond the patio is a great view of the sea. Along the seawall that rims the patio are several tables covered with necklaces and small carvings. An entrepreneur has set up a gambling game at one end of the plaza. The action there is fast, wads of Jamaican money are rapidly being handed back and forth across the table.

The Ark Band is on stage. They're tight, hammering out traditional roots reggae to the appreciative crowd. They're practitioners of a Jamaican cultural aberration called 'Wheel and Wheel Again'. This is the annoying custom where a band or a Dee-Jay starts a song, lets it run for 20 seconds or so, stops it and then starts it up again, and then repeats the cycle several times over. I've asked but I haven't been able to get a good explanation for this practice. One fellow smiled and gave me the old Jamaican axiom, "In Jamaica, if it's nice, we do it twice." Yes, I agree with that, twice is nice, but thrice is a vice. It's kind of like an annoying facial tic that won't go away.

The Ark Band members are bouncing on the stage and their dreads are flying. The lead singer's are the longest, swinging well below his waist. These guys are good, very good, but their music doesn't have the Trenchtown hurt that imbibes the music of the old reggae masters. Perhaps that genre has seen its days.

The night air is filled with music, laughter and the jumbled banter of a hundred conversations. I sit on a stool near the bar, lean up against a bamboo post, sip on my beer and take in the crowded scene. Beyond the bright lights of the club, a spray of stars, like glittering diamonds on black velvet, decorate the night sky. I look out over the dark sea, just then a BIG fireball meteor glides across the sky leaving a long lumpy orange trail. Its passage leaves me awestruck. I look around to see if anyone else at the bar has seen it, but apparently no one has.

'Is this place for real?'

From the corner of my eye I catch a flash of red near the bar. Whoaa! A beautiful young Jamaican woman in a short skin-tight red dress is looking at me. She smiles. She's gorgeous. I can't help but smile back. She slinks over, locking her shining eyes with mine. She lays her small warm hand lightly on my bare thigh midway up.

Okay, I'll admit it, I know she's a working girl, but I am enjoying the moment purely for its face value, I can't help it, I was born male . . remember? The gold straps on her dress flash against her perfect chocolate skin. I feel like biting into her shoulder. She is an African queen.

"Hi," she says, pushing closer to me. Pheromones drift up from her skin triggering my basal instincts.

"What's you name?" she coos.

"John," I say, "yours?" But I already know; it's Temptation.

"Exotica," she says. Well, I wasn't that far off. She rubs my inner thigh, higher this time. We exchange small talk. I wallow in her beauty. She moves beside me, placing her free hand on my shoulder, then she rests her head there. Delicate waves of scent from her perfume wash through my nostrils, it's like breathing ambrosia; exquisite torture.

Then she pops the question that I knew inevitably would come. "Do you want some company tonight handsome?"

'Oh yes, I thought you'd never ask', I think, but don't vocalize.

Beelzebub: *'Go for it!' Remember what they say -- 'what goes down in Negril stays down in Negril'.*

"Don't tempt me darlin'," I say instead.

Virtue: *'Good boy.'*

She backs away a little and looks up at me, tilting her head and pouting slightly, "Come on."

"I really can't . . . honestly . . my wife is back at the room . . and she's expecting me."

This doesn't discourage her. Instead, she carefully purses her lips, redistributing her red lipstick, and then puts her ringed index finger on my chest making little swirling movements, "Maybe I should come back to your room with you and we can both wake her up?"

Several images filled with intertwined naked torsos, one of them black, immediately and involuntarily flash through my mind.

Exotica, seeing my hesitation, raises her eyebrows, "Hmmm, how about it?"

"Ahhh, no...no, thanks, I don't think so," I sputter, but the images persist and become increasingly more erotic.

She presses a small scrap of paper into my palm.

"Call me if you change your mind honey, we'll have fun." She moves away, her hips catching the humping rhythm of the Ark Band.

I take this as my cue to leave.

The parking lot is a jumble of rent-a-bikes and taxis. There's one with the name *'Salti Bwoy'* stenciled in big silver reflective letters across the top of the front windshield. I grab it for the quick ride back to the hotel.

I fall asleep to the gleeping sounds of the little tree frogs.

Donald Sangster International Airport and the Impenetrable Door

'Tis a foolish dog, bark at the flying bird.'
Jamaican Proverb

 We're cruising down the Hip Strip in MoBay a couple of miles from the Donald Sangster International Airport. It's been an uneventful, albeit bumpy, trip from Negril. I'm daydreaming about hordes of sand crabs when suddenly, the bus intercom comes on with a click and a loud squeal, "Did you all 'ave a good time in Jamaica?" the driver asks, his voice rising when he says 'Jamaica'.

"Yessss," we all reply in unison, like kids on a school bus.

"Den you will 'ave to come back to our beautiful island again."

"Yessss."

"Hear me now, de road from Negril is poor an' dere are many very bad accidents all de time," the driver says. "An' if you don' drive very careful it's easy to get into an accident. But you are here safely an' on time . . . 'cause I am de best driver in de company!"

I get this creeping feeling that I know where the driver's soliloquy is taking us.

"So don't be shy about leaving a tip of two or t'ree dollars for de driver, jus' to show your appreciation for a job well done . . . an' dose Jamaican dollars are no good where you are going, so you can leave dem wit' me an' I will take care of dem for you."

This brings a few laughs from the riders.

"But if you don't have any Jamaican money left, U.S. dollars will be accepted. T'ank you all very much and come back to Jamaica."

When I disembark the driver is standing outside the door with his hand out as if he's collecting the fare. I normally do tip drivers, and I almost feel obligated to tip this one, but I don't respond well to being berated so I walk past his outstretched hand without making a deposit.

The drop off area in front of the terminal is chaotic, chock full of buses, taxis, cars and vans. I check my watch, which will be going back into storage this afternoon, and see that I'm a little late, if the flight from Toronto was on schedule it has already arrived.

Before proceeding to the arrivals area to meet with the others I go to the Air Canada check-in counter to pick up a box of Jamaican flowers that I'd ordered for Amy earlier in the week. The inside of the terminal is crowded and busy. A message is broadcast over the PA system but it is so loud and distorted that I can't tell if it's a pre-boarding announcement or a weather report. The puzzled looks on the faces of several people around me confirm that I'm not the only one having comprehension problems.

I retrieve the box of flowers, which is long and heavy. I add it to my already heavy collection of baggage and hustle across the concourse to the arrivals area only to discover that it is not accessible from the inside of the terminal. I exit the building and ask directions from the first skycap that I see. He points to a big sign, 'Arrivals', which is mounted over a doorway. When I attempt to go through the doorway, through which I can see the arriving passengers and the bus yard beyond, I'm blocked by a big woman in a blue uniform with some kind of official looking badge on her bosom.

"Yu caan't go tru' suh," she intones, only paying half attention to me.

"Why not?" I ask.

"Yu caan't pass by heah suh," she replies, still totally disinterested.

"I'm supposed to meet my wife and kids over there," I point to the people milling around behind her, a mere thirty feet away, "and I have to catch a bus, which is probably waiting for me right now."

"No suh, yu caan't go tru' dis door suh," for the first time she actually focuses on me and in that moment I realize that my chances of getting past her and through that door are about even with my chances of becoming a professional hockey player, which are zero.

I become exasperated. Not being allowed to go through that door just doesn't make any sense to me, but in the back of my mind I'm convinced that it has got to have something to do with ganja.

"Alright, if you check with the Air Canada rep to see if my name is on the arriving passengers list, would that make a difference?" I said.

"I'll check suh, wait heah," with that she turns around and disappears into the crowd. Then I realize that she didn't take my name: Another guard, a younger woman, takes her place.

"Can I help you suh?" she asks with the same distracted air.

Oh no!, this is déjà vu all over again. "No... ah, I think the other woman is helping me . . . I hope."

A full five minutes pass and the first guard is nowhere to be seen. Getting desperate, I decide to attempt an end run by walking around the outside of the terminal building to the bus yard. I leave the door and head down the sidewalk dragging all my stuff behind me, thanking the Samsonite Company for putting good wheels on my big suitcase. To my dismay, there's a guard shack at the road at the end of the terminal and the whole area is enclosed in with a high chain-link fence, topped with rusty barbed wire.

Knowing full well what the answer will be, I point back around the terminal building and ask the guard inside the house, "Can I walk around to the bus yard?" She shakes her head and stares at me expressionless.

I'm bewildered and don't know what to do next. The old adage, "You can't get there from here," repeats like a tape loop in my head. I trundle slowly back to the terminal, pondering my dilemma.

I check the impenetrable door as I walk by, number two guard is still on station. There's a beer vendor's stand near the door. Maybe a drink will help me to think this out, besides I'm a little dry from all the to'ing and fro'ing, so I get a cool Ting.

"Thomas!" I hear my name being called. I look at the impenetrable door and Amy is standing there waving at me.

She looks gorgeous. I rush over to her and scoop her up and plant a wet kiss on her lips. We hug and I tell her how much I've missed her.

Her long, straight natural blonde hair falls across her shoulders. She's wearing a pair of low cut jeans and a tight black, sleeveless T-shirt with the word Princess written across the chest in sparkling silver letters. Her pink painted toenails are peeking out of her sandals.

I step back and admire her, asking out loud this time a question that I so often ask myself, "How did a guy like me end up with a babe like you?"

"You just got lucky I guess," she answers. We embrace and kiss again.

Amy and I have been together for eight years. We always knew that someday we would get married and one night seven months ago I asked her to be my wife. She said yes right away (pheww!) and we started planning. It took us about two weeks to decide on a simple, small wedding in Negril. A traditional wedding was never considered for many reasons, one of them being that none of our family lived in Ottawa so anyone attending our wedding would have to travel. So we reasoned, if they have to fly half way across the continent and stay in a hotel, why not fly to an island, stay at a resort and make a real holiday out of it? We chose an all-inclusive resort, which also eliminated all worries about meals and entertainment.

We picked Point Village in Negril because it offered a wedding package, was moderately priced and was family oriented. We sent out invitations to our relatives and close friends, the only catch being that people would have to get themselves to Point Village in Negril if they wanted to attend. In total, fourteen will be in our wedding party, which is more than we thought we would have. In addition to Amy and I, of course, my daughters Erin and Hannah, my brother Doug, his wife Donna and two of their boys, Cameron and Seamus are coming. Also, my sister Anona and her friend Wendy, Amy's mom and dad and her twin sisters, Linda and Michelle will attend.

As most weddings do, ours took a lot of planning with the additional task of fulfilling the Jamaican documentation requirements, all of which had to be notarized and in proper order. The resort has a wedding coordinator who looked after all of the on-site details. We communicated with her frequently via phone and fax and I did a final check with her a couple of days ago to ensure that all was prepared and in readiness.

"We've been waiting for you, the bus is ready to go," Amy tells me.

"They won't let me through this goddamn door," I explain. The guard looks impassively through me. "See if the bus driver will come around here and pick me up."

"OK, I'll be right back," she says.

I stand in a shady spot drinking my Ting and getting excited about seeing everybody. Soon the bus rolls up and I see a whole crew inside waving and smiling at me. I jump in and hug and greet everyone. Missing are my brother Doug and his family as they will be flying in from Houston and Amy's mom and dad won't be arriving for two more days.

We're sharing the bus with a group of first year students from Brock University near Toronto. As we approach the ganja bridge, I see a guy with a full head of dreads coming up to the bus. He's holding up an exceptionally large bud of ganja and waving it around. One of the students spots him and soon they are all crowded to the one side of the bus, trying to get a better look at the weed. The ganja guy comes right up to the open window that Erin is sitting at and he shoves the bud in. She leans back a little. The students "Ohh!" and "Ahh" and reverently extol the beauty of the bud. The dread holding it is a sight to behold, with a righteous set of locks down past his shoulders. This is the first close up encounter of a true set of dreads that the girls have had. They're both wearing identical, "Oh, my God!" looks on their faces. "He wants you to buy his weed," I say from the seat behind them.

The bus rolls across the narrow bridge and by the time we get to the other side the girls have recovered enough to start giggling. For the next couple of miles they titter and whisper and cover their mouths during repeated fits of giggling.

Everybody is in a relaxed and talkative mood and the trip to Negril passes very quickly. I point out things along the road to my girls. Erin, the older of the two, is openly excited, she stares wide-eyed at all that passes. Hannah, ever the cool teenager, is attempting to hide her excitement but is having a hard time doing so. When we pass through the Saturday market in Lucea the hustle and hubbub is too much and her façade suddenly drops. Her mouth opens a little and she becomes totally engrossed in the passing scene.

Before we know it, we are passing through the security gate at the Point Village Resort.

Getting Hitched

I see trees of green, red roses too
I see them bloom for me and you
And I think to myself what a wonderful world.
Louis Armstrong - 'What a Wonderful World'

Saturday

 We check into our rooms and are issued a map of the grounds. Point Village is a huge, spread-out resort, probably the largest property in Negril, encompassing eighteen acres and occupying most of Rutland Point. The resort's guestrooms are housed in clusters of low-rise buildings that are interconnected by a network of asphalt walkways.

We have a one-bedroom suite on the second floor of a room cluster on the northwest side of the resort overlooking the sea. There's a living area, a kitchenette and dining room and a king-size bed in the bedroom. Since we are on the all-inclusive plan we won't be using the kitchenette but we unpack the two bottles of Möet & Chandon that Amy brought with her and put them in the refrigerator. There's a balcony that can be accessed from the living room or the bedroom. The room is bright and comfortable and we are very happy with it. It's quite a stark contrast from my accommodations last week but there's also a major price difference.

Erin and Hannah have a small main floor room with two single beds in the cluster next to us, which is close enough for us to keep an eye on them but not so close that they will be keeping an ear on us. We hear someone calling Amy's name from the direction of the kitchen window. Looking out we see her sisters Linda and Michelle waving at us from a balcony across a small courtyard.

We're finishing our unpacking when Hannah bursts through the open door.

"Dad, come and see what's on our beds!" she says.

I go down to check it out. Sitting in the middle of each of their beds is a graceful white swan sculpted from a big white bath towel. At the foot of one of the beds, written by the chambermaid in long segments of Puss Tails, is the welcome message, 'One Love'. On the other bed is written 'Respect'.

Puss Tails are long fuzzy, flexible maroon colored fronds that grow on the bushes around the resort and throughout Jamaica. They look and feel like thin cat's tails.

There's a small TV on a nightstand in the room.

"You girls remember the agreement that we have on TV?" I ask.

"Yes dad," they both reply, annoyed.

Prior to coming down, I'd extracted an agreement from them that they wouldn't spend any time watching TV while we were here. Also, since they're missing a week of school while on this trip, they brought down some schoolwork with them and they've agreed that it will get done.

"Well I'm going to remove you from temptation," I said. I unplug the TV and disconnect the cable from the back of it, placing it in the nightstand drawer. The girls grimace. I leave the TV turned around with the screen facing the wall.

Shortly thereafter we meet the rest of the group at the resort's main dining lounge and entertainment area that's marked as 'The Village Connection' on the map. From there we set out on a walking tour of the grounds.

Rutland Point is an outcropping of land that juts into the sea at the extreme north end of the seven-mile beach. This places Point Village somewhat off the beaten path, in fact it's about as far from the town center and the cliffs as you can get and still be in Negril. Due to its isolated location, Point Village is quiet and has a secluded ambiance. On its south side, it borders on the notorious Hedonism II property, infamous for its nude beach, wild parties and shenanigans. (Amy and I will be checking into Hedo next week for the first part of our honeymoon, but nobody else knows this.) There's a high fence along the property line between Hedo and Point Village and it's impossible to see around, over or through it. There is also a checkpoint at an opening in the fence on the beach with a guard shack on either side. There's a small crescent shaped beach on the Point Village side of the property that's posted with a sign that reads, **'Adult Beach'**. A few naked people are sunning on the small beach as we walk by.

Beyond a small outcropping of trees that marks the end of the little beach there is a water sports shack sitting above a small rocky cove. Here the resort's guests can borrow snorkeling gear, kayaks and sailboats.

I walk up to the edge of the cove and I'm suddenly overcome by a strong flashback of sitting here some twenty years ago. At that time there was no Point Village and Rutland Point, crisscrossed by a latticework of footpaths, was totally uninhabited. On the north side of the point were deliciously secluded coves with small private sandy beaches. It was in those coves where the whole nude thing that eventually took over Hedo got its start. In those days a trip to Bloody Bay, on the north side of the point, was like an adventure trek into the backcountry.

On that first trip a Jamaican friend showed me this spot and we went there many times to sit and talk and meditate while we looked at the sea and drank warm Red Stripes. Now I'm back to the very same place with my girls. I have a fleeting mental image of two shimmering time lines meeting and forming a nexus. A karmic circle has been closed.

"Da snorkeling boat leaves from dere." I snap back to the present, the water sports attendant is pointing to a cement pier to the side of the shack.

"An' de snorkeling is very good right from de shore here too," he says, now waving his hand in the direction of the shallow flats that start at the foot of the cove. We're planning a snorkeling expedition later in the week so we'll have the opportunity to find out firsthand.

Sitting just off shore across a three hundred-yard channel is Booby Cay, in all of its deserted tropical island alluring beauty. It's possible to swim across the channel to Booby Cay from the cove but it's actively discouraged due to the volume of motorboat and jet ski traffic that passes through there.

We continue our tour along the pathway that hugs the shoreline. The waterfront here consists of a natural low rocky coast. Little crabs scurry over the rocks that line the shore. They freeze in position waiting for the next wave to wash over them. Between the waves they move quickly to new clefts in the rock and then await the next inundation. We watch them go about their business. It must be tough to go through life in quick seven-second bursts.

Amy comments that there are hardly any people around, although we had been told that the resort is sold-out. The apparent lack of people is no doubt due to the sheer size of the grounds. We round the path to the western side of the point. Here there is a swimming pool and a shore bar and around the bar is the first concentration of people that we encounter. We stop at the bar and get 'walkin' drinks before continuing our tour.

A little further along is a sand volleyball court and another small crescent-shaped beach. There are several families with young children playing on the beach. Beyond the beach are two seaside cafés and another bar, which happens to be very handy to our room. My Pina Colada has gone down quickly so I grab a cold beer at the bar.

We approach a flat grassy area that overlooks the sea to the northwest. The sea is rougher here and the waves are splashing up against the rocky shore. There's a fresh breeze blowing inland.

"This would be a beautiful spot for our wedding," Amy says. The setting is tranquil and we are at the far end of the grounds, away from most of the rooms and the resort activities. The location is naturally breathtaking.

A few yards beyond the grassy area we come across what is marked on the map as 'The Rock Pools'. They're situated on a rocky area that's raised about eight feet above the sea, right on the shoreline. We walk onto a large section of coral that has been leveled off and paved over with cement. Here several little swimming pools have been carved down into the coral and lined with smooth cement. Because this area is exposed to a rough sea, the pools are filled with salt water that has washed over the rocks in the form of high waves. I dip my foot into one of them. The water is bath warm.

"Last one in buys the next round," I said. Ten seconds later we are all sitting in the warm, cozy little pools. The hot Caribbean sun has heated the water resulting in natural salt-water hot tubs. It is absolutely delightful. We sit there sipping on our cool cocktails, overlooking the clear emerald waters of the ocean. Occasionally a larger wave washes over the rocky shore and cooler water from the sea spills into the rock pools.

We are truly in paradise.

The rock pools are so inviting that we stay until our fingers turn pruney. Reluctantly, one by one, we exit the pools and presently we are on the last leg of our tour. But we know it won't be long before we will be back to the rock pools.

North of the rock pools is a tiny cove that is sheltered from the sea, its waters calm and clear. On the north side of the cove is a cliff wall that's about twenty feet high. We walk around and stand at the top of the cliff. From here we have a good view of the shallow and tranquil Bloody Bay. Nestled at the base of Bloody Bay is The Grand Lido, Negril's most luxurious resort, its property abutting that of Point Village along its northern flank. A graceful looking yacht is moored out in the middle of the bay. It's the 147 foot M/Y Zein, the wedding gift from Aristotle Onassis to Princess Grace and Prince Rainier of Monaco. They used it as their honeymoon yacht. Later it was acquired by The Grand Lido and it is now used for sunset cruises, weddings and other special events.

The Grand Lido has a connection with the chick-flick *'How Stella Got Her Groove Back'*. The movie is about a middle-aged African-American woman who is on vacation at a Caribbean resort and meets a much younger hunk of a Jamaican waiter at breakfast one morning. They fall in love and live happily ever - - (yeah, right, and the cow jumped over the moon.) The movie is based on a real life event that is supposed to have taken place at The Grand Lido.   The movie, however, was filmed in Port Antonio on the north coast of Jamaica.

We finally reach the back lot of the resort where there are tennis courts and a full size soccer field, the end of our circumnavigation of Point Village. A goat is tied up to a stake at one end of the soccer field. We go over and scratch him behind the ears and tell him how handsome he is. He nudges us with energetic little head butts in an apparent show of affection. After feeding him several clumps of grass we bid him goodbye. As we are walking away he lets go a loud sonorous billy goat fart. Erin and Hannah start to laugh so hard that they practically fall over each other.

Sunday

The next morning Amy and I meet with the Point Village wedding coordinator, Carol, to finalize our arrangements. She takes us on a tour of the resort's wedding venues. We don't tell her that we already have a place in mind. The first one she shows us is the little nude beach. Since we aren't doing a nude wedding, we decline. The next is a spot on the lawn on higher ground overlooking the ocean. The view is spectacular, with Long Bay and Booby Cay in the background. We tour a couple more venues, all of which are very nice, but we hold off until she takes us to the grassy spot near the rock pools.

"This is the place," Amy says.

"Yes, this is one of our most popular spots," agrees Carol, "it's about a private as you can get on a big resort like this." She points to where a wedding arch will be erected and describes how it will be decorated. We will stand under the arch as the minister performs the wedding ceremony. Off to one side of the arch location, the tables for our cake cutting and toasts will be arranged in a T pattern. We look around, envisioning the layout.

"Yes, this will do just fine," Amy says.

So it's decided, on Friday afternoon at 4:00pm we will be wed on a grassy flat a mere garter belt throw away from the sea.

Amy's parents, Keith and Ann, arrive in the afternoon. We meet them in the lobby where they are sitting waiting patiently for their room, which we are told, will soon be ready. We talk and the minutes tick by. Keith begins to get frustrated. Forty-five minutes pass and there is still no room. Finally he gets pissed and goes to the front desk and raises a minor ruckus. When he comes back he has a key and a map of the resort with their room location marked on it.

It was a minor coup to get Amy's dad to come to the wedding. Although her mom was keen on the idea from the very beginning and said that she was coming hell-or-high-water, Keith doesn't like flying and hadn't been on an airplane in many years. This is a little surprising since he is a licensed pilot himself and used to rent small airplanes to fly the family around the country on vacation trips. Initially he was a little put off by the arrangements, feeling that the wedding should have been held closer to Vancouver, where they live, or at the very least, on the mainland. Since he wasn't willing to get on a plane, he explored the possibilities of driving from western Canada to Miami and then taking a boat to Jamaica. Ann told him that she was flying and that he could drive across the continent and take a boat by himself if he wanted to. Eventually Keith relented and agreed to fly into Montego Bay. The flight apparently went well.

My brother Doug, his wife Donna and his two boys also arrive in the afternoon.

Amy and I are relieved that Point Village has turned out to be a good choice. It was a big risk choosing the place sight unseen, and to do so for the whole group raised the ante even more. But it has proven to be a great venue for a wedding gathering and other than little complaints, everyone seems pleased with it. We spend the rest of the day hanging together in a loose group, relaxing, re-acquainting, sunning and playing. My brother's sons, Cameron and Shamus, are water rats, they spend their entire time swimming, snorkeling, sailing and windsurfing. Since everyone has taken the all–inclusive option, gone are the pressures of preparing meals, planning entertainment and the myriad other logistical problems that usually have to be dealt with when invited guests arrive. Upon arrival we merely unpacked and started to relax and enjoy.

Later on we gather for dinner at The Sun Drenched Café, a thatched roof, airy, open dining room that overlooks the sea on the northwest shore of the property next to one of the beach bars. It's a quiet place to dine, away from the commotion of The Village Connection. We await our meals, bathed in the warm red rays of the sinking sun. The surf surges quietly against the rocky shore. The setting could not be more perfect. By the time the sun slips below the sea we are one big happy, relaxed family.

After dining we retire to the patio between the bar and the café. We talk away the hours in the warm of the star-filled night. One by one the members of our group drop out and make their way to their beds until only my brother and I remain. The gleeping frogs and the sounds of the waves lapping at the shore accompany us.

Monday

This morning Amy and I walk into The Village Connection for a late breakfast. We are surprised to see Cameron up on the stage with a microphone in his hand. Several other guests and a couple of the club's entertainment staff are on stage with him. Cameron is attempting to sing 'O Canada' but he's having problems. His cheeks are puffed out, his mouth apparently stuffed full of something, and he's laughing as he sings. When he finishes he passes the mike to another guest who first crams three cookies into his mouth before he attempts to sing 'The Star Spangled Banner'. The next contestant is an Italian who also attempts to sing his own national anthem similarly handicapped. Somehow Cameron wins the competition. For his efforts he walks away with a small bottle of Tia Maria, the native Jamaican coffee liqueur.

Like most of the all-inclusive resorts in Jamaica, Point Village employs a staff of entertainment coordinators whose job it is to organize activities and motivate the guests to get involved. Bottles of liquor and T-shirts being the prime motivators.

The practice of keeping such staff was started back in the seventies by Club Med. The Club Med animators, called GO's, which is short for Gentil Organisateurs, keep the guests participating in club activities. I watched a GO at work one afternoon on the beach at the Club Med in Guadeloupe. In this case, he was the designated 'Club Fool'. His role was not to get guests involved in any activity but rather to entertain them, and he did this by acting out solo skits designed to amuse. On that particular afternoon he was busily engaged in dragging various articles that he had gathered from around the club down to a spot on the beach. He worked alone and in silence, industriously lashing things together until it became apparent that he was constructing a raft. A loose crowd gathered to watch and urge him in his efforts, which he continued as if unaware of their presence. Occasionally an onlooker would help out by providing a piece for his raft or by holding a couple of parts while he lashed them together. By and by, with the final addition of a flagpole flying the French tri-couleur, he completed his raft, which he then dragged with much feigned difficulty to the sea's edge. He pushed the raft into the water, boarded it and began to paddle furiously. The raft promptly broke apart and sank, leaving the Club Fool floundering in the water. The spectators cheered and the Club Fool, soaked and defeated, waded back to shore.

At Point Village the animators are called 'The Friends'. They are a young, helpful, friendly bunch of multi-talented people who do a good job at keeping things lively with organized activities like volleyball, scavenger hunts and numerous other competitions.

There's a small craft market within a five-minute walk of the resort. Amy and I are planning an excursion there to look for a couple of seashells and we want the girls to come with us, but first we have to find them. They aren't in their room and nobody in our group has seen them for a while. Acting on a hunch, we go down and check the rock pools. There we find them, sitting in the warm water, sipping on their colas. They are unwilling to get out and accompany us.

Erin and Hannah have fallen in love with Negril. I can't say that I'm surprised. How can one not fall in love with paradise? This being their first trip to the Caribbean, they are enthralled with everything they see. It was the same for me on my first trip and I'm enjoying seeing things new again through their eyes.

We enter the craft market, our quest is to acquire a couple of sea shells that we are planning on using as ring-bearing platforms. Back home Amy bought a couple of tiny satin pillows, about the size of a small lemon, and wrapped them in lace. Then she sewed a short length of ribbon on top and tied it in a bow. Our plan is to tie our rings to the ribbons and then stuff the little lace pillows into a seashell with the right size opening.

Erin and Hannah are our ring bearers. They'll carry the seashells in the wedding procession.

We look in several stalls searching for the right shell. I had wanted to use conch shells, because I love them so, but their openings are not suited for the little pillows.

We go into one stall that has quite a broad selection of shells. Amy and I are examining one when we hear the girls talking in hushed whispers and giggling behind us. They're inspecting a display table upon which there is a squad of different sized Ready Freddy's, all lined up and standing erect. There are also several other interesting pieces on the table, figures of naked women complete with large pendulous breasts, thick pubic hair and prominently sculpted buttocks. There are a few small but detailed pieces depicting couples entwined in various sexual positions and there is one explicit carving of three couples who are engaged in an orgy. I thought it considerate of the shop owner to have arranged all of the erotica in one easy-to-peruse department.

We move on to another, less risqué stand and it is here that we find what we are looking for; triton shells. The tightly spiraled shells have openings that are the exact fit for the ring cushions. Triton shells are very pretty, decorated with thin swirling bands of mottled color ranging from light to dark brown. We buy two medium sized shells that fit nicely in the girl's hands.

We are crossing the road on the way back to the resort, happy with our find, when Amy says, "What about the souvenirs for our guests?" This results in another tour of the market, which we had already circled three times. In the end we leave with a flock of little carved birds with tiny red beads for eyes. The vendor, who thought that we were bargaining for just one carving, was floored but very happy when we cleaned out his stock.

Tuesday

Today we are going on a snorkeling trip out to the nearby reef. It's the perfect Caribbean day, calm, sunny and hot with a few billowy clouds floating about, just enough to provide occasional and much appreciated shade from the blazing sun.

We all pile into the glass bottom boat, chatting happily, several other guests from the resort board with us. A plywood awning shades the boat. Along the bottom of the hull, on either side of the keel, are thick panes of glass mounted into a framework of wood. The seabed is clearly visible through the windows, although here at the dock the bottom is sandy and uninteresting. Water is slowly leaking in through a couple of places in the glass framework, but not enough to be concerned about. Several plastic bailing pails are scattered about the boat. It's obvious from the large beads of silicone that are plastered into several of the window joints that leaks are a common problem.

The Jamaican crewman yanks on the cord to start the outboard. It doesn't respond. He cranks it again, still no results. Two of the resort's water sport staff who are standing on the dock watching the crewman simultaneously begin to shout instructions in rapid fire patois while we all sit patiently watching them. The crewman makes a couple of adjustments on the side of the motor and again gives it a pull. It still won't start. One of the guys from the dock jumps into the boat and takes the cowling off the outboard. He works on it for several minutes and then gives it a pull. It sputters a couple of times and then reluctantly comes to life, emitting a choking cloud of oily smelling blue smoke that drifts over the passengers. My sister Anona gasps and covers her nose with her towel. The engine cowling is replaced, the mooring lines are cast off and we are on our way. The outboard motor, which is a 15 horsepower, is far too small for the size and weight of the boat. It's revving at top speed and producing a lot of noise and smoke, but in spite of it all we are moving very slowly through the water.

Eventually we plow our way out to the reef and tie up to a buoy. The water is incredibly clear and inviting, it literally calls out for us to jump in. Mother Ocean calling her children to come home.

We get our briefing from the crewmen. He encourages us to stay inside the reef by telling us that they have an agreement with the local sharks that they can eat anyone who ventures outside.

We leap in, eager to explore. The first thing that I notice is a sunken cannon and anchor, obviously placed there as underwater attractions. I wave the girls over and we circle around the artifacts. They're encrusted with coral, sponges and sea fans, but still very recognizable. A school of small, black and white striped fish, called sergeant majors, is stationed around the anchor. The reef is in about ten to fifteen feet of water and it's teeming with life. We see hundreds of little, rainbow colored reef fish darting about the coral in small schools. I spot a puffer fish cowering in the eelgrass on the bottom. I dive down and gently trap it in under my tented palms. Puffer fish can't move very fast, I've caught them before while scuba diving. The puffer immediately inflates into a cantaloupe-sized ball of thorns. I buoy him carefully up to the surface and show him to the girls. I carefully pass him to Erin and she gingerly accepts him. She examines him and then passes him off to Hannah. A woman in a one-piece flower print bathing suit who is snorkeling around in her life jacket comes over to see what we have.

The puffer's little eyes are open wide and its tiny mouth is slowly gaping open and shut. Try as he might, his frantically moving fins can't propel his engorged body fast enough to escape from us. He looks absolutely helpless and adorable. We can't help but smile widely when we hold him up close to our masks and look into his cute little face.

Our big smiles break the seals on our masks and water leaks in. Finally we let the little guy go and he sinks slowly back to the bottom, happy to escape from the big, noisy, bubble-blowing monsters.

We're hovering over a clump of brain coral when I feel something kicking at my legs, the woman in the flowered suit and life jacket has swum close to me and her fins are battering my knees. She is becoming quite a nuisance. The girls and I swim rapidly off to another location.

Black sea urchins with long sharp spines are nestled in the nooks and crannies of the coral. One can tell just by looking not to touch these little critters. Their spines are needle-sharp and very brittle and will break off in the skin leaving a welt that hurts like hell and itches for several days. But for all of their prickly, menacing sharpness, the black urchins are extraordinarily beautiful. Examined close up one can see delicate threads of bright purple running in and around the base of their slowly articulating spines.

We also see a couple of lobsters hiding under rocky ledges, their antennae poking out from beneath, sensing us in the water as we pass. We see several ochre-colored starfish and many sea cucumbers. I pick one of them up and gently stroke its silky back. A small trumpet fish floats vertically beside a tall, tubular-shaped sponge, attempting to camouflage its long slender body. The girls are having a great time, hamming it up and snapping pictures with their disposable underwater cameras.

A bright blue parrot fish takes quick bites out of the coral with its hard beak-like mouth. We hear a little 'crunch' each time he makes contact with the coral. I've been diving when many parrot fish were grazing in the area and the sea was filled with a cacophony of loud crunching sounds. The sound of their grazing reminds me of a movie theater full of popcorn munchers.

Parrot fish consume a lot of coral, which they excrete as coral sand. Each parrot fish produces hundreds of pounds of sand per year. Most people don't realize that when they are lying out relaxing on the beach, much of what they are resting on is parrot fish poop.

A small, white and black spotted eagle ray swoops gracefully beneath us. It's about 20 inches across, wingtip to wingtip. Its long black tail, about two and a half feet in length, snakes sinuously behind it. It makes a wide banking turn, and heads back out to sea. One moment it's there, the next it's nowhere to be seen.

This excites Erin so much that she surfaces, takes the snorkel out of her mouth and yells, "Dad! I saw a stingray!" Because her nose is trapped in her mask, her voice sounds comically high and nasally. I tell her that it's not a stingray and not to worry about it. Eagle rays cannot harm people.

The woman in the flower print suit is back again! She bumps into me and gives me a little apologetic wave. The ocean is very large, I can't understand why she has to stick so close to us. I'm beginning to get annoyed with her.

Hannah, who doesn't have a lot of meat on her bones, gets chilled and climbs back into the boat, her skin covered with goose bumps. I swim under the boat and peer up through one of the windows at her. She starts to laugh and points at me, which makes me laugh and again seawater leaks into my mask, stinging my eyes.

A few minutes later I hear the boat hand whistling, he's waving us back in. One by one we reluctantly leave the water. Once aboard, I join in the animated discussion, everyone is talking about what they've seen on the reef. A woman says that she saw a dogfish, which is a small member of the shark family. She holds her hands apart, showing us how big it was. Several people are excited about seeing the ray that passed through the area.

I look around trying to spot the flower print bathing suit of the annoying woman. It's my sister Anona! I didn't recognize her with the life jacket, mask and snorkel on.

Linda is rubbing the heel of her right hand. I take a look at it, there's a small black dot with a red welt around it. It looks to me like she's had a close encounter with a black sea urchin. I tell her that vinegar or urine, applied to the puncture point, will provide relief from the sting. I then offer to pee on her hand, but she demurs.

Later in the evening I go down to the girl's room to visit them and see what they are up to. Approaching their room, I see the telltale blue moving light of a TV shining through the frosted glass panel in the door. I knock on the door and shout, "Hey girls, it's me, open up."

I hear muffled talking, then, "Just a minute, we're getting dressed!" This is followed by shadows scrambling rapidly behind the glass. The TV light winks out. There's more movement and a few moments later Hannah opens the door. I look at the TV. The screen is turned toward the wall, just as I had left it, and the cable is nowhere to be seen. Schoolbooks are spread out on each of the beds and the girls are in their nightclothes. I walk over to the TV and put my hand on the grill. It's hot.

"Hmmm, the TV is hot, I wonder why that is?" Neither one of them replies and they both keep their noses buried in their schoolbooks.

Erin employs the 'change of subject' diversionary tactic. "Guess what happened to me today Dad?" she says.

"Ummm, you stayed in the rock pools too long and turned into a prune?"

"No! One of the Jamaican guys who works here asked me to marry him!"

"Yeah, right, and the cow jumped over the moon."

"No Dad, I'm serious. And he put his ring on my finger to see if it would fit too, didn't he Hannah!" she turned and looked at her little sister for support.

Hannah, her nose still buried in a textbook, nodded almost imperceptibly and kept on reading.

"So, what did you say?" I asked. I knew that female tourists often got marriage proposals when visiting Jamaica but I never expected one of my babies to attract that kind of attention.

"I told him I would think about it and answer him later," Erin said.

"That's my girl, always keep your options open, but be sure and say no."

"I was thinking I might say yes, he's kind of cute Dad," Erin said.

"Never mind that, tell him thank you but no. And you girls should turn the lights out soon."

I gave them a hug and left them to their devoirs. On the way back to the room it occurred to me that I'd soon have to start thinking of my girls as young women; time had done an end-run on me again.

Wednesday

Today we feel the need to escape from the resort for a while so we decide to go for a group walk along the beach. We discuss starting out on the road first and then cutting down to the beach at the first opportunity in a maneuver to avoid the nudes at Hedo so as not to shock the girls.

"Oh, don't worry about Erin," Michelle says, "we went through Hedo together yesterday."

"Yes, but I kept my head down and didn't look," Erin replied quickly in her defense.

"Oh come on Erin, I saw you looking around when we went through there!" Michelle teased. Erin's face turned deep red and she looked away.

It's a hot day and we don't get too far down the beach before Hannah complains about the heat. I take her up to the road and we head back to Point Village. As we walk we keep an eye out for a discarded bottle that's suitable to carry a message. Amy and I have written a note on the back of one of our wedding invitations and we're planning on putting it in a bottle and throwing it into the sea after the wedding ceremony. Before long we come across a small pile of trash in the ditch by the side of the road. I see an intact bottle and pick it up to examine. It's an empty coconut rum bottle, complete with the screw cap.

"Hey mon, dat's my bottle!" I look up and see a young Jamaican guy approaching us. In this country, where jobs and money are scarce, no single opportunity to make a buck is left unexploited.

"How about the rest of this trash, is that yours as well?" I ask.

"Yeah mon." He points to the bottle in my hand. "You can 'ave dat bottle for a dollar," he says.

A woman standing across the road from us in the shade of a tree, apparently waiting for a bus or a taxi, yells a short phrase in patios at the young man. He looks across to her and responds plaintively, his hands spread at his sides. She replies, this time louder and in a much sharper tone. He shrugs his shoulders and moves on down the road without looking at us again.

"What was that all about?" asks Hannah, wide-eyed.

"I didn't understand a word of it," I reply.

We continue our trek back to the hotel, message bottle in hand.

My brother Doug and I are engaged in an impromptu game of lawn darts when I spot a small patch of mimosa growing in the grass. I had been introduced to the mimosa, a fern-like plant that grows everywhere, during my first trip to the island. The mimosas in the resort's lawn only grow to about two inches in height before they get mowed back down. I bent over the plants and called Doug over.

"Watch this," I said. I gently stroked the spine of the plant with my index finger. The tiny leaves folded in on themselves, like hands held together in prayer, as my finger passed between them.

"You have got to be kidding me!" Doug exclaimed.

"Go ahead, try it," I said, pointing out another mimosa frond that was open.

Doug gingerly ran his finger over its spine, the leaves closed with a rapidity that is astonishing for a plant.

"I have to video this!" he said and trotted off to get his camera. He returns with several of our group in tow. Feeling like a magician, I demonstrate the phenomenon again to the amazement of all. Everybody has a try at it and soon we've exhausted the little patch of plants. They all sit with their leaves tightly folded.

The mimosa is not indigenous to Jamaica, it is found in the tropics all over the world where it is often referred to as the 'sensitive plant'. Jamaican's also call it 'shame-me-lady', interpreting its reaction to being touched as that of hiding in shame.

I got quite a different reaction when I demonstrated the timid mimosa plant to a couple of fellows back in the '70's. It was shortly after I had learned of the plant's neat trick. I was sitting on a grassy knoll, passing the time watching a group of bikini clad young women playing volleyball, when a couple of guys that I had met at the hotel walked up and sat down beside me. They were brash, loud-talking assholes whom I didn't have much use for. If I remember correctly they were from Ohio. They had just returned from a trip to town and they were obviously high on something.

"What're you guys on?" I asked.

"We had some of Mrs. Brown's mushroom tea," one of them said, then they both began giggling uncontrollably. Tea made from the highly potent psylocibin mushroom is widely, and legally, available in Negril. I've never tried it but I've seen several people who have taken a little too much and have paid the price in bad trips.

I thought I would have some fun. "Look at this," I said, and stroked my finger down the spine of a nearby mimosa plant. The effect on the mushroom boys was instantaneous. They both stopped giggling and one of them scrambled to his feet and quickly retreated to a safe distance. The other grabbed his head with both hands and said, "Ohhhh, don't fuck with my mind man!" His bulging eyes were transfixed on the little plant.

"Look at this! It's black magic!" I said, and stroked another one. It obligingly clasped its leaves together.

"Holy shit man . . . stop it, you're fucking with me!" He rolled away from the plant, got up and stumbled over to join his buddy. They sat on the grass there, huddled together, occasionally casting wary looks in my direction.

After dinner at the resort we hire a van to take us down to Risky Business for some dancing. There are a couple of taxi-vans parked in the resort lot and we try to make a deal on one of the vans but the driver isn't willing to budge. He wants to charge us a per-head price of three dollars US for the one-way trip. That's thirty dollars for the ten of us for a four-minute ride. Knowing that there are always taxis waiting just outside the gate we take a short walk and hire three cabs at five dollars each.

There's a good-sized crowd made up of a mix of locals and tourists at Risky's. The dance floor is a wooden platform raised above the sand. There's a second story open deck overlooking the dance floor and the beach beyond. Tonight the music is supplied by a deejay sitting in a windowed booth beside the dance floor. Out on the beach a large bonfire is blazing, sending streamers of embers and smoke into the night sky.

We get drinks and go up to the second floor deck to look down on the action. The smell of ganja is thick in the tropical night air. Linda, Michelle and Amy can't sit still for long. They're in a party mood and the music grabs them. The three of them rush down the steps and hit the floor together forming a dancing triangle. Several tourist girls with braided hair are gyrating in another group beside them.

I lean back in my chair, take a deep breath and look up into the sky, the Milky Way arcs from horizon to horizon, filled with a billion dazzling points of light. Erin and Hannah laugh out loud and point down at the dance floor. Three young Jamaican guys, dressed to kill and weighted down with gold jewelry, have moved in on Amy and her sisters. The one dancing with Amy is doing the 'bamboo thrust' at her. She giggles but continues to dance.

We hang around for another hour or so, dancing and drinking and partying, then head back to the Point just before midnight.

Thursday

Amy and I are up earlier today so we take the opportunity to go for a jog along the beach in the cool of the morning. We cut through the gap in the fence at the Hedo checkpoint. Even though it's early there are already are quite a few people sunning in the nude. There's something unsettling about nakedness in the slanting rays of the early morning sun. There was an episode on Jerry Seinfeld's TV sit-com where the subject of nakedness in certain situations gave rise to the term 'bad naked'. As we move through the nude area of Hedo we see several examples of 'bad naked' sprawled on the beach lounges. When we check into Hedo next week we'll have the opportunity to examine this nude thing in hairy detail.

Five days into the week and Erin has already spent every last dollar that she came with. Given that we are at an all-inclusive, I can't figure out how she's managed it. Hannah still has most of her Jamaican money. I expect this is a pattern that will probably ever be so.

My daughters have taken well to the all-inclusive concept. There are no meals to prepare, no housework to do and unlimited soft drinks. Here, they don't even have to make their beds in the morning. Amy and I hardly ever see them during the day as they are keeping themselves busy with their cousins. Occasionally we'll see them slowly walking along one of the asphalt pathways that crisscross the resort. They always have drinks in hand, which I take on good faith to be non-alcoholic. Although if they wanted, they could drink legally here since there is no minimum drinking age in Jamaica.

We meet the girls for lunch at the Paradise Café, another idyllic seaside spot. This is also a popular hangout for the local cats, which are scrawny timid waifs compared to our big, well-fed Kahuna-sized cat back home. Amy and her sisters are cat lovers and somehow the cats seem to know this. Suffice to say that the cats are being well fed and are getting lots of attention this week.

Today Anona treats the girls to a parasail ride. We go down to the cement pier where a big powerful boat has pulled up. The girls and Anona board it and it rumbles out into the bay. Soon Erin and Hannah are suspended in a double seat under a large red, white and blue canopy. When they arrive back at the pier they are still beaming at the experience.

We spend the rest of the day sunning and relaxing. Cameron and Shamus play volleyball on the beach in an international tournament arranged by The Friends. I wander around the resort taking photos.

Tomorrow is our wedding day.

Friday

We wake up on our wedding day to the sound of rain slashing hard against the walls. It's a tropical downpour. In due time it passes, leaving some clouds and a brisk northerly wind. The sea is up and almost every wave is crashing over the sea wall at the rock pools.

But the day is warm and the sun is shining. We go to the administration office to check with Carol on arrangements. Amy frets over the weather but Carol assures her that a little rain on the wedding day portends future prosperity.

Several vendors from the big craft market in town have come to the resort today to set up a mini-market near the volleyball courts. I'm checking what they have on display when I come across a most awesome looking angel fish carving.

"Wow, this is beautiful!" I say to the vendor.

"Yea mon," he says smiling, "it's carved from de root wood from de ironwood tree."

The fish is sculpted frozen in the middle of a sharp turn, its mouth open. Each of its scales have been individually and intricately carved into its sides. It stands about twenty inches high. Most of the wood in the carving is dark but there is a lighter colored band running diagonally through the body and the tail. I pick it up. It's very heavy, weighing about forty-five pounds. I want it.

"How much for the fish?" I ask.

"How much would you pay for it?" comes the reply.

"Depends how much you want for him," I answer.

"Well, if you buy today, I will let you have it for one hundred dollars."

"I'll think about it," I said.

I'm feeling a little out-of-sorts today, I don't really know what to do with myself. The wedding ceremony isn't until 4:00pm, but I'm already antsy. Amy is off spending the morning with her sisters. I go to the room to do some reading and I'm out on the balcony when Hannah shows up. She tells me she's bored. We get the little souvenir birds out and tie silver ribbons around their necks.

Hannah and I go down to the rock pools where the waves are pounding up over the edge of the rocks, creating ten foot geysers of warm salt water. We stand where the water is spraying and get gloriously doused over and over again. The thunder from the water drowns out our laughter. In the manner of the ocean, approximately every tenth wave is much bigger than its predecessors. We await the big ones and when they come, they almost knock us off our feet.

It's early afternoon and the wind continues to blow hard so we decide to move our wedding venue downwind a little to a more sheltered location near the beach bar. We will still be on the grassy flat but we'll be further away from the rock pools.

After lunch Amy hugs me and says, "The next time you see me I'll be coming down the aisle."

"You mean you'll be coming down the path," I answer.

"Yes, the path. Are you sure you want to go through with this?" she asks.

Beelzebub: *'This is your last chance mon! Take it! Say NO and run!"*

Virtue: *'Gwaan, doan listen to him, do it! It's the right t'ing to do'*

"Yeah mon, it's the right t'ing to do," I say.

"OK, don't say that I didn't give you a chance!" she says. "I'm off to get my hair and nails done." She pecks me on the lips, waves, leaves the room and I'm alone again.

I amuse myself by lining the little souvenir birds up like soldiers and then circling them. Then one pecks another in the rump and they get into a scrap and a bird-melee breaks out, which I mediate.

Time drags. I check the champagne in the fridge, yup, it's cold. I read a little and write in my journal.

At about 2:30 I get dressed. I'm wearing beige silk dress shorts, a new pair of leather sandals and a blousey white, short-sleeved rayon shirt, no tie. I've asked all of the men in the wedding party to dress in shorts as well. I buff the triton shells and tie Amy's wedding band to the pillow in one of them.

There's a knock at the door, it's Linda and Michelle. "Thomas you have to leave now! We're going to get Amy ready and you know it's bad luck to see the bride in her dress before the wedding."

Erin and Hannah dart past me carrying their dresses as I go

through the door. They've had their hair and makeup done and they look absolutely darling.

I go down to the beach bar to have my last drink as a single man. From the bar I can see the ironwood angel fish carving that I was looking at in the morning. I walk over to the vendor.

"I'll give you seventy for the fish," I say, picking up where we left off.

"I need at least ninety dollars. Look at it, it's a very nice piece."

"Yes, he's beautiful, I'll give you eighty, no more."

"You can have it for eighty-five."

I offer my hand to the vendor, "It's a deal," I say. We shake on it.

I tote the heavy carving over to the beach bar and plunk it down on the bar top. Soon Doug, Donna and the boys show up. Doug admires the fish.

"What do you think I should name him?" I ask.

"Why don't you call him 'Irie'?" he suggests.

"Perfect, Irie he shall be!" I said.

Originally, the term 'irie' was used by Rastafarians to mean "I free", as in free from repression and Babylon. The pronunciation gradually evolved to Irie. Now 'Irie' is used as a salutation, as a positive affirmation of good vibes.

Amy's mom, Anona and her friend Wendy all show up at about the same time and we walk over to the wedding venue. The archway is draped with white lace and a big pink crepe paper wedding bell is hung from its apex. The white-skirted tables are set with champagne glasses and silverware upon a royal blue tablecloth.

Carol comes down with a boom-box and places it near the tables, a Jamaican man dressed in a black suit and carrying a bible is with her.

"This is the minister, Father Avery," she says. I introduce myself and shake his hand.

"Amy and the other girls are ready," Carol says, "we'll be right down!"

I go back to the bar, get Irie and carry him over to a stump beside the tables, he becomes the fifteenth member of our wedding party. The minister moves off to be by himself, he stands near the wedding arch, looking contemplatively out to sea.

"Here they come!" says Amy's mom.

Erin and Hannah, in the blue satin dresses, are leading the procession, each holding a triton shell in front of them. They're followed by Linda and Michelle. Behind the twins are Amy and her dad, walking arm in arm. Keith is wearing shorts.

Amy looks ravishing in her knee-length, simple white dress. She's carrying a bouquet of colorful flowers. Her long blonde hair is pulled up and held back with a flowered hair wreath. She is a vision of beauty, I have to work at catching my breath.

Carol turns on the boom box and the traditional wedding march begins to play. Amy stops the procession and says something to Linda. Although I can't hear her, I know what she's saying. She had told me on many occasions that she didn't want to 'walk down the aisle' to the traditional wedding march. We replace Carol's tape with the one that we recorded at home. Unfortunately when it starts to play, instead of the 'The Wedding Song' by Kenny G, we hear 'Don't Worry, Be Happy' by Bobby McFerrin. Amy shrugs and the procession continues.

We all arrive and position ourselves under the arch, my brother Doug stands beside me as my best man, repaying the favor from twenty-five years ago.

The minister performs the ceremony and all goes well. When I'm asked the question I answer "I will", resisting the temptation to answer "Yeah mon" as I had been threatening to do. Amy also answers "I will", falling through on her threat to answer the question with "No problem".

We both remember our vows, and with the sound of the surf in the background, we are pronounced man and wife at 4:30pm.

We go off with Glenroy, the photographer, to have some pictures taken at various settings around the resort. He looks at me and then takes a lingering look at Amy.

"How did you get such a woman?" he asks me.

"I ask myself the same question all the time," I answer truthfully.

He poses us in front of the wide trunk of a Banyan tree. Again he takes a look at Amy in her form-fitting white dress, decorated with rows of pipe sequins, "My lady's dress is tight like a cabbage," he notes.

Amy whispers, "These Jamaican guys are such flirts!" She shows me one of the nails on her right hand. "Look at this," she says. "When I was getting my nails done a Jamaican guy was flirting with the esthetician, and he said, 'I want to take you for a walk and kiss you all over' and she started to giggle and messed up the polish on this nail. See?"

Glenroy leads us to the adult beach, which thankfully is deserted at this time of the day. He takes several pictures with the sea as a backdrop. We do back-to-back poses and then he takes a couple of shots of me lifting Amy, her one arm draped around my shoulders, the other holding her bouquet, one leg straight, toes pointed skyward, the other bent at the knee.

We work our way back to the group, posing for more photos as we go.

There's a traditional Jamaican wedding cake on the table. It's a spicy chocolate fruit mélange that has been marinated in rum and glazed with almond paste icing. Amy and I make the ceremonial cut, Glenroy takes a photo.

"You have to do the 'bird feeding' now," Carol tells us. This entails holding a large chunk of wedding cake in one's teeth and feeding it to your partner, mouth to mouth as a mother bird feeds her chicks. No hands are allowed. We do this several times feeding each other, sometimes successfully, other times dropping pieces of cake on the table. We toast our way through the two bottles of champagne that were supplied by the resort and then start in on the two bottles of Moet et Chandon that Amy brought down.

We pose for a photo where I am down on one knee peeling the garter off of Amy's outstretched leg with my teeth.

I toss the garter belt, flicking it like an elastic band. Cameron bowls Shamus over to catch it. Then Amy tosses the bouquet. Linda adroitly plants an elbow into Michelle's side and maneuvers into position under the airborne bouquet, snatching it deftly from the air. While doing so she has a concentrated and deadly serious expression on her face.

Amy rolls up the invitation, ties it in a silver ribbon and places it in the empty coconut rum bottle that Hannah and I found on the road. We go out to a little point of land that protects the beach and hurl the bottle as far out to sea as we can. We watch it bob in the waves for a while then bid it a good trip to Africa and rejoin the group.

Erin and Hannah pass out the little souvenir birds and Amy and I toast everybody and thank them for sharing our day with us.

We finish the champagne and cake, and as the sun is barely touching the horizon Glenroy poses us for a final group photo with the sunset as a backdrop.

We move over to the bar, bringing Irie with us. Reggae is playing and we have more drinks and dance on the patio in the fading sunlight. Next door at the Sundrenched Cafe, the tables for our dinner are being set up. Linda and Michelle are getting blitzed. Nobody has to worry about driving tonight.

We're served a pasta and seafood dinner. More toasts are proposed and Amy and I are called to our feet so many times by the clinking of silverware on glasses that we get dizzy.

Later we wander to The Village Connection and join in the festivities. We enter a reggae dance contest and Cameron wins, adding a bottle of rum to his growing collection.

This week at Point Village four couples have 'tied the knot' and for the final dance of the night all the couples are called to the floor and we're introduced to the other guests.   Then one of the resort's entertainment staff takes the mike and in a very respectable and gravelly Louis Armstrong voice he sings 'What a Wonderful World'.

As I'm dancing with my new bride, I think back on the splendid week that we have spent with our families and what the future might hold for us, and I can't help but agree with Mr. Armstrong. It really *is* a wonderful world.

Saturday

The next morning goes by in a rush.   We have a quick, late breakfast and help the girls get their bags down to reception for the trip home. Then there's a flurry of hugs, kisses and hand shaking and back thumping.   Last-minute group photos are taken and a few of The Friends come down to say goodbye. Some of the women cry.   Then everyone except Amy and I and her mom and dad pile into the mini bus and it pulls away, Hannah's arms waving out the window as it goes.

I watch the mini-bus exit the parking lot and I feel a little wave of loneliness creep over me. I'll miss my girls. They'll fly to Toronto with Linda and Michelle and then on to Ottawa where they will stay with their mother until we get back home.

Amy and I pack our bags in preparation for our move to Hedonism next door. Although they know that we will be checking out of Point Village and moving to another hotel in Negril, nobody knows exactly where we are going. We've left emergency numbers in a sealed envelope.

Ten minutes later Amy and I are hightailing it over to Hedo dragging our luggage behind us. Irie has severely taxed our carrying capacity. We exit the Point Village gate, walk a short distance down a lane and pass through the Hedo checkpoint.   The guards are bemused to see new guests arriving on foot.

Yeeee! Haaaa! The serious partying is about to begin!

Down an' Dutty at Hedo

'Mi com yah fe drink milk, mi noh com yah fe count cows.'
Jamaican Proverb

Let's take a walk on the wild side. Take the following ingredients: a vacation, no responsibilities, hot sun, a cool pool, a limitless supply of booze, bountiful high-grade ganja and a big group of uninhibited naked people. Mix them all together on the shores of the Caribbean, add a dash of music and Creole spices and what do you have? In a word, Hedonism.

Its infamous reputation precedes it. To those who have heard of the place, the name conjures up images of naked people cavorting in Eden-like gardens and wantonly engaging in group sex with abandon. That image, in fact, is not that far from reality. When a red cap at MoBay airport hears that a couple is headed for Hedo, he's likely to call out, "Two for the zoo!" as he tosses their bags onto his cart. And if the airline loses the bags of a Hedo-bound traveler, not to worry, clothes are not necessary.

The Hedo credo is *'Be wicked for a week'*; experience shows that it only takes a couple of days to get down and dirty.

At Hedo, everything is included; meals and snacks (all day and all night long), cocktails, wine and beer, nightly entertainment, all land and water sports facilities, including equipment and instruction, and there's absolutely no tipping allowed.

John Issa, the chairman of the Super Clubs chain of exclusive resorts, introduced the all-inclusive concept to Jamaica in 1976 when he opened The Negril Beach Village, which later became Hedonism II in 1981. There never was a Hedonism I, unless you count the original Negril Beach Village.

We spent a week at Hedo, but it seemed a lot longer.

Saturday Afternoon

We check in to the resort and are given a sheaf of briefing papers, an activity list, a rundown on entertainment, a list of excursions and information on Jamaica. There's a lot of paperwork to go through. We take our tote bags to the room; our big pieces will be delivered by one of the luggage haulers. Hedo is laid out somewhat like Point Village, with rows of low-rise buildings connected by pathways, but the foliage here is much, more lush.

Amy and I are beyond excited to finally be here. On the way to the room we are asked by no less than three different people if we need ganja, which I thought was very considerate of them, they really do take care of your needs here. Our room is on the second floor of the west wing overlooking the gardens. Although all of the rooms at Hedo are identical, a premium is charged for those that have a view of the nude areas of the resort.

I unlock the door and we enter the room. It's medium-sized and dominated by a king-size bed in the center. Amy lets out a squeal of delight, "Look! There's a mirror on the ceiling above the bed!" She drops her bag and makes a flying leap onto the big bed. She jumps up and down on it a few times like a little kid and then flops down, laying spread-eagled looking up at the mirror.

"Look how long my left leg is!" she laughs. The mirror has a bulge in it that produces remarkable distortions. I hop onto the bed beside her and maneuver my forehead into the distortion area of the mirror. The effect is akin to standing in front of a full-length fun-house mirror. In the reflection my brow extends to Frankenstein proportions and my body shrinks to a length of three feet.

"You monster!" Amy says, and rolls on top of me. Looking up, I now see an enormous blonde head topping a tiny doll's body mounted astride a baby Frankenstein. The big blonde head bends down and nuzzles at baby Frankenstein's neck. I quickly lose interest in the mirror.

The room has a big bay window overlooking the garden. There's a sitting area in the bay, but there is no balcony, which is too bad. A balcony is such a handy place to hang wet beachwear, it never seems to dry completely when draped on the shower rod in the bathroom. There is no TV in the room, which probably helps to keep more people out of their rooms mixing and mingling, since that is what Hedo is all about. We won't miss the TV, but we do appreciate the mini AM/FM radio and CD player, I brought down a collection of Bob Marley CDs. The FM will be tuned to IRIE whenever we are in the room. The bathroom is small and disappointing. There's nowhere near enough counter space for the hundreds of little bottles and tubes and other cosmetic do-dads that Amy travels with. It's in the bathroom that Hedo shows its twenty-five year plus age, the fixtures are old, the tile work could be better and the slat window above the shower is definitely a relic.

Our bags are delivered. It feels strange not to tip the guy who lugged them up the stairs. With Irie packed inside, my big Samsonite is enormously heavy. I pull him out and put him up on the dresser.

Junior's Rasta-Lion is carefully packed away in a tote bag and remains so.

Amy and I go for a tour of the property. Our first stop is the main bar, which is adjacent to the central dining area and abuts the pool deck. Amy orders a Bloody Mary, she tells the barman that she wants it hot. He adds a splash of Jamaican hot sauce, smiles and hands it to her. She takes a sip. "Wow! This is hot!" she exclaims, exhaling through 'O' shaped lips, "It makes my eardrums sting!"

The bar is ringed with colorful pictures and short descriptions of the cocktails that are offered. I debate between 'Sex on the Beach' and 'Dirty Banana' and finally chose the later. It's a blended concoction of crushed ice, crème de banana, crème de cacao, Kahlua, two scoops of vanilla ice cream and a whole ripe banana, essentially an adult milkshake. I take a sip, it is delicious and very smooth.

We walk toward the beach and enter the disco that's situated on the terrace below the swimming pool. There's a welcome party for newcomers going on, pallid skinned people are swilling rum punch and dancing to loud music. I have a two-week tan and Amy is turning nicely brown after her one week in the sun, but we manage to pass ourselves off as newcomers anyhow and join in. Mounted in the wall behind the disco bar are two big portholes that provide a view into the deep end of the main swimming pool.

We spend some time in the air-conditioned coolness of the dark disco and them emerge back into the heat and brilliance of the day to continue our tour. There's a well-equipped gym, open on one side to shuffleboard courts. A couple of buff Jamaican guys are working out in the gym, but no guests. I'd feel intimidated working out beside those guys too. We head down to the southern beach area, called the prude beach as this is where guests who prefer to remain clothed hang out, or rather don't hang out, as the case may be. Dominating the prude beach area is an enormous tree with a bar built around it. It looks like something from Fantasy Island. At one end of the bar is a self-serve daiquiri machine offering pina colada and strawberry flavors. My Dirty Banana has evaporated, so I help myself to the pina colada spout. The barman adds a generous dollop of rum and we are on our way again.

The guests at this resort are definitely more outgoing than those at Point Village and the grounds are more populated. It's not that the Point Villagers were unfriendly, but everybody here seems to walk around with big smiles on their faces and they greet us with cheery hellos.

"Oh! I'm going to try that!" Amy points to a circus trapeze rig set up on the upper part of the beach. It's complete with ladders, high platforms and a big net. This is another one of the activities that's offered at Hedo. Under the guidance of experts, guests can try their hand at the trapeze. The artists also put on an after-dinner circus show once a week.

The prude beach is fairly deserted, so we head north toward the nude beach area passing the dock where the big catamaran that I saw at Rick's is tied up. There's a water sports activity shack and a couple of massage huts along the way. We pass a sign saying;

Nude Beach
No Photography or Video

In the distance is a field of naked bodies, some lounging on the beach, some crowded around a snack-shack and others milling about. We continue into their midst, feeling rather conspicuous in our shorts and tank tops. There are bodies of every size and shape here. Most of the nudies seem to be around 40ish and I guess-timate that 90% of them are American. One fellow gets up to adjust the position of his lounge. In doing so he thrusts his large flaccid butt up into the air in our direction. Amy lets out a stifled gasp and quickly averts her eyes, which was the proper thing to do. I attempt to do the same but find myself transfixed, staring into the fellow's hairy nether region, which is decorously punctuated by a wrinkled, dangling scrotum. This particular view was not one of the sights that I have mentally catalogued under potential 'nude beach scenes'. I felt as if I'd just been sucker punched in the solar plexus. Again, Seinfeld's 'Bad Naked' comes to mind.

We reach the extreme end of the property, marked by the high fence that completely blocks the view of Point Village next door. More accurately I expect, it blocks the view from the Point Village side into the nude area of Hedo. The nude pool and hot tub are located in this area. We had walked (hastily) through the beach part of this section last week when we were staying at the Point, but dared not dawdle to study the layout. There's a swim-up bar at the beach end of the pool and it's crowded with nudies, standing cheek to cheek, many are obviously and happily inebriated. Not wanting to be left out, I sidle up to the bar and order a shot of twenty-five year old Appleton rum, neat. In the pool there are several built-in water-level tables that are surrounded by people. The tabletops are covered with a litter of empty plastic glasses. The whole area is jam-packed with people, which explains why the prude beach was literally deserted. There's a party atmosphere here, people are laughing and talking in loud voices, jumping into the pool. Music is blaring from somewhere. At one end of the pool is a raised mini-pool that waterfalls down into the main pool.

There's a group of nude young ladies cavorting in the mini pool. They're caressing each other, giggling and splashing around in the water. There are several guys gathered around intently watching the girls.

Beelzebub wakes up and grunts satisfaction in my left ear.

I check my mental 'nude beach scenes' catalogue. Ahah! There it is! I lick the tip of my mental pencil and satisfyingly tick off one of the images.

On the other side of the mini pool is a shallower section and to one side of that there's a grotto constructed from fieldstones. Water spills off the roof of the grotto, creating a waterfall curtain across the entrance.

We continue our tour, picking our way through the crowded pool deck.

I mentally pinch myself, *'Is this place for real?'*

Amy casts me a 'How about this?' look, her eyebrows arching above her dark sunglasses. I reply with a mini shrug.

"Hey! Get naked or leave!" someone yells. I look around and see a middle aged guy with a big paunch standing on the other side of the pool, a drink in each hand. Mentally I give him my best Al Pacino; *'Are you talking to me!'* but outwardly I ignore him and continue walking.

We later found out that if you take too long to disrobe while hanging out around the nude pool, an attendant will inform you nicely that you will have to strip or leave. I can't see why anybody would want to remain clothed while at the nude area anyhow.

We reach the nude hot tub. It's huge and it's jam-packed with naked people. The hot tub is laid out in a four-leaf clover shape. At the apex of one of the clover leafs a woman, head bobbing vigorously, is leaning over a moaning man who is sprawled half in, half out of the hot tub. They have a large and appreciative audience. Amy and I look at each other, she tilts her head in the direction of a path that leads off between two room complexes, away from the nude area. Once beyond earshot of the pool deck she bursts out giggling, "Well! I never!" she says, fanning her hand rapidly in front of her face.

From what we've seen in our first couple of hours here, it appears as if the Hedonism reputation is pretty well spot on. We are not prudes, but the transition from the family atmosphere of Point Village to the sybaritic character of Hedo is a bit rapid and unanticipated. For a simple boy from the Bible belt of the Canadian prairies, it would take a little getting used to. But I feel compelled to give it my best.

At the intersection of two paths, we come across a lacquered tree stump about eight feet high. In it are carved initials and names and dates, presumably of guests who wanted to leave their mark. We lean closer and see that there are also carvings of penises and little figures engaged in sex in every imaginable position. In fact, the tree stump itself is a large phallic symbol, somewhat like a 3D Kuma Sutra carved out of wood.

Everywhere we walk there is soft background music. Curious, we track it down and discover that it's coming from the rocks. Or what initially appeared to be rocks are in fact speakers ingeniously camouflaged as small, weathered volcanic looking stones. Our tour continues to the accompaniment of an assortment of Bob Marley and Jimmy Buffett tunes, it couldn't be more perfect.

We meander our way through the grounds. The vegetation is astonishing in its variety and lushness. Plants that grow to 10 inches in pots back home vault thirty feet up the sides of tree trunks here.

"This must be what the Garden of Eden was like," Amy says.

I remind her of the scene back in the hot tub.

"Okay," she corrects herself, "perhaps Sodom and Gomorrah then."

We wend our way through the garden and back to our room block. I dare not turn to look back in the direction of the hot tub lest perchance my gaze alight on something that may turn me into a pillar of salt.

"God-damn-it!" Amy yells over the sound of the running shower from the bathroom.

I go to the bathroom door, "What's up?"

"The temperature of the shower keeps changing, I had it adjusted just right and then it got cool and then it fucking near scalded me."

Just then the spray from the shower suddenly reduced to a dribble. "Well that's great," Amy says, poking her head out of the shower. Her hair is covered with shampoo suds. I start to laugh. The shower comes back on and she dives back under it.

Later I take a shower and although the pressure is up, there isn't a drop of hot water. So I rinse in cold water, which isn't so bad since it really isn't any colder than going for a dip in the ocean.

We agree that future showers will have to be taken during 'off-prime' hours. The antiquated plumbing system of Hedo doesn't seem to be capable of handling 500 people hitting the shower at the same time.

When we leave our room to go to dinner. It's dark and the little frogs have started into their nightly chorus of gleepings. Dinner at Hedo is served buffet style, or alternatively, advance reservations can be made at The Pastafari, the resort's Italian style restaurant.

We walk into the main dining area and, as moths to a flame, head directly to the buffet. It is humungous! The food is artistically presented on several different terraced islands and there is way too much to choose from.

Amy settles on rib roast, green beans and roast potatoes, all cooked and spiced to perfection and served at the right temperature. I peruse the buffet's salad section, which consists of more than twenty types of salads, and I'm delighted to find a big bowl of cold conch salad nestled inconspicuously there. I help myself to multiple servings. In fact, the conch salad is all that I have.

Dinner at Hedo is more than a mere culinary event. Many of the guests, the females in particular, dress to express. Looking around I see more glitter, sequins, netting and audacious finery than the queens sport at the annual pride parade.

Amy comes back from the dessert table, eyes agog, "You have to go and check out the desserts, they are to-die-for! And now that I'm a married woman, I can eat as many desserts as I want!"

I walk over to the dessert table. There's a detailed ice sculpture of a jumping dolphin displayed on a raised dais in the middle of the table. It's surrounded by a colorful and dizzying array of cakes, pastries, pies, chocolate creations, puddings, custards and ice creams. I quickly turn away before temptation gets the better of me. There are items on the dessert buffet table that I'm certain contain at least 8,000 calories per individual serving. I believe that the concept of the dessert buffet is fundamentally flawed. It's akin to giving brain-wired lab rats unlimited access to a button that stimulates orgasms. Overindulgence is inevitable.

Sunday

The guests at all-inclusive resorts tend to stick around the property because they don't want to miss out on any of the meals or non-stop organized activities; after all, that's what they have paid for. While that's fine for many, for me it's a problem. I miss the local vibes and color and I find that after staying at an all-inclusive resort for a while I feel a strong need to 'escape' the compound and go out for a dose of reality. Although as I've said before, I'm still not completely convinced that Negril *is* real.

As it's our eighth day in all-inclusive captivity, Amy and I are planning a walk down the beach toward town, which happens to be the only direction that you can walk the beach from Hedo. But before we go we write a big stack of postcards. I do my friends and family and Amy does hers. She takes care, writing personalized notes to all the addressees, explaining what we are doing and how much fun we are having. I finish mine quickly writing the same message on each, *'Ha, Ha, I'm in Jamaica and you're not!'*, which, in the end, conveys the same message as the little notes that Amy is writing.

As Amy finishes her postcards, I relax in the window seat overlooking the garden, thoughts of my first trip to Hedonism in the '70's, when it was still The Negril Beach Village, come back to me.

◄◄   ◄◄   ◄◄

At that point in time, it was still in the process of evolving into an all-inclusive resort. It used to be known as a hangout for singles, way before the current 'uninhibited couples' clientele took over. I was attracted to the club because scuba diving was included, which made it a very good deal, and by all counts it seemed like a relatively laid-back environment. At that time the dive operation was run out of a water sports shack that was located a short distance down the beach, toward the south end of what is now the Sandals property. I was new to scuba diving then and my top priority was to make sure that I got in my allotted two dives a day, regardless of anything else that may have been going on. Diving in the clear waters of the Negril reefs was exhilarating and glorious. It was then that I became hooked on scuba for life. In the evenings I chummed around with Errol, the first mate on the twenty-eight foot dive boat. Toward the end of my two-week stay he let me drive the boat out to the dive sites. I fell so naturally into the Negril lifestyle that on one of the latter trips a diving couple from the States asked me how long I had been living on the island.

Back then drinks were not part of the resort package and each drink had to be individually purchased. But cash wasn't handled at the bars so drinks were purchased with little plastic tokens, acquired at a central kiosk, which came in the form of plastic shark's teeth. These could be snapped together to make a bracelet, or, for the high rollers, a necklace. The shark's teeth came in bronze, silver and gold, with the gold ones being the most valuable. To buy a drink one would snap off a couple of shark's teeth and slap them down on the bar. The shark's teeth could also be used as currency with some vendors on the beach, depending on how thirsty they were. I think the management borrowed the idea from Club Med, who were using snap-together beads as drink tokens in that era. In those days the Negril Beach Village grounds weren't cordoned off as they are today and everybody had unfettered access to the beach, although there were always a few security guards on patrol.

That first trip I came alone and, not wanting to pay the single supplement, I took my chances getting billeted with a stranger. I was reading in my room early one afternoon, as yet unassigned a roommate, when the door opened and a very attractive young lady walked in carrying her luggage. She saw me and stopped dead in her tracks.

"Are you staying in this room?" she asked, quickly checking the key in her hand.

I considered a smart repartee, like, 'No, but they let me read here in the afternoon,' but instead I answered, "Yes, I am." And then hopefully, "Are you my new roommate?" Mentally, I had already formed an image of her in a tiny bikini.

"Er... ," she paused for a moment, glancing around the room, her eyes lingering on the two single beds spaced a mere 18 inches apart. I wanted to think that she was considering staying. But instead she said, "Ah . . . I think there's been a mistake. Sorry to have bothered you." She backed out of the room, the door slammed shut and I never saw her again, though not from lack of searching. Perhaps the whole episode was just a mid-afternoon Negrillian daydream.

My assigned roommate did show up later that day. Funny thing is, I never saw the guy. From the tags on his baggage, I knew he was from New York. We never crossed paths during that day and I crashed early so I would be fresh for the morning dive. I was sleeping when he retired to the room for the night. At around 1:00am, I awoke to the sounds of a wild boar being strangled to death in the bed next to me. The wretched beast was struggling for its life, choking, squealing and grunting, its throat bubbling with phlegm. It was hideous. Had I not heard it for myself, I would never have believed that a human being could produce such tortuous sounds. I bailed out of the room right then and there and went to the reception and demanded a room change. The night clerk was unapologetic, exhibiting a kind of 'You pays your money and you takes your chances' attitude.

"I'm sorry mon, but dere's nuting I can do 'bout it tonight."

So I crashed out on the rattan couch in the reception. The clerk told me that I couldn't do that, but I stayed there all night anyway. In the morning the guest relations manager saw me laying there as she reported in for work. She looked after me right away and I got a new room on-the-spot. I went back to my old room and cleared all my stuff out as quietly as I could. I needn't have worried, the beast from New York didn't stir.

My new room was on the ground floor of the room-block at the extreme south end of the property overlooking the sea. At night I left the window open and instead of guttural throat sounds, I was serenaded by the steady rhythm of the waves washing the beach. It was heavenly. I had the room to myself for the rest of my stay.

⏭ ⏭ ⏭

"Hey daydreamer, are you still with me?" Amy had finished her postcards and was standing beside me.

We cross the security checkpoint at the border between the Hedo and Sandals properties. Our names and room number are recorded on the Hedo checklist. There's an older Jamaican guy hanging around the guard shack, he looks like he might be a friend of one of the security people. He looks at me and says, "You're an ole timer my friend."

"Yeah, got a few good years left in me though."

"No, I mean you bin comin' here a long time, haven't you?" he responds.

"I have, but how do you know that," I ask.

He points to the black coral amulet that I have hanging on a leather cord around my neck. "Dat's an old piece, you got dat a long time ago."

He's right, I bought the Y-shaped piece of black coral on an early trip to Negril from a vendor on the beach about fifty yards from where we're standing and I've been wearing it on every visit that I've made to the Caribbean since. The guy that I bought it from said that the more I wore it close to my skin the more of its power would transfer to me. It's a beautiful, silky smooth, ebony black piece that over the years has worn to a deep luster. Small gold flecks are suspended in it just below its shining surface. I wear it when I go diving as a good luck talisman and to bring it back to visit the deeps from whence it came.

Today it's illegal to harvest black coral in Jamaica, as it should be, but back in the 70's the attitudes toward such things were just beginning to change. However, on recent trips to Hawaii and Las Vegas I was quite surprised to see items of black coral for sale in some mid-priced jewelry shops.

"Yes it is, and I bought it right there many, many years ago," I point to a spot on the beach in front of Sandals. "In front of the Sundowner Hotel."

"I remember the Sundowner," he says, nodding and smiling. "Who did you buy it from?"

"I don't remember his name, but he walked around with a briefcase full of black coral pieces."

The fellow nods and smiles. We bid him and the guard good day and cross onto the Sandals side of the fence.

The guard there comes out of the little shack and makes a note of our passing. He then radios his counterpart at the far end of the property, "One male, black top, one female, blonde, topless, commin' t'ru." This is a common practice for all of the big all-inclusives. Access to the beaches in Jamaica cannot be restricted, as they are public property. However, the all-inclusives are concerned with security and go to great lengths to prevent scroungers from freeloading on their facilities. All that being said, it is mildly annoying to be stopped and questioned by uniformed guards at every checkpoint. Fortunately this only occurs at the all-inclusive end of the beach. Closer to town there are no such checkpoints.

The first time Amy and I approached the beach in front of Sandals we looked forward to seeing scores of attractive, athletic young people engaged in volleyball and water sports, lounging, laughing and sipping on drinks from coconuts garnished with hibiscus blossoms. We expected that all the men would have ripped athletic builds and be sporting six packs and flashing dazzling smiles of perfect teeth. And the women, we expected, would be playfully cavorting in the ocean, tossing heads full of long, thick shining hair, all of them wearing tiny bikinis, the tops of which would be overflowing with bouncing breasts. These were not unrealistic expectations because that's exactly what we had seen in the colorful Sandals advertising brochures.

Needless to say, we were disappointed when confronted with the stark reality of the situation. The Sandals clientele is not made up of young athletes and beautiful models. If fact, they are just your average cross section of quasi-affluent holiday goers, complete with an ample complement of large butts, bulging bellies and hairy backs. What ever happened to truth in advertising?

Today we walk by Sandals without high expectations.

We get as far as Beaches Inn, a lovely looking resort a short stroll from Hedo. The day is hot so we go for a plunge in the ocean. The waters of Negril are so swimmer-friendly that one doesn't have to search out a place for a dip. Wherever the mood strikes all one need do is turn and walk into the water. Other than a short stretch or rocky bottom where the trees come down to the water near Long Bay Park, the entire seven-mile beach is eminently swim-able.

I come up from being dunked by Amy when she says, "Hey look, it's my mom and dad!" I look shoreward and see Keith and Ann walking by. They have obviously seen us but are trying to 'sneak by' unnoticed as they are both holding their sandals up to hide their faces. Apparently they don't want to disturb the 'honeymooners'. It occurs to me that, since no one knows the identity of our honeymoon hotel, Keith and Ann probably now think that we are staying at Beaches Inn. Amy and I have a good laugh over this.

We exit the water and walk down the beach a little further. There we see a spanking-new parasail boat sitting on a trailer. Its paint is shiny and all the running gear is rust-free and appears fully functional. This is a rarity in Jamaica. Here, mechanized things break down rapidly from heavy use, salt water and the relentless heat and humidity and they are in a constant state of disrepair. To make matters worse, replacement parts are expensive and come from afar. It's normal for boats, vehicles and anything mechanical to be generally run-down. I admire the freshness of the new boat, knowing that it won't look this way for much longer.

We move a few paces down the beach and become engaged in a discussion with one of the vendors on the quality and variety of the seashells that he has on display. I take this as a sign that we have truly slowed down to island time. Pausing to examine boats and discussing the minutiae of the conch shell are subjects of suitable depth and interest that befit our present frame of mind. Amy tries on a necklace of little leaves carved from mother-of-pearl. The vendor holds up a mirror for her, she decides it looks good and buys it. As we are about to leave the vendor says to Amy, "Do you need another boyfriend?"

"Another boyfriend?" she replies.

"Yeah mon, you an' me an' I can get a nice Jamaican girl for your boyfriend," he offers.

"No . . . we're okay for now, thank you," she says.

He then tells us that he has several girlfriends and five children with different 'mommas'. I assume this is a type of sexual pedigree that he's offering in an attempt to get Amy to reconsider. He then adds, matter-of-factly, that tourist women often pay him for his sexual services.

Amy declines again, in spite of the man's evident sexual prowess. Remarkably, this turn in the conversation does not seem out of context with our seashell discussion. We wish Ready Freddy a good day and continue on our way down the beach.

Soon the heat of the day commands that we take a break. We find some shade under a sea grape and sit down, the waves lapping at our feet. We spend the next hour relaxing there, daydreaming, talking, watching people walk by, squinting out over the sparkling water and digging our feet into the wet sand.

Sunday Afternoon in the Nude Hot Tub

There's a party in the Hedo nude hot tub every afternoon. It's not an organized club event, it just turns out that way. Curious as to what really goes on there, we head down to the nude pool a little early to settle in before the party really gets going. Even though the nude hot tub is very large, it can hold over 100 people, in the afternoon it fills up fast.

We take the walkway that goes through the 'au naturel' section of the grounds. Not unexpectedly, on our way we pass a few people strolling around in the buff, but at Hedo one quickly becomes accustomed to naked bodies and flopping body parts, so we hardly take notice. We observe that the doors to several of the guestrooms are propped open. This, we've been told, is the Hedo way of signaling, 'feel free come in and join us'. Before entering the hot tub pool deck we stop to admire the Kuma Sutra tree phallic symbol again, it's truly an amazing work of art, a totem pole perfectly suited for the location.

There are already quite a few people in the hot tub, mostly couples gathered together in groups, but there are also numerous single guys. The woman sitting across from us has an enormous set of boobs that are bobbing in the water in front of her. Her nipples are peeking just above the waterline, looking like a set of predatory alligator eyes. We drop our towels and slip in. It's not as hot as it could be but it's comfortable. Amy snuggles up to me, in the water her skin feels like slippery silk against mine. We embrace, enjoying the warm closeness, unencumbered by bathing suits.

I notice that a couple of the single guys are sculling their way closer to us. We'd been warned about the single men here. Hedo couples refer to them as 'Vinnies' or 'Wallys'. These are not complementary nicknames. Vinnies can be seen lurking in the hot tub any time that there are naked women present. Besides the opportunities to gawk at tits and ass (and how can I fault them for that?) they also come to Hedo hoping to get in on some action as a third or fourth (and how can I fault them for that?). As they move stealthily through the water they remind me of sharks, slowly prowling around with watchful, hungry eyes, sniffing the air for the scent of perfume. Not every single male is a Vinnie, it's his attitude and behavior that determines if he is so branded. Occasionally a Vinnie will try to take pictures in the hot tub area with a small camera that he has sneaked into the area. Woe betides the wretched Vinnie who is caught with a hot camera in his hand.

One of the Vinnies paddles to within a couple of feet of us. He's submerged up to his chin. He says hello and we reply politely but otherwise ignore him. Several minutes later, another couple arrives and sits down on the edge of the tub, Vinnie sets his sights on them and slowly drifts off in their direction.

There are not a lot of single women at Hedo. I've heard that the ratio of single men to single women is around seven to one, not great odds for the average guy but very promising for the ladies. However, hope springs eternal (as do other things), especially in the mating game, and all things considered, Hedo is probably not a bad place for single guys as long as they don't have high expectations of getting laid. After all, there are nude women around everywhere and there's the occasional free sex show, what more could a libidinous male ask for? As long as there's a handy supply of lubricant and if mother thumb and the four sisters are cooperative (and they always are), I think the chances of a single guy finding the solitary form of happiness at Hedo are quite good.

There's a large 'lifestyles' club banner strung up on the side of the stone grotto. For several weeks during the winter season large groups from American swingers clubs descend on Hedo like a pack of randy rabbits on a lettuce patch. A naked woman is posing for a picture beneath the banner. By the quality of the equipment that he has set up the photographer looks like a pro. I don't know what publication the photo will appear in but I am quite sure that the young lady is not going to be a poster girl for the Mormon Tabernacle Choir.

"Oh...my...God," Amy breathes in my ear. "Look at that guy!" she tips her head slightly, indicating a man standing on the pool deck. At first glance, I thought he was wearing a metal pouch around his scrotum, which, around here, would not be considered out of place. Then, with mild shock, I realize that the entire surface of his scrotum is covered with......scrotum rings? In spite of the hot water that I'm sitting in, which normally has a relaxing effect, I feel a strong, involuntary, empathetic clenching sensation between my legs. The fellow has also shaved off all of his pubic hair, which makes his penis look like that of a big baby. How he managed to navigate a razor around his forest of adornments, I shudder to think. Perhaps he lathered his scrotum with hair removal cream.

To add injury to insult, he has another ring dangling from the tip of his penis. This one is looped through the pee-hole and pokes out the underside of the head about a half an inch up. The clenching sensation in my crotch becomes more intense. I later learned that this particular adornment is called a 'Prince Albert'. I confess that prior to this shocking introduction, the mere concept of penis jewelry was totally alien to me.

I do a quick scan of the nudies around the pool deck and note that there are several other visible piercings. Nipple rings and dangling labia charms abound. It's odd, but sitting buck naked in the nude hot tub, I suddenly feel conspicuously underdressed.

I appoint myself judge and mentally award the guy with the silver encased scrotum with today's blue ribbon for genital jewelry. In my imagination, I have one of my female assistants pin it to his penis, I doubt that he would mind. I have three questions that I ask the winner;

1. *'Why did you do this?'*
2. *'Is there a spraying and dribbling problem when you void?'*
3. *'What happens when you pass through airport security?'*

"This water is kind of cloudy," Amy says, her nose scrunched up a little. She's right, I hadn't noticed it with everything else that was going on, but when I look down into the water, I can't even see my feet.

"And what's this floating crud?" she asks, pointing at a swirl of unidentifiable scum that's drifting by.

"Uhh . . . I don't know," I answer, but an idea is forming in the back of my mind is pushing its way forward.

Amy points to the couple across the tub from us. "Are those people boinking?" she whispers.

I look across at them, they are either boinking or the lady is having a nice horsy ride. With the murky water, it's hard to be sure.

I turn back to say this to Amy but she's already bolted from the hot tub and is walking quickly toward the shower. Her shoulders are hunched over, which I recognize as a clear signal that she is on a mission. I follow her. One of the resort's pool workers is stacking towels in a rack near the shower. When I catch up to Amy, I hear the guy saying, "I'm sorry Miss, guests is not supposed to be fuckin' in de hot tub." He looks exasperated. "Dey's supposed to do that only in der rooms. You can complain about it at de front desk."

"I'm going to," Amy assures him. With that she marches the rest of the way to the shower, opens the taps wide, and stays there, scrubbing herself down, for the next ten minutes. I use the shower next to her. One of the many, many things that I admire about my wife is that she doesn't stay upset for very long. She vents, and then moves on. When she emerges from the shower she's smiling. She comes up to me and hangs her arms around my neck. "I have a treat for you," she says.

Immediately images began forming in my mind.

"Follow me," she says and walks over to a long bench upon which she spreads a fresh towel. My mind is now churning out a steady steam of erotic visions. "Lay down on your stomach."

Poof! Most of the visions evaporate into the hot afternoon air.

"I'm going to give you a massage," she announces and with that she extracts a bottle of strawberry-scented oil from her beach bag.

She squirts the warm oil on my back and slowly begins to work it in with long sensuous strokes, warm slippery oil, strong hands kneading flesh . . . soft skin sliding against my side. . . Bob Marley singing 'Three Little Birds'. . .

. . . relaxing, loosening . . . *a huge sand crab?* . . . the hot sun on my calves . . . warm air over my body. . . muscles. . . jelly . . . drifting. . . dozing . . .

"Hey you... wake up." I open my eyes to dazzling sunlight. There's a beautiful naked woman with long legs and flaxen hair standing beside me. Her body is glistening in the sun and she's gently pushing on my shoulder. She looks very familiar.

I sit up limply on the bench, waves of grogginess wash over me. "Thank you," I hold my arms out to the shimmering angel and we embrace.

Later I accompany Amy to the front desk where she complains about the activities in the hot tub. The complaint is noted in a logbook. The attendant reaffirms that the resort actively discourages that type of activity. (Yeah, right.) He tells us that there are security people (called the sex police) who do regular patrols. They often have to stop couples who become over-amorous in public, which happens virtually everywhere on the resort; on the beach, on the pool deck, on the benches and lounges and in the hammocks.

Frankly and honestly, I could not care less about couples or groups of consenting adults or whomever having sex anywhere or anyhow. But doing it in the pools and hot tubs is inconsiderate and disrespectful, if only for the obvious sanitary and health reasons. I would wager that the hot tub boinkers would bail out if I jumped in beside them with a gaping, festering wound on my body. It amounts to the same thing and anybody that has an iota of respect for others will recognize this. I'm sure that there are many Hedo-goers who will vociferously disagree with me, (and I care not a fiddler's fart) but to them I say, fine, just don't complain the next time a diaper clad baby takes a dump in the pool that you're swimming in.

All that being said, Amy and I never got back into the nude hot tub again and we met several other couples who stayed out of it for the same reasons.

Monday

Hedonism is the adult equivalent of a kid's day camp, except that the hours are 24/7.

This morning we go down to the tie-dye T-shirt clinic that's set up near the water sports shack. Amy has a white T-shirt that she's willing to sacrifice. Sparrow, one of the entertainment staff guys, is running the clinic. Sparrow is a very gregarious fellow and, judging by his effeminate mannerisms, I conclude that he's gay (not that there's anything wrong with that).

Jamaicans, and I'm generalizing here of course, are intolerant of gays, as is evidenced by the widespread use of the derogatory patois term 'batty mon'. This intolerance is supported, and probably engendered to some extent, by the state, since male homosexual intimacy is currently classified as a criminal activity in Jamaica. The Offences Against the Person Act prohibits 'acts of gross indecency', which has been generally interpreted as referring to any kind of physical intimacy between men, in public or in private. Gay activists have, with some success, been lobbying the Jamaican Parliament for amendments to the Constitution's bill of rights that would see sexual orientation protections added.

Sparrow has an assortment of paints arranged in rainbow order on a picnic table. I consider asking him if he arranged them that way intentionally, but I leave it to my imagination. Amy tells Sparrow that she wants her T-shirt done in reggae colors; red, green and yellow. She doesn't want to get paint under her fingernails so I volunteer as Sparrow's assistant. We attack Amy's shirt.

Tie-dyeing is a long process and Sparrow takes it seriously. He has me hold the collar end of the shirt tightly in my fingertips, then he twists it lengthways into a tight cigar shape. Holding it taunt, he dips his fingers into the red paint pot and draws his hand several times over the long tight shaft of cloth, spreading the paint. He then closes his fingers over the shaft and strokes it slowly from end to end. This he does with a wry little smile. When he's satisfied, we untwist the shirt and Sparrow shakes it out. Random streaks of bright red run the length of the shirt. The shirt is then re-twisted from another anchor point exposing virgin white cloth. The smearing and stroking process is repeated using green paint. Several passers by stop to watch the process. After numerous twists and re-twists and applications of colors, the shirt is finished. Sparrow shakes it out and holds it up. It looks great! A couple of the people who were watching applaud and Sparrow curtsies and smiles demurely. He slings the T-shirt onto a wire clothes hanger and hangs it in the sun on the frond of a nearby palm.

"Now you have to let it dry for at least two hours. When you get it home soak it in vinegar-water overnight to set the colors before you wash it," he instructs.

To top off the day-camp experience Amy and I go to the self-serve ice cream bar and make ourselves a couple of triple-decker cones.

There's a group of four single black guys staying here who really stick out. We've never seen them down at the nude area so they're obviously not Vinnies. They all stand about six foot six and look like they would weigh in at a muscle-packed two hundred seventy-ish pounds. One of the other guests told us that they are pro football players who are here on a post Super Bowl vacation break. Mostly they keep to themselves, just hanging out together around the main pool, talking in deep voices, laughing loudly, drinking beers and smoking big Cuban cigars. Amy and I walk by the main pool area where two of them are sitting down in the middle of a crowd of young women. The girls are taking turns having their pictures taken while sitting on the guys' laps, wearing nothing but bikini bottoms and big smiles. The guys are good sports about it but they project an air of being unwilling accomplices.

For lunch we go down to the nude end of the beach to get hot dogs from the self-serve machine there. It's funny, eating hot dogs when all that high quality buffet food is available for the taking, but sometimes the mood strikes and a hot dog is just the thing. And when it's combined with a side of French fries from the nude beach grill and a dollop of Jamaican hot sauce for dipping, the dish measures a nine on the Epicurean Richter scale.

On the way back after lunch we encounter a body-painting contest at the nude beach. As we have no pressing appointments this afternoon we join in. Amy is a good artist and she uses the tempura paints to draw a cat on my chest and stomach and a monkey sitting in a coconut tree eating a banana on my back. For the finishing touch she puts blue paint on her hands and smacks my butt cheeks. My artistic talents have not advanced much beyond drawing stick-men, but I manage to paint a flowerpot on her stomach with two yellow daisies sprouting out of it whose petals surround her boobs. On her back I draw a big green, yellow and black banded 'IRIE!'

The contestants line up for judging, which is a measurement of the applause from the small crowd that has gathered around the contest area. Amy and I come in second. In spite of the fact that we are standing near the 'Nude Beach – No Photography' sign, several people have their cameras out and attempt to take pictures of the line of contestants. We turn our other cheeks to them at the last moment before we hear the little 'clicks' of their cameras.

The main dining lounge area is a sea of people tonight. In fact, the hotel is overbooked and some guests who have confirmed reservations at Hedo are 'billeted' at The Grand Lido, which is kitty corner to Hedo and an affiliated Super Club resort. 'Billeting' may not be the correct term when referring to The Grand Lido. It's a relatively new hotel and is much, much more luxurious than Hedo. Even so, when we talked to a couple of Hedo regulars who had been turned away they were furious, even though they were given full access to both resorts. It's ironic, but some Hedo regulars are too embarrassed to tell friends and family members that they are staying at Hedo, so they say that they're staying at The Grand Lido and make arrangements with the understanding management of the resort to have any messages forwarded to them at Hedo.

There are so many people down for dinner tonight that we make several circuits of the dinning area before we find a table with two empty chairs. It's a table for four and another couple is already seated. They invite us to join them and introduce themselves as Brian and Joni from Detroit. They're an attractive young couple, she has long honey blonde hair and he has dark, All-American, good looks.

Dinner is enjoyable and we discuss the resort and our lives back in the real world. Brian owns a bicycle store and Joni works as a dietician at a federal prison.

When the entertainment starts we are so far from the main stage and there are so many people in the dining room that we can't even tell what's going on. Joni suggests that we go to Veronica's, the on-site sing-along piano bar.

We enter Veronica's and find seats near the piano. The piano player nods to us in welcome and we pick up songbooks that are laying on the table. An inebriated lady on the other side of the bar calls out a page number from the book and the piano man starts to play 'Kansas City'. She howls her way tortuously through the song, with a little help from her soused girlfriend, but it's all in good fun and they get a round of applause when they finish, or perhaps the applause is because they've stopped singing, I can't be sure. We sing along with the next singer who does a good job on 'The Gambler'. The bar is packed and the atmosphere is merry; we order more drinks.

A heavyset man in his fifties, sitting directly beside us, calls out the page number for 'You've Lost That Loving Feeling'. He starts to sing and midway through the first line it's obvious that he's no ordinary Joe. He belts out the song with astounding force and passion. When he finishes the place goes wild. "MORE! MORE!" the patrons yell, pounding on the bar top, but the singer declines and passes the mike on.

We ask him where he learned to sing. It turns out that he's an old guitar-picking rock-n-roller who has a couple of albums out. He tells us that his old records are currently very popular in Japan, where he travels occasionally on promotion tours.

Veronica's closes but we aren't ready for bed yet, so we go to the disco where we party until our ears are numb from the thumping music. We crash in the wee hours of the morning.

Tuesday

I open my eyes and see a bedraggled, naked, hairy me staring down at me from the mirror on the ceiling, not a pleasant experience first thing in the morning. Initially I thought that the fun-house mirror over the bed was a little over the top, figuratively speaking, but it has turned out to be the source of amusement for us.

After breakfast we take a long walk down the road then back along the beach to the zoo. When we arrive at the monkey house the inmates are running amok. There's a scavenger hunt in progress, the men against the women. The teams are standing in front of the stage, breathless, waiting for the next item on the announcer's list.

"Now . . . we need . . . A PAIR OF WHITE SHORTS! . . . A PAIR OF WHITE SHORTS . . . WAVING IN THE AIR!" the announcer shouts.

There's a flurry of activity and in short order, a pair of white shorts are being waved in the air above the head of a member of the men's team.

"TEN POINTS FOR THE MEN . . . TEN POINTS FOR THE MEN!"

The men's team erupts in self-congratulations and the supplier of the white shorts pulls them back on.

"Now . . . THE BIGGEST BAMBOO! THE BIGGEST BAMBOO!" Members from both teams run and grab the nearest black guy that they can find who will cooperate and drag him up to the stage. Two are found and, facing the stage, they discretely reveal their units to the emcee. Members of the women's team gather around for the judging. They squeal and cover their mouths when one of the guys undoes his pants. The emcee points to him and awards ten points to the women's team.

And so it goes. The biggest boobs, a white bra, a dildo, the hairiest chest, a condom and then he calls for a true blonde. I look over at Amy, but she is already running toward the stage, electing to support the men's team. She shows the bare minimum to qualify and the men's team rejoices.

The next call is for the best fake orgasm. A member from the women's team takes the mike and does a long, screaming, stage thumping, hair flailing, slowly climaxing multiple orgasm. It is very convincing, almost as if she had practiced before hand. Next the representative from the guy's team grabs the mike. He closes his eyes, scrunches up his face and grunts "Ugg!" and that's it. The girls get ten points.

Down on the beach the trapeze clinic is underway. Amy gets a briefing from the professional artist. He's from France and when Amy answers him in his native tongue all further communication between them is in French. She climbs up the skinny rope ladder and swings herself onto the narrow platform, all under the supervision of the pro. I sit on the grass nearby and watch. Amy is handed the trapeze and, on the shouted command "HEP!", she swings out over the net hanging from her hands. On the next swing she brings her legs up and hooks them over the trapeze bar and releases her hands. She does one swing hanging from her knees and them grabs the bar and unhooks her legs. I'm amazed that she can do this. The pro shouts "HEP!" again and Amy drops to the net, slowed by a safety line attached to a belt she's wearing that's manned by a crewman on the ground.

I clap for her as she comes up to me. "That was a lot of fun, you should try it," she says.

"Yeah, maybe tomorrow," I reply.

In addition to the trapeze, Hedonism offers an exhausting list of sports activities, sailing, water skiing, diving, snorkeling, sea kayaks, sunfish, Hobie cats, windsurfers, fitness walks, tennis, table tennis, billiards, gym, volleyball, cycling, squash, badminton, shuffleboard, basketball, dancing classes, and a games room.

It's after sunset and we're lounging in the room. Outside the light is fading from the sky and it's quiet in the garden. Suddenly through the open widow we hear someone laughing like a madman. I go to the window to look out but it's already too dark to see any details outside of the lighted areas. The laughing, which verges on hysterical from time to time, continues unabated. It's obvious to me, a survivor of the 70's, that someone is having a trip, having probably partaken in a little too much magic mushroom tea. I can hear people asking the laugher if he's OK, he just laughs louder in reply. The hysteria continues for about twenty minutes, rising and falling in volume until it finally ceases all together.

Tonight we have reservations at the Pastafari, an elegant Italian restaurant on the resort that provides an opportunity for guests to get away from the madding crowd. We made reservations for four for eight o'clock. Brian and Joni will be joining us.

Receiving guests at the door is the maitre de, a tall young Jamaican who's dressed in a long sleeved white shirt, black tie and black pants. "Good night," he greets us. In spite of my many trips to the island I'm still not used to the salutation. I'm always tempted to say, 'You mean 'Good evening', but I return a 'Good night' and Amy giggles as we are shown to our table. Joni and Brian are already there.

We order our five-course meals from the menus. Our conversation meanders around the things that we've been doing and the things that we are planning on doing. The food, the service and the ambiance are all exquisite. Midway through the main course Brian asks, "Do you guys ever go to any of the lifestyle clubs back home?"

"You mean, like swinger's clubs?" I ask. 'Lifestyles' is the softer, euphemistic, conversational term that has come to be synonymous with 'swinger'.

"Yeah," he says, "Are you two into the lifestyle?" This is a legitimate question since a fair percentage of the club's guests are 'into the lifestyle'.

"No, we just came here out of curiosity and convenience. We don't even have a swing-set in our back yard," I answer.

"OK, we were just curious. We're starting to do a bit of experimenting ourselves," Brian says.

Our conversation moves on to other subjects and the topic of experimenting and swinging never comes up again. But, during the rest of the meal, each time I look at Joni I see her from a new perspective. She features prominently in an ever increasing erotic series of images. Hey, I can't help it, remember? I was born male.

Tuesday is pajama party night in the Hedo disco. Anyone who comes to the door who isn't wearing something that can pass as pajamas is not allowed entry. Amy is wearing silk lingerie, a clingy, one piece, dark green number that sets her blonde hair off nicely. I'm wearing a pair of blue, dolphin print, silk boxers, a leather vest and a bow tie. One enterprising guy comes to the door wearing two pillows tied around his waist with a belt. He passes muster and is allowed in. Others came prepared, like the couple that enters, walking regally, wearing only gold g-strings and covered from head to foot in gold body paint and glitter.

The pajama party is really just another opportunity to dress erotically. One fellow, bucking the erotic motif, is allowed in wearing two Ohio vehicle license plates strung around his hips with a length of cord.

The disco is wall to wall people and it gets very, very hot and stuffy on the packed dance floor. Occasionally we see naked people looking into the disco through the portholes to the lighted swimming pool.

We party until we almost succumb to the heat and then make our escape to the comparatively cool air outside. There are a couple of inebriated Vinnies hanging around the exit. One of them asks me if I share, as if Amy was my chattel.

What day is it - Wednesday?

The breakfast buffet varies at Hedo and today I'm lucky, I spot two of my favorite Jamaican breakfast foods, ackee and callaloo. Ackee is the national fruit of Jamaica, it grows in clusters of pods on an evergreen tree. When it ripens, January through March and June through August, the ackee's skin turns bright red and cracks open. The flesh of the ackee is golden yellow. Although it's a fruit, ackee is cooked as a vegetable. When prepared, it and looks just like scrambled eggs. I help myself to a big mound of it. Callaloo is a leafy green vegetable that looks like spinach but tastes way better, especially when prepared Jamaican style with added spices. I help myself to a good portion.

Amy has eggs Benedict. Halfway through breakfast, a scrawny cat walks nonchalantly up to our table and sits down beside Amy, they always find her. She immediately gets up and goes to the buffet where she makes a suitable selection and delivers the cat his breakfast.

I'm hungry today so for 'breakfast dessert' I feast on a chocolate Belgian waffle with thick syrup topped by a big wad of melting butter.

There's a photo stand set up each morning in the central area where guests can view photos that have been taken around the resort the previous day. Today there are some very interesting shots of the PJ party last night in the disco. The company that runs this enterprise is the same one that we hired for our wedding photos and they had told us that we would be able to view the wedding party proofs today. We check in with them and are mildly but pleasantly surprised when we are handed a thick envelope with our names on it. We rip the package open and spend the next forty-five minutes examining the proofs and making selections and deciding on the size and number of prints that we want. The most amazing photo of the lot is the group shot with the setting sun as the backdrop. It has turned out beyond perfect. As we are admiring it, Brian and Joni walk up and join us.

Joni is wearing a small blue bikini, her hair is tied up in a bob on the top of her head. She has a pair of blue tinted sunglasses pushed back on her forehead. It's a hot day and there are several small beads of perspiration on her upper lip. She has a pearl stud in her navel that I had never noticed before. She looks incredibly sexy. My mind goes back to dinner at the Pastafari.

Amy hands the group-wedding photo to Joni. Brian asks where it was taken. When we tell him it was taken on the beach he can't believe that the backdrop is natural, and it takes some time to convince him that it's for real.

Later Amy and I go for a walk down to the dock. A cool wind has picked up and is blowing inland as hard as I have ever experienced in the tropics. The Hedo beach is somewhat in the lee due to Rutland Point, but still the waves are washing well up onto the beach.

We watch the crew of the big catamaran struggle to get the boat untied and away from the dock. Apparently they've decided that there is a better place to weather the storm. They're having a difficult time as the boat is pitching violently in the waves and threatening to smash into the cement dock. They finally get it away and motor slowly to windward.

The water sports shack is closed. There's a handwritten sign out front that says;

No water sports today due to rough seas

We move up the beach a little toward a flat area where some crafts are on display. A familiar looking old Rasta is sitting at a picnic table there.   He has some musical instruments made from short lengths of bamboo with rows of longitudinal ridges cut into them. He's singing and playing one of the bamboo instruments by stroking a short stick back and forth over the ridges. There are a few American guys (sharks I think) standing beside the Rasta and singing along. Suddenly, I recognize the old guy, he's the one that was aboard the big cat when it made its pass through the cove at Rick's during the Wild Thing cruise. We go over and talk to him. He introduces himself as 'Ralphie the Rasta'. We join in on the next song, which is Bob Marley's 'Buffalo Soldier'.

On the way back up to the central area we walk by a couple of Jamaican guys, Hedo employees, who are kicking a soccer ball around on the grounds near the volleyball pitch.

"What are you doing today?" one of them asks.

"Not too much, just hanging out, relaxing," I answer.   "Are you cold?" I ask him, as he's wearing a jacket and toque.

"Yeah mon, it's cold today," he says. "Hey listen up, do you want to take me back to your room for some hot fun?"

"I don't know," I say looking at Amy, "do you want to Hon?"

"Ah, not right now, maybe this afternoon, though," she answers.

"OK mon, check you later," he says and goes back to his soccer game.

We continue on our way back to the main dining area, seeking a hot coffee and some shelter from the cool breeze.

One of the entertainment staff is on stage soliciting women to join in the wet T-shirt contest.

"You should go up Amy, just for the fun of it," I say, half-joking.

Amy takes a gulp of her coffee, gets up from her chair, pecks me on the forehead and answers, to my surprise, "OK, wish me luck."

In total, twelve women have responded to the call. The 'judges', mostly Vinnies and sharks, are sitting on a step that rims the sunken dance floor in front of the stage. The girls have access to a shower and ice cubes back stage. They come on the floor wearing wet T-shirts and bikini bottoms, gyrating to the music and doing their best to earn points with the judges, who sit there roaring, clapping their hands stomping and yelling for the tops to come off. About half of the girls oblige, to the raucous appreciation of the judges, and end their act topless.

But it's more than a wet T-shirt contest. Each of the participants is also tasked with some sort of act. Three of the girls are each tasked with selecting men from the judge pool and then arranging them into as many different sex positions as they can. The winner is the one who comes up with the greatest number of positions. It's hilarious, and instructive, to watch. The eighth girl is instructed to lie down. Chocolate syrup is poured on her belly and a volunteer is asked to lick it up. Amy is the ninth performer. She comes out doing her best bump and grind and gets the sharks worked into a feeding frenzy. Sitting at the table on the second terrace, I'm impressed, wondering where she learned to move her hips like that. A chant of "TAKE IT OFF! . . . TAKE IT OFF!" rises from the judge's ranks. Amy teases them by pulling her T-shirt up to expose her belly, twisting it into a knot between her breasts and flipping it up her back as she thrusts her butt at them, but she never shows them what they are yelling for. Considering the locale, it's odd that the men are calling for the tops to come off, since all of the contestants can be seen totally naked any day down at the nude pool.

For her 'skit' Amy is told to pick two men from the audience. She looks at me, points with a high arched arm and then does the 'come here' movement with her index finger. Her next victim is one of the big pro-ball players who is sitting in the judges gallery.

The emcee instructs her to lie on her back and then crumbles cookies on her, laying them in a line from her knees, between her tightly pressed thighs, on her crotch, across her belly and up between her breasts. The big football player and I are then told to start eating the cookie crumbs, as fast as we can, with him starting at her chest and me starting at her knees. At the signal we both start. The cookies are good, chocolate chip flavor. I work my way quickly up between her thighs, lapping up the cookies and munching them down. Amy is lying rigid but her whole body is jiggling from suppressed laughter. I eat my way up to her crotch and I'm in the process of digging a large crumb out from the deep crevice between her legs when I'm bowled over by the football player who is moving down her belly like he's driving for the goal line. His head, sitting atop massively muscled shoulders, butts into mine. It's so hard it feels like he's wearing a helmet. I'm knocked sprawling on my back. The pro then effortlessly scoops Amy up off the floor and, to the cheers of the judges, carries her to where he was sitting and sits her on his knee.

In the end, inevitably, the two girls with the biggest boobs, both of whom had taken their tops off, come in first and second in descending boob size order. Amy is awarded third, even though she isn't third in boob size, and she's presented a bottle of Tia Maria for the fun of it.

We're awakened from our mid-afternoon nap by a tremendous clap of thunder. Torrents of rain and huge gusts of wind pound mercilessly at the window. Given the hour, it's peculiarly dark outside. The garden is periodically lit by brilliant flashes of lightning, revealing a phantasmagoric scene of wet trees, stark shadows and sheets of rain. This is not a normal afternoon rain shower, it's a serious blow. The trees in the garden are being lashed about wildly by ferocious blasts of wind. We sit in the window alcove watching the spectacle. The window rattles with each crash of thunder.

Having little else to do, we retreat to the king size bed, put on a Bob Marley CD, light a couple of candles and play ceiling mirror games.

That night the circus show, which is normally given on the trapeze equipment on the beach after a beach bar-b-que, is moved inside the main entertainment area due to the inclement weather. Not surprisingly, under the circumstances the show is less than spectacular. The highlight of the act occurs when the French artist who had given Amy her trapeze lesson falls from a rope on which he's twirling onto a mat from about 10 feet up. Fortunately he gets up quickly, unhurt, and does a little bow for the audience.

We go to Veronica's, the piano bar, which is turning into our favorite haunt. Brian and Joni are there and so is Jack, the old rocker. The stars tonight are a group of young Russians, who speak little English but know the tunes and words to many songs. We're surprised when the singer from Point Village walks into the bar. I wave him over and ask him if he'll sing 'It's a Wonderful World'. He complies and sings it again in his excellent Louis Armstrong voice. The crowd in Veronica's loves it. Amy and I decide right there to adopt 'It's a Wonderful World' as 'our song'.

Next Day, Thursday I Think

Next morning the weather breaks clear and warm. We are up early so that we can be sure to get a couple of the club bicycles, which are limited in number and in great demand, for an excursion into town.

Amy is dressed in a yellow bikini and she's wrapped in an orange, hibiscus print sarong.

"I'm not sure if this is okay to wear into town," she says.

"Based on what I've seen people wearing . . . and not wearing, I'm sure you'll be alright," I assured her.

"Well, I'm going to ask someone anyway."

Sparrow, the gay tie-dye T-shirt-meister, happens to walk by as we are discussing Amy's attire.

"Sparrow . . . do you think I'll be okay going into town like this?" Amy asks.

Sparrow pauses, tilts his head and places a hand contemplatively to his chin. After a moment he says, "Turn around sweetie." Amy obliges. He reaches for the sarong and pulls it open, examining Amy's bikini beneath. It occurs to me that he's misunderstood her request, he's doing a fashion assessment rather than a check to see if her outfit is appropriate dress for town.

"Yeah," he says slowly, glancing at her sandals, "that should be fine." With that he wishes us a good day and moves along, throwing off a cheery "Good morning darling" to a woman sitting at breakfast.

We get the bikes, which are road-weary single-speed, coaster brake models that should have been replaced long ago, and head off down the road for town.

Debris from last night's storm is strewn all about. Branches have been ripped from trees and bushes have been stripped of their blossoms.

We pedal for about five minutes and then pull off the road at Long Bay Public Beach, incredulous at what we see. It isn't the same beach that we walked along a couple of days ago, because the beach is no longer there. In its place are drifts of ocean debris piled three feet high. This area obviously took a direct hit from yesterday's storm. Way out to sea, big waves are still breaking on the reef in huge geysers of white water. We park our bikes and walk out to the debris.

The drifts consist of washed-up eelgrass, sponges and thousands and thousands of small sea urchins mixed with sand. The urchins crunch under our sandals as we walk carefully over a smaller mound to approach the water. Several Jamaicans are standing in the shallows, scanning the surface.

We are astounded at the scene before us. The beautiful white beach has been taken out to sea and the crystalline waters that we swam in have been replaced by a thick slurry of dark sea debris. And it stinks. Bad.

In spite of the debacle, I take the opportunity to look around in case something interesting has been washed up. I use the toe of my sandal to prod around in the debris. The drifts also contain many dead fish and small conch shells with the animals still within. There are also numerous oyster-ice seashells. These are delicate translucent fans about six inches long that are extremely fragile, most of them are broken.

I see something that looks odd and pull it out of the drift. It's a wafer-thin fan-shaped piece about 4 inches across that's slightly tented along one axis. I recognize it as tortoise shell.

A voice from behind me says, "Dat's a flake from de back of a hawksbill turtle."

I look around and see an old Jamaican man standing calf-deep in the mucky water. "Oh really? Do you think the rest of him is around here?" I ask.

"No, de sea lick it off him back an de storm wash it up. You're lucky to find it."

"Uh-huh," I nod my head in agreement.

"I can polish it up for you and make a hair piece for the lady," he offers.

"No thanks, I think I'll keep it natural. What are you looking for?" I ask.

"For de conch," he says turning his attention back to the sea. I notice that he's holding a fist sized conch shell in his hand.

"How often does this happen?" I ask, pointing at the smelly mess where the beach used to be.

"Oh, bout ev'ry two or 'tree years. De sea come an take de beach away, but after a time it come an takes dis away and puts de sand back again," he answers.

How long does it take to come back? I ask, thinking that we will be returning here after our trip to the north shore in a week.

"Oh, perhaps a month or two, maybe sooner, it depends on de mood of de sea," he says.

At the southern end of the public beach a front-end loader is filling a dump truck with the smelly stuff. I wouldn't want to be downwind of wherever it is they're dumping the stuff after it has sat in the sun for a couple of days.

After our uneventful trip to town, we take a short walk to see how much damage was done to the hotel beaches. The Hedo beach fared well due to its relatively sheltered location, but all the hotel beaches further south were severely eroded. The beach in front of Sandals is gone and all that remains is a pathetic spit of sand upon which a dozen shell-shocked guests are sitting. To speed the recovery of the beach, a raft outfitted with a sand pumping rig is anchored about 100 yards offshore, sucking sand up from the bottom there and sending it shoreward through a thick hose. In the shallow water near the shore, a geyser of sandy water is gurgling up.

On the way back to Hedo we saw a huge blue-gray ocean crab walking sideways down the wrecked beach, looking dazed. This guy too was probably washed up during the storm. I recognize the type of crab as being one that normally lives in the deep water of the reef, as I see them often when diving. On one dive I was examining a big barrel sponge and when I poked my head to look inside of it I came face-to-face with the grand daddy of ocean crabs. He was looking at me with his stalk eyes, his claws were up and open and he was being very territorial about his hidey-hole. He gave me quite a start and not wanting to lose a thumb I quickly got the hell out of there.

Before leaving the beach I take one last look at it, I still find it hard to accept what I'm seeing. I feel sorry for the people who have recently arrived as I'm sure the beach will take more that a week to come back. It's just as well that we'll be leaving for Runaway Bay tomorrow morning.

Thursday night is toga night at Hedo. No sheet, no eat, and that's no bull-sheet.

Extra sheets for the event are left folded on the bed and toga-tying demonstrations are given on the stage during the afternoon. Around sunset Amy and I pick items from the Hedo Garden of Eden to accessorize our togas. She dresses me in a standard Roman style toga and I fashion a bandoleer from a long, narrow two-colored green leaf that I picked off of a huge bush in the garden. Big beautiful pink blossoms have dropped from a flowering tree on the grounds. We gather several of these and stick them in the bands around our waists. Then we both make head wreaths from sections of a crawling, vine-like green plant.

Earlier this morning Amy had braided her hair when it was still wet. Now I help her to undo the braids and she shakes her hair out. The result is a head full of kinky hair, it takes five years off her already deceivingly youthful looks. One of tonight's toga categories is 'Most Virginal' and in her white toga, kinky hair and becoming head wreath, Amy looks convincingly vestal.

We walk down to the main dining room, I carry the trail of Amy's toga behind her as we enter. We catch the attention of some guests seated nearby and they take our picture. The dining room is a sea of togas. We find Brian and Joni and join them. Joni's toga is hanging loose over her shoulders and when she moves the material shifts to reveal parts of her chest. I find myself tracking the disposition of Joni's toga, thinking that perhaps I might be treated to a glimpse of her breast, which is odd, since I spoke to her yesterday at the nude pool and she was completely naked.

There are several Hedo regulars who have brought their own

costumes for toga night. One couple is outstanding in royal blue matching satin togas. Of the approximately 250 couples in the dining area, we see only two who are not dressed in togas, and they are probably late arrivals. The evening is a blast, we cruise the buffet in our outfits and everyone is admiring and commenting on each other's attire. The contest and the parade of togas commences after dining. There are many categories; best traditional, most daring, sexiest, most original and best overall. We become so engrossed in conversation with Brian and Joni that Amy misses her opportunity to enter the 'Most Virginal' contest.

There's a couple in their 70's who have been participating in all of the club events throughout the week. They've become quite popular with the other guests. People admire their energy and zest for life. They prove to be crowd favorites tonight as well and win the best overall toga couple, this in spite of their unspectacular outfits. The runner-up couple, Hedo regulars who had come equipped with custom togas and body paint, did not appear to share the crowd's enthusiasm for the old couple.

The winning septuagenarians leave the stage to clamorous applause and whistles. Amy leans over to me and says, "We should come back when we are old and gray and try for the best couple prize!" I say "okay" and then she leans over to me with her lips wrapped over her teeth, making like she has no teeth and tries to kiss me, but I dodge her attempts.

DAY - OH!

'Man noh done cross riva, noh fi cuss alligator long mout.'
Jamaican Proverb

 I wake up humming that old Animals tune, 'We Gotta get Outta this Place!'

The urge to move on is very strong this morning. We're headed for Runaway Bay on Jamaica's north coast, where we'll be staying at Hedonism III for a few days. As far as Amy is concerned, she believes that we are going to Runaway Bay for the scuba diving, which is true. What she doesn't know is that Bob Marley's final resting-place, the hamlet of Nine Mile, is about an hour's drive from Hedo III.

We finish packing and have our last buffet breakfast at Hedo, one for the road.

Sparrow walks through reception as we are checking out. He comes over, gives Amy a big hug and tells us to be careful on our trip.

"When will you be coming back?" he asks, as if that were a forgone conclusion.

"We'll be back in Negril next week but we're staying on the cliffs," I answer.

"Well, you have a good time and come and visit us soon again," Sparrow replies and sets off to spread more of his unique brand of hospitality. Funny, but as he leaves I realize that I'm going to miss him.

Our driver, a gentleman whom I estimate to be in his late sixties, waves us over to the taxi. He's wearing long pants, a nylon jacket and a green 'John Deere' cap with a picture of a tractor embossed across the front. He introduces himself as Basil.

Our ride to Runaway Bay should be about four hours, barring any roadblocks, accidents or excessive road construction, all of which are not uncommon along the coast road.

Usually I feel morose upon leaving Negril, but we'll be back soon, and we have another ten days in Jamaica, so today I'm feelin' irie.

On the flat stretch of road north of Negril we pass a dump truck filled to overflowing with workers heading off to a job site; mass transportation Jamaican style. Some of the men on the side that we pass on lean over, look at the blonde in the back and make catcalls as we go by.

About fifteen minutes into the ride I look into the back and see that

Amy has drifted off to sleep, she's flat out on the seat. All of the familiar 'road to Negril' scenes pass by. It's quiet on the road this morning and I too feel myself getting drowsy in the hot morning sun. Indeed, I drift in and out of sleep.

I wake up as we pull to a stop at a construction site. We are there only for a few minutes. A bulldozer is being offloaded from a flatbed to do some land clearing. Some day, with a little bit of luck and good management, this road will get finished.

Soon we are descending the hill to the south of MoBay overlooking the city. Amy's head pops up as we slow for the roundabout. Basil pilots us through the city and we stop at a gas station on its northern edge. While he fills up we get drinks and snacks from the store. I do a quick conversion from Jamaican dollars to the Northern peso and see that the price of gas is about the same as it is back home.

There's a string of fancy hotels and a glitzy looking shopping mall along the ocean side of the road to the east of Montego Bay. Basil notices that we are now both alert so he starts to give us a running commentary of everything we pass in his peculiar patois-drawl.

At first his remarks are kind of interesting, he points out Rose Hall, one of the original and greatest of the plantation houses. Constructed of limestone and whitewashed, it stands majestically overlooking the sea from a high bluff.

"Look waaay up dere on de hill. Dats Rooose Haalll. . . A HAUNTED HOUSE!" Basil exclaims. Legend has it that the house is haunted by the ghost of Annie Palmer, one of its earlier inhabitants. She was a 'white witch' who was taught voodoo by her black nannies. Apparently all three of her husbands and the several slaves that she had taken as lovers died mysterious deaths. Her reign of terror ended when she was strangled in her bed during a slave uprising in 1831.

Basil keeps on talking, pointing out cows and green fields, apparently believing that we don't have these back home. "Look . . . a cow!" he says and points it out for us. "Lots of cows in the greeeen fields of lovely Jamaica!"

Each time that Amy and I try to have a few words between us or point something out to the other, Basil jumps in and adds his two bits worth. Normally I would think this amusing and take it in stride, but after twenty minutes of non-stop commentary, Basil is starting to annoy me.

By Jamaican standards, the highway along the coast east of Montego Bay is good. Basil picks up speed until we are really flying down the road. He continues to talk and wave his hand around pointing things out. From what I've seen so far, I'm not overwhelmed in confidence with his driving abilities.

"Flamingo Beach!" Basil announces suddenly, "bee-ooo-tiful white sand beach for swimming in bee-ooo-tiful Jamaica!"

The car is now moving so fast that I'm feeling very uncomfortable. "We're not in that much of a hurry Basil, you could slow down a little, we have all day," I tell him.

"O Kaaaayy, I can sloooow down," he lifts his foot off the accelerator and we slow to an acceptable speed. But the car continues to decelerate and soon we are moving at a crawl relative to the other traffic. "Now we're moving slooowly . . . I can drive slowly and we are taking our time today."

"How would it be if you drove at about fifty?" I suggest.

Basil accelerates the car up to fifty. "Look! Babylon going the other way!" he says. He sticks his arm out the window and waves at the police car that passes us going in the opposite direction.

Basil has to be the weirdest driver that I've ever had, he's like a moving sideshow.

Next we pass through Falmouth, an old town with many historic buildings and a small but bustling market located adjacent to the main drag. The road through the core of the town is very narrow with several sharp turns.

Back on the highway, Basil shouts, "LOOK! LOOK! . . . Rafting on the Martha Brae!" "You can go waaay up in de mountains an' raft all de way down! The Maaarrrtha Brae!" he points to the river as we pass over the bridge.

We pass an inlet and I see what I've been looking for, Bush Cay. I lodged at the Trelawny Beach Club, a couple of miles down the road from here, on my second trip to Jamaica. Every morning of my two-week stay I would take a hike from the resort up the beach to the sandy spit that's known locally as Bush Cay, which lies on the tip of the peninsula that frames the inlet we are passing. I remember it being absolutely and gloriously deserted. I would go there and spend hours walking on the pristine sand, sunning, swimming and indulging in Robinson Crusoe fantasies. Occasionally fishermen would land on the spit and cast their nets into the sea. I would help them to drag the nets back in, excited to see what beasts the sea had offered up for their efforts.

Soon we pass the hotel where I stayed and I'm besieged by a flood of memories of my time there. Memories that I didn't even know I had come flooding back.

"DAY - OH! . . . . DA – AY - AY OH! . . . . DAYLIGHT COME AND ME WANT TO GO HOME! Dats where Harry Belafonte used to live!" Basil points energetically at a building on the side of a hill next to the road. We're passing through the Duncans area. Because of his music, many people believe that Harry Belafonte is from Jamaica, but he was actually born in New York and only spent some of his childhood in Jamaica. His father, however, was Jamaican.

Next we come to the Bengal Bridge which spans the Rio Bueno River gorge. It is the worst bridge that I've ever had the displeasure of crossing. Its surface is so tortured, pot-holed and uneven that it reminds me of snow moguls on a heavily-skied slope. We lurch painfully across, the car's suspension heaving enormously and squeaking in protest at every mogul.

At the other end of the bridge there's a police roadblock. They have a car stopped with the trunk open. As we pass slowly an officer of the Jamaican Constabulary Force bends to look into our car. Satisfied, he waves us on.

"Columbus Park, dis is where Columbus discovered Jamaica!" Basil points to a sign at the side of the road that declares the fact. We are getting close to our destination now, Discovery Bay and Runaway Bay share the same stretch of coast.

The Discovery Bay region is steeped in rich and colorful history. Christopher Columbus landed here on May 4, 1494 during his second voyage to the Caribbean, claiming the island for Spain. Shortly after arriving, he encountered the very first Jamaicans, the peaceful Arawak Indians whose history in Jamaica dates back to 800 AD. It was the Arawaks that originally gave the island its name. The word 'Jamaica' is an adaptation of the Arawak word 'xaymaca' which means 'land of wood and water', a term that is used by many people to describe Jamaica to this day.

The Arawaks' canoes were constructed by chiseling out the trunks of silk cotton trees until they were hollow, a method that is still used by native Jamaican fishermen. And it was the Arawaks that originated the local dish called bammy, a thick pancake that's made from cassava.

Columbus didn't hang around Discovery Bay for too long, as he had a lot more discovering to do. The Spanish, however, did stay on. They began arriving in large numbers in the early 1500's for what turned out to be a 160-year stay. The Arawak Indians didn't last half that long. They were totally wiped out during the first 75 years of the Spanish occupation. Their pastoral lifestyle was disrupted and they were murdered and plundered by the occupiers. Those who survived the initial onslaught later succumbed to the diseases that were introduced by the Spanish to which they had no resistance. It has been reported that many Arawaks drank poison and killed their own children to escape enslavement by the Spaniards.

Thus, the cycle of oppression and violence that plagued the island for centuries got its start.

The Spaniards were interested in gold but found none in Jamaica. So they used the island primarily as a jumping-off and support base for their plundering missions to other parts of the Americas. They brought in a limited number of slaves from Africa to toil on their plantations, raising only enough food for their own sustenance and to re-supply the ships of their navy. Consequently, the Spanish population and that of their slaves remained relatively small. However, the slaves that the Spaniards brought to Jamaica later played a very important role in the history of the island.

The Spanish built Jamaica's first town, Sevilla Nueva, near St. Ann's Bay between Runaway Bay and what is now Ocho Rios, in 1509. They stuck it out there for about 30 years and then abandoned it due to the location and swampy conditions. They set up in new and better digs in the southeastern part of the island where they founded the town of Santiago de la Vega, which is the important city now called Spanish Town.

Negril was also named by the early Spanish settlers. They called it 'Punta Negrilla' referring to the land mass that's now called the West End. 'Punta' means a geographic point of land and 'Negrilla' connotes the diminutive form of 'black' or 'dark' in Spanish. However, there is some debate as to why the Spanish chose to call the area Negrilla. What 'black' thing or characteristic was it that compelled them to do so? Some say it was because of the ubiquitous black conger eels that used to inhabit the local rivers. Others claim that 'dark' was a reference to the remoteness of Negril's West End. And there are others who argue that the 'dark' refers to the dark color of the waters of the South Negril River, which picks up a dark pigment when sluicing through peat bogs upstream.

Some Spanish names have survived and some buildings bear unmistakable Spanish architectural influences, but it was the British that had the most influence in Jamaica's development. In 1655, the British navy was roaming the Caribbean looking for islands to conquer. They tried to drive the Spaniards off the island Hispaniola, where the present day countries of Haiti and the Dominican Republic are located, but were repelled. They moved on to Kingston Harbor in Jamaica and tried their hand against the Spanish garrison there. This time they were successful, and claimed the island in the name of the British crown. Therefore it can be said that Jamaica was actually a consolation prize for the Brits.

The defeat of the Spanish ended their involvement in Jamaica but opened the page on a very interesting chapter in its history. When the Spaniards fled to other islands ahead of the Brits their slaves escaped into the mountainous Cockpit Country area of Jamaica, forming a group called the Maroons. The word derives from the Spanish 'cimmaron' which means savage or feral. Other slaves who managed to escape from their British slave drivers joined the Maroons. The Maroons were fierce fighters and for many years they waged guerilla warfare against the British, who were virtually helpless against their stealthy hit-and-run attacks. Raiding parties of Maroons would sweep down from the hills, attacking plantations and kidnapping women for their pleasure. The English eventually capitulated and signed peace treaties with the Maroons, granting them large tracts of land in the Trelawny area and central parts of the island where their descendants still live today.

However annoying and effective they were, suppressing the Maroons did not fully occupy the British, who succeeded in turning Jamaica into a huge sugar plantation, bringing in vast numbers of slaves from the west coast of Africa to do all of their work for them. The slaves were emancipated in 1838, and most of them took up sustenance farming on their own small plots of land, a practice that survives to this day.

In the 17th century, the then capital of Jamaica, Port Royal, had the dubious distinction of being the headquarters for some of the world's most notorious pirates and buccaneers. They were led by Captain Henry Morgan who, besides having a fine dark rum named after him, did a very commendable job of plundering the treasure ships that sailed the Spanish Main.

In 1692 a major earthquake struck Port Royal causing 1700 deaths and sinking two thirds of the town into the sea. Some say the quake was God's revenge on the townspeople, many of whom spent their lives in a drunken fog of debauchery, gambling, drinking, whoring and thieving.

In addition to its rich history, the Discovery Bay area is also the home of the Green Grotto Caves, an extensive labyrinth of natural limestone caverns that run along the coast. The caves were initially used as shelter by the Arawaks, and later on, by escaped slaves hiding from slave drivers. The vanquished Spanish too took to the caves, seeking refuge from the British conquerors. The caves also served as a haven for pirates who attacked shipping along the north coast of Jamaica. During the period between World Wars one and two, smugglers running arms to Cuba operated out of the Green

Grotto Caves, making use of a natural outlet to the ocean as a means of slipping to sea unnoticed.

The Green Grotto, after which the caves are named, is an underground lake located 120 feet below the surface that can be accessed by descending stairs that are carved into the rock.

"An dis is where de slaves raannn away!" Basil waves his hand expansively as we round a hill and are treated to a splendid view of Runaway Bay.

At the bottom of the slope we pass a decrepit looking dock where a rusty ship is being loaded with bauxite. A large conveyor belt is constructed on the side of the higher ground that overlooks the harbor, connecting the bauxite processing plant that is located atop the hill with a holding shed on the loading dock. Bauxite, from which aluminum is made, is one of Jamaica's main (legal) exports. The others are sugar, bananas, rum and coffee.

There is some disagreement as to how Runaway Bay got its name. In 1655, the ragtag remains of the defeated Spanish garrison, who had worked their way across the island from Kingston, escaped their British pursuers by sailing north to Cuba from a small fishing village in Runaway Bay. Some say that it was from that 'running away' event that the bay got its name. It is also true that escaped slaves used the bay as a jump off point to paddle their way to freedom and some say that it was those acts that the bay is named after. Still others claim that the bay got its name from the local trade in slaves who had runaway from north-coast sugar plantations only to be re-captured and sent to other plantations in Cuba.

Basil seems to be picking his way along this final stretch, carefully reading all of the signs along the road. I believe that it's probably his first trip to this relatively new resort. "Here we are . . . Hedonism!" he announces triumphantly as the road sign for the resort comes into view. The hotel entrance is painted a jaunty yellow and white and it and the vegetation, both still wet from a recent rain, look Technicolor fresh in the bright sun.

After more than four hours on the road, we finally pull into the circular driveway of Hedonism III. We offload our gear and tip Basil, bidding him a safe ride back to MoBay.

We go to reception and check in for what promises to be an interesting stay.

Bare Nuptials

'Chicken merry, hawk deh near.'
Jamaican Proverb

The rooms at Hedo III are far and away nicer than those at Hedo II. The big difference being the size and the newness of everything. There's a mirror above the king size bed here too, but unfortunately it produces no distortions. The bathroom is enormous with modern fixtures and lots of counter space. It too has a mirror on the ceiling strategically located above the two-person Jacuzzi tub.

I turn on the TV. It provides news and movie channels plus one unexpected bonus, the Playboy channel. I think we'll be comfortable here.

We take a tour of the grounds, which are expansive. Things are more spread out here at Hedo III than at its sister resort in Negril. Because the resort is located on a rocky shore, there are no natural beaches. There is a small manmade beach, but it's a poor facsimile of the real thing. The grounds are roughly divided into the prude and nude areas. There are the other familiar Hedonism themes, but everything here is newer and somehow it seems less decadent than at the Negril Hedo. The clientele is made up of a younger crowd and although it's only a feeling, there seem to be fewer 'swingers' here.

About half and hour before sunset we go to the manager's cocktail party. (Somehow the word 'cocktail' conjures up different connotations at Hedo.) The party is staged on the sundeck atop the Scotch Bonnet seaside restaurant, where local Jamaican fare, including jerk chicken, curried goat, meat patties and rice and beans are served. The restaurant is named after an extremely hot local Habanero pepper that looks like a miniature pumpkin. It rates way up there on the 'Holy wow! This is hot!' scale. One should have to sign a waiver before purchasing it. And if you think it's hot going down, just wait until its fiery exit. Remember, in Jamaica, *'If it's nice, we do it twice*!

The view from the deck atop the restaurant takes in a magnificent sweep of Runaway Bay and the coastal hills. The sea can be rough at times on the north coast and today three-foot rollers are breaking on the shore. The air is warm and humid and the surf crashes on the rocky shore below the deck as the sinking sun paints the sky with broad pastel strokes of yellow, pink and turquoise. It's an exquisitely romantic setting.

We stand at the railing, mesmerized by the rhythmic pounding of the surf. I put my back up against the railing and pull Amy toward me. Her skin is glowing pink in the slanting light of the setting sun and her eyes are sparkling and alive. We embrace, I could not be more contented. Just another day in paradise.

A steel band is assembled at one end of the deck and they start to play. The small but hungry crowd is mounting an assault on the hors d'oeuvres, and we quickly make our way over to the buffet tables, not wanting to miss out on the shrimp, which as every experienced buffet-goer knows, always go first. While elbowing our way up to the buffet for our second helping of delectable pepper shrimp, we strike up a conversation with another couple, Jenny and Bill, who are from the L.A. area. She's tall, slim, pretty, has long, straight dirty blonde hair, a great smile and a major set of hooters. Bill looks like Jimmy Buffett did when he was in his mid-thirties and was wearing that big bushy blond moustache. Our conversation wanders up and down the usual avenues; introductions, where are you from? How do you like it here?

"Why did you decide to come here?" Amy asks Jenny.

"Oh, we're getting married on Valentines Day. . . in the nude, with eight other couples," Jenny replies, matter-of-factly.

"The nude wedding is here?" Amy asks, barely containing her excitement. Last week, while listening to IRIE FM back in Negril, we had heard reports about the upcoming mass nude wedding, but we didn't realize that it was to be held at Hedo III. There had been some talk on a call-in show about it. A publicity stunt, some had said, and a blatant attempt to get into the Guinness Book of World Records. The callers to the show were pretty well split between those who were upset about it, feeling that it debased the holy sacrament of matrimony, and those who were quite blasé about the whole thing and couldn't care less what people did in private. One caller felt that it was good to exchange vows in the nude because that way the couple couldn't hide anything from one another. Another lady called and said, *'People gettin' married in da nude don't do nuthin' to change da price a buttah in my town.'* Which I thought spoke volumes to the generally liberal attitude of Jamaicans and the respect that they have for people's privacy. A spokesman for the Jamaican government tourism agency called the show and criticized the event as 'improper and offensive'.

Jamaica does have laws against public nudity, but they are obviously enforced selectively, as a walk along the beach in Negril will attest. There is also disagreement as to whether the public nudity laws are applicable on private property.

"Are you having your wedding pictures taken while you're naked?" Amy asks. Her curiosity has been piqued and Jenny and Bill could be in for a long line of questioning.

"We're having two sets of photos done, one in the nude that we can show our 'horizontal' friends and another set done with our clothes on that we can show our families and 'vertical' friends," Bill explains, revealing the fact he and Jenny are swingers. I can tell from Amy's lack of reaction that she had already come to that conclusion, as had I.

Whoever the audience, I don't think I would be particularly inclined to pass out photos of myself with my 'Happy Banana' right out there, front and center. Besides, even when given a fresh shampoo and brush-up, when you get right down to it, male genitalia really aren't that photogenic.

Bill elaborates; "Our trip is sponsored by a 'Lifestyles' club that we belong to."

"What do you plan on wearing for the ceremony?" Amy asks Jenny, which I thought an odd question considering that it was, after all, a nude wedding.

"I have a veil, high heel spikes, a bouquet and I'm getting a paint job," Jenny replied.

The next morning, after a short workout in the small but well equipped gym, I head for a dip in the massive swimming pool. On my way there I walk past the open-air games room area and see that a body painter has set up shop in one corner.

I go over to see what he's up to. He's outfitted with a large case of paints and brushes and a compressor powered airbrush system. The painter is a tall, thin white guy. He's wearing a long ponytail that hangs down to his waist. His shirtless body is generously decorated with colorful tattoos and he has a couple of face piercings. He's working on a pretty young woman who is sitting ramrod straight on a stool wearing nothing but her bikini bottoms. The artist is about half way through painting a matching bikini top on her chest. Here is yet another case of a tough job being done by a tireless dedicated professional. Sheesh! And I chose business over the arts? I lean up against a post and watch for a while. "Put your arms up over your head," the artist instructs. The young woman complies. He dabs paint on the underside of her boobs, tapping the brush up on the soft flesh making her jiggle.

Next he goes to work on her nipples applying a thick layer of paint, blowing on it and then adding another layer and blowing some more. The young lady doesn't seem to mind having a stranger poking and blowing on her, and neither, apparently, do her nipples. He adds texture to the 'cloth' of the bikini top by applying strategically placed runnels and blobs of paint and finishes the job by painting the neck and back straps, which are tied in bows complete with dangling strings. The end product is a very authentic looking bikini top that is a perfect match to her bottoms.

On a table there's a portfolio of pictures of some of the work that the artist has done. He tells me that he's from New York, that body painting is his profession and that he worked on the Broadway production of the musical CATS. The wedding organizers and Hedo have brought him here to paint the nude brides and provide some poolside diversion for the guests. As I'm flipping through his very impressive portfolio he asks me if I want something done. I accept the offer and, as I'm feeling B-A-D today, I opt to have a tribal pattern painted in black across my upper back.

It's a simple job that he finishes in about five minutes. It's strange, but even though I can't see it, my new decoration makes me feel suddenly dangerous and omnipotent.

I strut across the pool deck in search of Amy, who told me she was going to catch a few rays, to show her my new 'tattoo'. Halfway across I see the young lady who just had the bikini top job. Had I not seen it being painted on with my own eyes I would have never known it wasn't the real thing. I watch her very closely as she walks by. Of course, I do this only out of a keen interest in the arts. Yes, I notice that there is just a smidgen more bounce than one would normally expect for such a young, firm woman.

The swimming pool at Hedo III defies the term 'pool'. It's huge and meandering, more like a lake than a pool, with coves, straits, islands and bridges. It also has a fountain and a waterfall. One of the 'islands' in the pool, at the end of a long narrow strait near the piano bar, is covered in a patch of grass and features a single inviting hammock. The pool also comes with its own waterslide which starts at the tower above the disco, sluices through the disco itself, where the tube is transparent plastic, makes a couple of 90 degree turns and empties in a section of the pool near one of the bridges. Needless to say, the transparent tube running through the disco is all the enticement that's needed to assure a steady stream of naked sliders around midnight every night.

The preparations of the wedding site begin the day before the event.

Naturally (so to speak) it's located in the 'nude' area of the resort, well away from the 'prude' side. The spectacle, . . . or rather, wedding, is to take place in a large, open sandy area that normally serves as a volleyball court. It's situated in the elbow formed by two blocks of rooms, oriented to form a shallow 'V', facing the water. To one side is the nude pool, hot tub and beach area. At the ocean's edge, a railed boardwalk runs along a fifteen-foot drop-off to the rocks and surf below. The backdrop is the blue Caribbean Sea, framed by round-leafed sea grape trees. And for effect, along the boardwalk perched over the breaking surf, is a pink gazebo decorated with ribbons and lace, a perfect spot for wedding photos.

The volleyball nets have been taken down and the sand has been raked and groomed. A set of large chess pieces, borrowed from the outdoor chessboard, have been arranged to form the matrimonial aisle. Tables decorated with colorful bunting have been set up to one side.

Several film crews have shown up to document the big event. There's a crew from HBO who are doing a 'nude wedding special' and some other teams from American news networks. There's even a crew that has come all the way from Australia. Apparently the event has been promoted on The Playboy Channel, which may explain its availability on cable in the rooms.

In the afternoon we go down to the nude hot tub for a soak in the sun and some conversation. Unlike the Negril Hedo, the water in the Hedo III hot tub is crystal clear and there doesn't appear to be any foreign matter floating about. Jenny and Bill are there. I ask Bill if he believes in the old proverb about it being bad luck to see the bride in her wedding attire before the event. He laughs and responds by burying his head between Jenny's wet hooters.

The view from the nude pool is outstanding, providing a grand vista of Runaway Bay. The sound of the surf is a soothing match to the hot swirling waters of the tub.

"Oh! That's gross!" Jenny says. At one end of the swimming pool that's attached to the hot tub there's a raised circular dais with a fountain spraying straight up from a nozzle mounted in the center. A large fat naked guy is sprawled out on top of the dais. He's arranged himself so that his genitals are directly in line of the geyser. His penis and scrotum are flopping around as the water gushers up between his legs. It looks like some kind of new-age sexual hydrotherapy. He remains on the dais, ponderously repositioning himself periodically, for the entire time that we are in the hot tub.

What happens the night before a wedding? A stag party, of course! The wedding organizers put on a stag party for the grooms and a stag-ette party for the brides. The men's affair took place in the piano bar. Headlining were three Russian strippers who were brought in from Kingston for the event. The trio had created quite a buzz around the club in the days leading up to their performance, strutting their stuff on the pool decks and the beach, three very good looking young ladies who knew how to carry themselves. It wasn't until just before the event that the purpose of their visit became apparent to most.

The men's stag started at about 8:00pm in the Piano Bar on the second floor above a large patio next to the main bar. The stag goings-on were tantalizingly almost visible. From below, craning our necks to see more through the big multi-paned bay window, we could see only flashing lights, moving shadows cast on the walls, pumping silhouettes and glimpses of naked bodies. All very stimulating and erotically suggestive but nothing that we could really get our teeth into. After the stag several of the grooms were seen descending the steps from the Piano Bar with broad grins on their faces. The next day it was widely reported that the Russians' performance exceeded even the most optimistic expectations.

Unlike the men's stag, which was a groom-only party, the girls were allowed to invite one female guest each. Jenny invited Amy. The girls stag-ette was in the disco, which was virtually impossible to spy on.   There was no imported talent for the ladies, the entertainment was provided by selected male members of the staff who wore masks to hide their identities. The girls disappeared behind the closed doors of the disco. From outside, we could hear the music thumping and see the lights flashing through the windows, but that was all. The ladies emerged an hour later giggling and covered with perspiration. I asked Amy what happened but all she said was that it got quite wild and they had a lot of fun. In spite of my many pleas, she wouldn't reveal any details of what had transpired.

It's the day of the nude wedding and tensions mount. The organizers are seen rushing about, attending to final details, brows furrowed. Directions to workers are delivered in machine gun bursts of patois. A helicopter makes several passes over the site, ferrying dignitaries from MoBay and Ocho Rios. Dignitaries at a nude wedding? This morning I learn that the Chairman of the Board of Super Clubs, Mr. John Issa himself, will be in attendance along with several other high-ranking investors and assorted hangers-on. I am beginning to comprehend that this is a bigger deal than I had thought.

One of the guests who was out for a walk on the road reports that there are some protesters, mostly churchgoers from the local parish groups, picketing outside the entrance to the resort. He said that they're shouting and waving signs denouncing the wedding. There are also numerous police walking around the resort property today and several police cars parked in the entrance roundabout. A boat with 'POLICE' painted in large letters on the side can be seen patrolling offshore.

Amy and I walk out to the wedding site where the final preparations are underway. Rose petals are strewn along the chess piece pathway, three triple-tiered cakes are placed on the tables and huge colorful flower arrangements have been positioned at several locations around the venue. Large potted palms are arranged to form archways at the entrances to the area. A tall pyramid of glasses has been erected which will later serve as a champagne fountain. Several large banana leaves, decorated with gold glitter, frame the area where the betrothed are to stand during the nuptials. The wedding zone has been very well laid out and expertly prepared. It's obvious that this has not been done on a shoestring budget.

At the last moment, a large sparkling ice sculpture is brought out and placed on the table. It quickly begins to melt under the blistering midday sun.

At last, the moment arrives, the steel band, decked out in matching white pants and muti-colored tropical patterned shirts, starts to play.

The camera crews crouch in position. The spectators jostle for the best vantage points. But there's a problem. One of the organizers decides that all of the spectators are to be nude or they will not be allowed to watch the wedding. Perhaps it's being done at the request of one of the film crews. After all, how would it look to have a procession of naked brides and grooms walking against a backdrop of clothed spectators? It could entirely ruin the esthetics of the shot. Whatever the reason, all clothed spectators are given the option of either disrobing or decamping. About half of the clad and partially clad strip and are allowed to stay. For their reward, those in the front row are handed little bubble blowing kits featuring a pair of entwined doves on the bottle cap. The somewhat disgruntled remainder, presumably migrants from the prude side who are unwilling to pay the price of admission, retreat out of camera range to watch from afar.

Amy, already topless, removes her bottoms without any hesitation. She wouldn't miss this for anything. I don't respond well to orders so I step back a little distance into the shade cast by the rock wall of the nude pool grotto. From there I have a good view with the added benefit of being out of the scorching sun.

The grooms march into position, swinging to the music. What do you wear to a naked wedding? One of the grooms, choosing to be elegantly 'attired', is wearing a top hat and tuxedo jacket and nothing else. Another is wearing a fancy dress cowboy hat and a string tie. Bill, choosing a Playboyesque motif, is decked out in a set of cuffs and a matching bow tie, he's shod in a simple pair of open-toed sandals. A couple of the grooms are plain buck-naked.

It is my strong belief that when God created the male of the species, she never intended for him to walk around completely naked. We men, for the most part, are such ugly creatures, all of that body hair and flab and those hangy-down bits. Someone, a loin cloth, please! One of the guys is wearing a cummerbund. The oddest 'dressed' is the fellow who's wearing nothing but a floppy white bucket hat, like the one that Gilligan wore on his island. This chap looks strangely out of place, if you can imagine, and if I'm not mistaken, he's somewhat uncomfortable with the whole process. Perhaps the hat was a last minute addition, hastily added as something to hide under.

Let's not forget the best men. They've been supplied by Hedonism, picked from the club's entertainment staff, as were the maids of honor. One glance at any member of the entertainment staff and it quickly becomes apparent that the initial qualifier for employment is very good looks and a body to go with it. This is not to denigrate them otherwise in any way. Every one of the entertainment staff that I've had the pleasure of meeting is intelligent, talented, well spoken, outgoing and has a dazzling personality that befits their great looks and bodies. It's their presence and the atmosphere that they create that 'makes' the club. Without the excellent entertainment staff, Hedo III would be just another expensive, albeit nice, resort.

The best men are not nude, but clad only in tight fitting sequined G-strings, they're the next thing to it. Their black muscular bodies and prominent buttocks stand out in stark contrast to the assembled grooms. At this wedding at least, the 'best men', really are.

Eventually the party of grooms settles into position. A clothed ecumenical minister named Fred from The Universal Life Church in Miami stands in front of the men, holding his papers at the ready. A hush settles over the crowd. The surf, crashing on the rocks below, is the only sound to be heard. Now for the bridal party, and to say that their arrival is keenly anticipated would be a gross understatement. We wait, sweltering under the hot sun. Moments pass. Why do they always make us wait so?

A signal is given and the steel band bends eagerly to their chromed pans, hammering out a tropical rendition of the wedding march. Jenny, the first of the brides-to-be walks into view, accompanied by her entertainment staff bride's maid. An excited babble of 'Ohh's and 'Ahh's rises from the dearly beloved. Film rolls and cameras click. Jenny looks fabulous! Her simple outfit of veil, pumps and bouquet, sets off her extraordinary paint job. She's decorated with several large and colorful hibiscus blossoms that are attached to a single stem that winds down from her bosom, twists across her belly and finally roots in her crotch. Let me try that again . . . 'the stem twists across her belly and snakes in between her legs'. No, that doesn't work either. Ah well . . as a finishing touch, she has been dusted with gold and silver glitter. As she walks in the bright sunlight her body casts off a constantly changing pattern consisting of thousands of sparkling reflections. The effect is stunning. Jenny is the strutting sun goddess of Hedo III!

The other brides follow, similarly un-attired and decorated but none nearly as resplendent as Jenny. Some wear garters and stockings. They too, are escorted by entertainment staff bridesmaids. The bridesmaids are not naked, of course, but clad in bikini tops and G-strings, they add a dash of West Indies spice to the procession. Here again, with a couple of exceptions, the bridesmaids, who are also daubed with body paint, steal the show from their charges. To be fair to the brides, most of whom are on their second marriages and thus in their mid-thirties and older, it is unjust to be compared to erotically attired, twenty-year-old, long-legged hard-bellies.

Once the brides are in place, the marriage ceremony commences. The minister performs the traditional ceremony, but frankly, it is anticlimactic. From where we stand, we can't hear a word, just the crashing surf and the rustling of palm fronds. The minister's mouth moves and he gestures for several minutes. The couples exchange rings, more words are mouthed, and then the couples hold hands and kiss each other. At that point we know the deed is done, so we all start to clap.

The married couples link arms and stroll back down the rose petal aisle making their way to the registry table. A clutch of naked people bursts from the front rows of the crowd as the procession marches between the chess pieces, and blow streamers of bubbles above them. I wish I had my camera, because it's something that you don't see every day; nine beaming, naked couples, freshly married, walking on rose petals between rows of enormous chess pieces, surrounded by a horde of bubble-blowing nudies of all shapes and sizes, whose bums and boobs wobble and jiggle as they dip and blow and jump.

Above the scene, hundreds of floating bubbles glisten in the sun. It's a scene that is more befitting Alice in Wonderland than Jamaica. Again I ask myself, *'Is this place for real?'*

Immediately after the signing of the registry business, the newlyweds are assembled for a group photo. The big, gold spray-painted banana leaves are used as props, strategically placed so as to obscure naked body parts, which I assume, will allow for wider distribution and publication of the pictures.

We get tired of standing in the hot sun and, since the bubble-blowing scene could not possibly be topped, we go down to the little manmade beach for a cooling dip. About forty minutes later we come back along the boardwalk and run into Jenny and Bill, still outfitted in their matrimonial regalia. Under the direction of a camera crew they are walking slowly down the boardwalk, holding hands. They get to a certain point and then pause to look wistfully into each other's eyes.

Ahhh, to be young, in love . . . and naked.

A Pilgrimage to Nine Mile

"Facts an' facts, an' t'ings an t'ings.
Dem's all a lotta fockin' bullshit. Hear me!
Dere is no trut' but de one trut',
an' dat is de trut' of JAH RASTAFARI!"
Bob Marley, 1978

Amy doesn't understand how I can listen to the same Bob Marley CD's over and over and over . . . and over. She's never said it out loud, but I believe that she thinks I'm compulsive about Bob's music. She's good about it though, because she likes the music - - - kind of. Okay, she puts up with it. But for me it's much, much more than 'liking' the music. It's difficult to explain to someone who doesn't 'have it', Bob's music is a part of me, an important part, right down deep in my very core somewhere. I know there are others who feel the same way, others who 'have it', and there are a lot of us too. The amazing thing is, some of Bob's devotees weren't even born until after he left us. One of my daughter's guy friends, who is seventeen years old, has turned his bedroom into a Bob Marley shrine.

Bob once said, *"My music will live on forever."* He was right. In my mind and in the minds of thousand and thousands of his devotees around the world, his music is very much alive. Bob lives.

I saw him live in concert once. It was at the Montreal Forum on June 9, 1978, during the 'Kaya' tour. Leading off was 'The Tower of Power', a tight brass ensemble that did a good job of warming up the Forum, but everybody was there for the Wailers. By the time Tower of Power had wrapped up, the crowd had spilled over onto the open floor area in front of the stage. It seemed that the whole Caribbean population of Montreal had turned out and had staked out their rightful place smack in front of the stage. And no one was going to move them out of there either.

Then it was time. The lights went out. The rhythm guitar's sudden *'chuka... chuka... chuka...chuka'* leapt off the stage and homed straight into my gut.

"And now ladies and gentlemen. . . . ,"
the announcer said in a deep, booming voice,
". . . . coming to you all the way from Trenchtown, Jamaica . . .
. . . . . please welcome . . . .

.... BOB MARLEY AND THE WAILERS!"

The stage lights came on, the rest of the instruments joined in and there they were, the Wailers, and two of the 'I Three', Bob's female backup vocal group.   Later Bob introduced them as the 'I Two', explaining that one of the girls was sick that night, (Marcia Griffiths, if I remember correctly).

The Wailers were up there onstage, playing their instruments, the girls were bopping side by side, but Bob was nowhere to be seen.

"Until... the philosophy... which hold one race superior and another, ...inferior....."

His voice filled the Forum . . . people started to whistle . .

"Is finally...., and permanently...discredited...and abondened..."

Everybody was standing, I stood up looking for him, the cheering got louder, everybody's eyes were locked on the stage searching . . . waiting . . . anticipating . . . .

"H'everywhere is war......"

And there was Bob! Up on the front of the stage, bouncing his dreads, arms stretched out to the crowd. Pandemonium broke out! People around me were screaming. *I* was screaming. The crowd on the floor in front of the stage started dancing, heads bobbing in the sweeping spotlights.

For the next hour and a half, a natural mystic flowed through the air. We were in the presence of greatness. The messiah had come to town and we, his disciples, were receiving his benediction. Until my dying day, and then some, I shall never forget that concert, and whenever I hear the opening strains of 'War', goose bumps rush over my skin.

Erin and Hannah love Bob's music too. They know many of the lyrics by heart, and well they should; they've been listening to Bob since before they were born. When their mother was pregnant with them I would put headphones to her belly to wake them up and get them kicking when it was playtime. Erin was a little late in coming so I played "Exodus" to get her moving. It worked too, she came into this world a-wailin'. When I can't find my *'Confrontation'* CD, I know that it will likely be in Erin's mini-system.

So here we are in Runaway Bay, and I am keenly aware that Bob Marley lies in his mausoleum a tantalizingly short drive away. I intend to go, but I haven't broached the subject with Amy yet.

We're sitting in the Scotch Bonnet, watching the ocean rolling in, and Amy asks me, "Do you want to do any excursions hon?"

"Well, I was thinking of touring in the mountains a bit . . . . going up to Nine Mile maybe," I reply, keeping my eyes on the breakers, trying not to sound too excited.

"Oh, that sounds interesting! Nine Mile, that's where Bob Marley is buried isn't it?" She's a sharpy my bride, it's hard to get one by her.

"Yeah, well actually he's lying in a mausoleum."

Yes, we're going!

Cliff, our driver, picks us up at the front entrance early in the morning. Amy jumps into the back seat. We are planning on a route that will take us east along the coast to Ocho Rios, south through Fern Gully and up into the mountains, back east through the mountains to Nine Mile, where we'll pay our respects to Bob, then back down through Browns Town, Discovery Bay and back to the hotel. The route, when drawn on a map of Jamaica, describes a rough oval with one edge running along the north shore.

The drive to Ocho Rios is uneventful. Once there, we turn inland and drive up through Fern Gully, an old riverbed that was long ago converted into a road. It twists its way up through a gorge cut into the mountainside. Ferns smother the embankments and trees hug the road, towering above us. Even though the day is cloudless, Fern Gully is cool and steeped in dark shade. Cliff informs us that there are 350 different types of ferns here. He tells us that back in his childhood, cars driving this road had to use their headlights during the day. Now, due to the heavy traffic and overuse, a lot of the foliage has died off. Trucks are banned from driving through Fern Gully and efforts are being made to return it to its previous state. Craft stalls displaying colorful batiks flowing in the breeze punctuate the sides of the road as we climb the twisting, turning mountainside road. Suddenly the road straightens out and levels off and we break into brilliant sunshine along the ridge top. We all reach for our sunglasses. There's a large craft market located in a clearing and several tour buses are parked in the lot even though it's still early.

We turn west along the mountain roads, heading toward the town of Claremont. A small inconspicuous sign at an intersection indicates the way to Bob's place. The further we penetrate into the mountains, the worse the road gets.

I ask Cliff about the massive holes in the ground that scar the countryside. He explains that the excavations are left behind from where bauxite has been gouged out and hauled away. The soil here is red and shows at the edges of the holes where the vegetation hasn't completely grown back in yet, as if the earth was made of flesh and was oozing blood. The road meanders through the mountainous terrain. It's hot and the road is dusty so we stop at a roadside stand for a cold Ting. Cliff talks with the vendor, they speak in incomprehensible volleys of the local patois, laughing and slapping each other on the back. My patois ear is not tuned to the northern dialect and I only understand one word in ten.

We continue, passing through many small towns. Cliff deftly dodges the cows, dogs and goats that share the road. He tells us that the goats are very road smart and hardly ever get hit. If they get caught out in traffic, they will freeze in the middle of the road until it's safe to cross. It's the cows that you have to watch, "Cows, dey stupid," Cliff says.

Children in crisp school uniforms trot along the shoulder, toting their backpacks. We are getting deeper into the hills and the countryside is lush green and pastoral. The traffic thins out and soon the road narrows down to one lane. In places, portions of the road are so pot-holed and washed out that it can't properly be called a road. As we're jostling through a particularly bad spot, I ask who maintains the road. Cliff answers with a laugh, "Nobody mon!"

He beeps the horn as we approach blind corners, as if to put up a force shield to protect us, but he doesn't slow down any. When we encounter oncoming vehicles we slow to a crawl and scrape past each other. We meet a large tanker truck as we're descending a steep grade. There isn't enough room to squeeze by. Cliff backs the car up the hill until we reach a cutout in the roadside. The truck slowly edges by to the accompaniment of Cliff's shouted directions and waving arms. All the while the car radio, tuned to IRIE FM, blasts out an assortment of reggae and dance hall music. It seems that everything in Jamaica happens to the beat of background music.

I suddenly realize that we are on a road that Bob traveled many times and somehow that makes me feel closer to him.

Soon the only traffic we encounter are farmers leading donkeys loaded down with sacks bulging with vegetables. The clearings we pass are planted with patches of yams, each plant mounded high. Small groupings of banana plants abound. All the farmers that we see carry machetes, I ask Cliff about it. "To work de ear't, yuh know, dig holes, cut vines and rope and t'ings. An' to fight off de garden raiders an' protect der work", he explains. Everybody that we encounter waves and greets us as we pass. The terrain is extremely mountainous, wreathed in picturesque valleys. It's taking longer than I thought it would to get to Nine Mile, but the trip is very enjoyable and we are in no hurry.

We stop by the side of the road to stretch our legs and admire the view across a wide valley. Below, a narrow road snakes between the hills, modest farmer's homes dot the mountainsides. I take in the view, it is a scene of utter and complete tranquility. Cliff plucks a dry leaf from a small tree and bends it in two. "Smell dis," he passes it to me. It smells like spice.

"What is it?" I ask.

"Pimento," he says, "people crush de berries an' put it in dere porridge, some people call it 'all spice'."

We drive a little further and enter the tiny hamlet of Nine Mile. So named because, as John Crow flies, it's nine miles from here to St. Ann's Bay. The original name of the area is Rhoden Hall, but now everybody calls it Nine Mile. It's no different from any of the other small towns that we've passed through to get here, but I am finally here, where Bob was born and grew up as a young boy. We pass Bunny Wailer's house, one of the original Wailers, just across the road from the gates to Bob's mausoleum. There are no signs indicating that we are at the mausoleum. It looks like the rest of the town, sun-baked and understated.

A pair of high wooden doors in the fence surrounding the property are opened and we are directed in. Several Rastas are in the parking lot and they greet us with the fist tap. There is only one other car in the parking lot. Nine Mile is definitely off the beaten tourist path. Anybody that makes this trek does so with conviction. The mausoleum is perched on the side of a mountain, which, we are told, Bob called Mount Zion. We walk up to the reception area where there's a small gift shop with the world's largest collection of Bob Marley T-shirts. There's a bar and a veranda overlooking Nine Mile and the surrounding area. I go out on the verandah. Across the road is a concrete rainwater catchment covering the side of a hill. It drains into a large cistern that provides fresh water for the town's people. Small hills stretch to the horizon, simple homes and shacks are scattered on the hillsides. Below the verandah is Bob's grandmother's house, where he was born.

In the bar are a couple of visitors and another Rasta behind the counter. A TV above the bar is showing a video of Bob. It's turned up loud and his music echoes off the walls.

We meet our guide, Bongo Jo (his real name is Anthony, but like many people in Jamaica, he has a character-fitting pseudonym). Bongo Jo's head is covered with thick, long dreads. He leads us up the trail to the mausoleum. We pass through a gate swinging from tall, cone-shaped stone posts. On each wing of the gate there's a picture of Bob. I recognize it as the photo from the front jacket of the 'Kaya' album. Across the top of the gate are two signs, 'Respect' and

'Exodus'.

We slowly mount the path, as we go Bongo Jo gives us a brief summary of Bob's life, all the details already familiar to me. At the top of the path, about a third of the way up the mountainside, there's a small, level clearing where Bob's mausoleum and his second house, built by his mother, are situated.

It is quiet and serene here; we're alone. The house is narrow and very small, the walls are made of stone, the roof of corrugated metal. The wooden trim is painted in the Rastafarian colors, red, gold and green. We take our shoes off and enter the house. There are two small rooms and in one the bed that Bob slept in as a child is still there.

"We'll share the shelter of my single bed."

Bongo Jo tells us that Bob's children still sleep in these beds when they visit Nine Mile, it helps them to connect with their roots, he says. Outside the little house there's a medium sized boulder half buried in the ground.

"Cold ground was my bed last night and rock was my pillow too," Bongo Jo sings quietly, pointing to the rock.

The mausoleum, a few steps away from the house, is a narrow whitewashed building with a high vaulted ceiling. Three tall windows run up its side filling the high gable. We enter and although we are the only ones inside, there is a presence here. It's very quiet, candles and incense are burning, sunlight streams in through the windows. A large marble crypt dominates the center of the small narrow room. There's just enough space to walk around the crypt. I put my palm on the marble. It's warm.

"My music will live on forever..."

A lump grows in my throat and tears well up in the corners of my eyes. The walls of the mausoleum are adorned with photos and memorabilia including photographs of His Imperial Majesty Haile Selassie, the great African-American civil rights leader Marcus Garvey and a detailed needlepoint of a lion. There's a picture of Bob's brother propped up at the base of the crypt. Bongo Jo speaks in hushed tones as he tells us that the body of Bob's brother occupies the lower part of the crypt. He was killed in Miami in the late '80's. At the head of the crypt, on the eastern wall, there is a large circular stained glass window, gloriously back-lit by the sun. We are told that Bob is lying with his favorite guitar and a stalk of Sensemilla, his favorite herb, the species that he used when he wanted to meditate.

Bongo Jo tells us that Bob is laying with his head to the east, toward the rising sun, but that it wasn't always so. Several years back, after Bob's mother and some parish priests had independent visions that Bob had been mistakenly laid to rest with his feet to the east, the crypt was opened and the coffin was taken out, turned around, and correctly replaced. We spend several minutes in the chapel, looking around at the objects within and absorbing the tranquility.

We leave the mausoleum. On the west side there's a sycamore tree, planted by Rita, Bob's widow. I stretch my neck to look to the top of Mount Zion.

"Bob climbed to the top to smoke an' meditate," says Bongo Jo.

We move into the clearing. The grounds of the mausoleum border on a yard belonging to a family who is related to the Marleys. There are a couple of young girls playing there. They see us, come over to the fence and start to sing 'Three Little Birds'. We listen for a while until the singing breaks up into laughter. Bongo Jo laughs with them and tells them that they can't sing.

We cross the clearing and sit on a rock in a flat area across from the little house. It is so tranquil here, the silence broken only by the singing of birds and the laughter of the children. This is a spiritual place. The words of 'Redemption Song' echo in my mind. I look over at the mausoleum and wonder what would have become of Bob if he were still with us. What more could he possibly have given us? Maybe it was destined that his message be short, sharp and loud, so as to ring clearly down through the years. After several minutes of quiet contemplation, we get up and head back down the path. I dab my eyes, Bongo Jo looks at me knowingly. He puts his fist up, we tap. "Respect, my friend," he says. He's seen this before.

On the way out of Nine Mile we pass a big sports field on the west side of town. Last week the field was the scene of the annual Nine Mile Bob Marley birthday bashment. Reports are that it was huge this year, blocking the road until 7:00 the next morning. The field is torn up and there's still some litter laying around, mute testament to the party that was. Bob lives.

Our ride back starts out in silence. I reflect on our visit to the mausoleum, we take in the sights and Cliff answers our few questions. About thirty minutes out of Nine Mile our thoughts are disrupted by the booming bass of amplified music. It gets progressively louder as we move down the road. We round a corner and the source of the music is revealed to us. Music, at an earsplitting volume, is blaring from two enormous banks of speakers that have been erected in a vacant, dusty parking lot. Each bank faces the other from opposite sides of the lot. A few young men are in the parking lot standing between the speakers.   They are apparently engaged in testing the sound equipment and they seem oblivious to the deafening volume. A couple of children are sitting at the side of the road watching the sound test and I fear for their tender ears. Each bank of speakers is about twenty feet wide and twelve feet tall, making the setup that I saw at Cuba's look like bookshelf units. We roll by the parking lot, the car vibrating from the music. Each time the bass thumps something inside the dash buzzes in harmony. Amy holds her hands over her ears.

"What is that all about?" I holler to Cliff.

"Dere's goin' to be a big bashment 'ere tonight!" he shouts.

A short distance down the road we enter the small city of Brownsville. It's a bustle of activity. We pass a school during 'shift change'. In Jamaica, due to the scarcity of classrooms and teachers, some schools have been forced to institute morning and afternoon shifts. The kids are dressed in school uniforms that differ in color and detail depending on their ages and the school they attend.

About two miles outside of Brownsville, the traffic, which has increased to a surprising level, slows to a crawl. The reason soon becomes apparent; there are two men in the middle of the road waving makeshift red flags. On closer examination I see that in fact they are not red flags, but bouquets of red hibiscus blossoms. Each of them is also holding a bucket. They're dressed in tattered clothing and are barefoot, so they're obviously not police or municipal road workers.

"Dere collecting handouts to do repairs on de road," Cliff explains. The road here is especially bad. We weave slowly around the deep potholes, pass the 'flag' waving panhandlers without making a contribution, and continue on our way. I wonder out loud if they might have made the potholes deeper and wider to aid their cause. Cliff shrugs in answer.

A little further on Cliff points to a cave on the side of the road. "Dats Sergeant Corner," he says. "Dere's a man living in dere, he's been dere for fifteen years." The cave mouth is festooned with bits of cloth and it looks very lived in. "He was in de army an' he got an honorable discharge and dat's where he lives now," Cliff adds.

It has happened to me again, every time I start to believe that I'm getting to know this country, it shows me something that I never would have imagined.

We descend toward the coast but my mind turns back to Bob's mausoleum, I'm already thinking about going back to Nine Mile someday. I wonder if they would let me climb Mount Zion?

Goin' Down at Hedonism

'Hog say, di fus water 'im cetch 'im walla.'
Jamaican Proverb

Amy and I walk down to the dock for our morning dive. The Hedo III scuba boat is tied up there. On the hull is painted a large picture of a woman scuba diver. She's wearing a set of fins, a mask and the tank on her back, and nothing else. Her long hair streams behind her, her ample boobs hang below and bubbles float above. The boat is specifically rigged for diving. It's about 35 feet long, powered by two 255 horsepower outboards and is equipped with a flying bridge. It has racks along the front gunwales for scuba tanks and a big open area in the center with padded benches along the sides. As we approach the boat I notice that one of the engines is tilted up out of the water, its prop a mangled mess. It looks like it has had a close encounter with a coral head and has come away the clear loser.

The dive staff lugs the heavy scuba tanks onto the boat and we carry our fins, mask and weight belts aboard. Hedo is all about pampering and that extends to the water sports as well. There are several other divers already on the boat; some are fresh graduates of the one-day resort course and others, like Amy and I, are certified. The certified divers are chatting among themselves about their underwater experiences, while the one-day wonders are sitting quietly, no doubt trying to remember all that they have learned.

As is always the case, there are two types of certified divers, which I classify as the 'minimalists' and the 'professionals'. The 'minimalists' are sitting in bathing suits and T-shirts, already wearing weight belts. When we get to the dive site they will put on their fins and masks, strap a tank to their back, bite down on the regulator and jump in. The 'professionals' are clad in full wetsuits, including booties and gloves and have extra-heavy weights to compensate for the buoyancy of their neoprene suits. They are busy strapping on knives, whistles, strobe lights, clipboards, fish identification plates, cameras, compasses and myriad other doo-dads. One fellow, sitting in front of a gaping gear bag that is larger than my big Samsonite, has pulled out a large apparatus that is apparently a wrist-mounted mobile computer. He's tapping away at it doing whatever it is that he has to do to set it up for the dive. The 'professional' diver's gear is expensive, top-of-the-line stuff in the latest colors and emblazoned with flashy logos. Between the four 'professional' divers on the boat, they have enough high-tech and high-cost equipment to outfit half of the Jamaican Navy.

Amy and I count ourselves among the 'minimalists'. She's wearing a blue spandex one-piece bathing suit with white trim. She looks splendid in it, I've noticed a couple of the water sports crew raking their eyes over her. I'm wearing the same outfit that I wear everyday while I'm in the tropics, quick-dry nylon shorts and a tank-top.

Our two dive masters, Max and Mitch, introduce themselves and do a pre-departure check, ensuring that everyone has all the equipment they will need to dive. Max is quiet and serious. He has a medium size muscular build. He exudes an air of confidence and professionalism. Mitch is more outgoing, moving about the boat, smiling and chatting with everyone.

The boat pulls out from the shelter of the dock and the small manmade cove into Runaway Bay under the power of its one good engine. Five-foot rollers are cresting close to the shore. We head directly into the waves. The boat pitches wildly as it goes over the tops and smacks into the troughs, sending sprays of salty water over us. It's great fun, most of us enjoy it and laugh but some of the neophytes look concerned. Eventually, we work our way out to the calmer water and make a beeline for this morning's dive site.

The nice thing about diving in Runaway Bay is the proximity of the dive sites. Here, they are merely minutes away. I've dived in other places where it's not uncommon to spend a half-hour running out to a site. We tie up to a mooring buoy and the engine is cut. Mitch stands up front and gives us the pre-dive briefing.

We are at a site called 'The Canyon', where we'll be diving in 35 to 45 feet of water. Mitch goes over the underwater signals, ensures that we are all paired up with a buddy and asks for questions. Being none, he says that there is only one more important matter to cover; sharks. Mitch tells us that if we see any man-eating sharks we are to form a tight circle around the dive masters, keeping them in the center as we surface. We are then to keep our bodies between the sharks and the dive masters as they exit the water. They will then help any of us that are still alive back into the boat. He tells us that this is important, as it's the dive masters who will have to fill out the paperwork and answer questions back on land. Most of us understand that Mitch is joking but an Italian woman who fails to see the humor in it needs to be carefully reassured that it was just a joke and that dangerous sharks are an extreme rarity in Runaway Bay.

The pampered treatment continues as the boat crew assists us in donning our vests and tanks. We sit on the padded bench with our arms outstretched and they haul the tanks over to us and buckle us in. They also do a gear check and ensure that the air valve is opened. My gear is strapped on and I check the pressure in my tank, which reads the maximum, 3200lbs. I got a good fill.

Max brings Amy's tank over to her. The top of his 'Farmer John' wet suit is pulled down to his waist. He has a large star-shaped scar on the upper left part of his chest. Amy asks him about it. "Gang fight in Kingston," he replies without turning his attention away from her gear.

The pros are suiting up amid a flurry of clicking, snapping and Velcro ripping sounds. It's beyond me how they can move in all that gear.

One of the one-day resort course graduates has decided that she is not going to dive today after all. She makes a comment about diving with 'professionals', apparently intimidated by the plethora of complicated looking gear. Mitch tries to reassure her, but she's adamant, she's not going down, and furthermore, she wants to go back to shore immediately. Max goes over and tries his best to convince her. He doesn't get any farther than Mitch did. A call is made over the radio and, from what I can gather, a runabout will be dispatched to pick her up.

It's my turn to jump in. The water looks very inviting. A small two-foot swell is running. I do an upright 'giant stride' entry off the rear of the boat. When performed correctly, this maneuver keeps the head above the water. I manage to do it right and the air in my vest keeps me floating shoulder-high on the surface. I stick my mask in the water. I can clearly see the sandy bottom about forty feet below. The visibility looks to be about ninety feet, which is very good for this location. Ahead of the bow several of the divers who entered before me are descending down the mooring line to the assembly point on the sea bottom.

Amy is sitting on the side of the boat preparing to do a back roll entry into the water. She spreads her right hand over her regulator mouthpiece and mask, holding them in place, puts her left hand on the back of her head to protect it from getting banged by the tank, then rolls backwards into the water. She bobs to the surface and looks around for me. We give each other the thumbs-up sign, dump the air from our vests and start our descent. Just before I go under I notice an ominous-looking bank of dark clouds that is rolling in over the coastal hills.

We hold hands and fin slowly toward the marshalling point, descending as we go. As we are one of the last pairs to enter, most of the group is already on or near the bottom. Streams of bubbles rise above them, slowly making their way to the surface. Mitch is there, counting heads and flashing the 'OK?' sign at everyone, paying special attention to his resort course grads.

Many experienced divers don't like diving with novices and some refuse to go down with them at all. I personally don't mind because I enjoy seeing the reactions of new divers to their first dives. In fact, some experienced divers can be a pain in the ass as they are so preoccupied with their equipment, their certifications and themselves that the dive itself sometimes seems to be of secondary interest. However, when diving with novices there are three things that the more experienced diver must keep in mind. First, novices often have trouble equalizing on descent. This means that they have difficulty in getting the pressure of the air trapped in the sinus cavities to equal the pressure that the water is exerting as they descend. This is invariably due to anxiety and is quite common, but it means that the experienced diver may have to wait on the bottom for a while until the beginner gets things under control. New divers also tend to kick up a lot of sand and silt with their fins when they do get to the bottom. Again this is due to anxiety. A group of novice divers can raise an enormous cloud of silt in a couple of minutes, drastically reducing the visibility on the bottom. Experienced divers will go to the bottom and hover almost motionless just above the sand, preserving energy, air and the visibility.

There's one last thing to watch out for when diving with neophytes, and it's the most important. Again, because they are excited and operating in an entirely new environment, novice divers are not always aware of their position in the water relative to others. I have had my mask kicked off my face, my regulator wrenched from my mouth by a flailing hand, and have been landed on when sitting on the bottom by a rookie who forgot that he was sharing the ocean with other divers. So I always keep an eye on the newbies and give them a wide berth.

We sink to the bottom and increase our buoyancy to neutral by pushing on a button that releases a tiny blast of air into our vests. I hover face down and let myself slowly sink to the sand, landing on my chest. The faceplate of my mask is about 3 inches off the bottom. Due to the magnifying effects of the mask I have an incredibly clear and close-up view of the individual grains of sand and the tiny pieces of broken shells that make up the bottom.

I hear the familiar sound of an outboard motor getting louder. The sound seems to be coming from everywhere at once. Underwater, sound travels faster than in the atmosphere and the human ear is not capable of detecting the origin of sounds under such circumstances. It's impossible to tell from what direction the boat is approaching, but I surmise that it's the launch arriving topside to pick up the reluctant student.

The group is all assembled; Mitch leading and Max following at the rear. We swim out over the sand flats to a clump of coral about twenty yards away. There are several long yellow tube sponges growing along the top of the coral head, waving gently in the underwater surge. Small sea fans sprout along the edges. I swim up close to a group of sea fans and scan their surface, on the backside of one of them I find what I'm looking for, a Flamingo Tongue snail. It's about an inch long and a half-inch wide and shaped like a tiny thumb. It's covered with a leopard print mantle that it retracts when disturbed, to reveal a marbled pink and white surface, but I don't touch it. It's feeding on the sea fan, leaving a dark trail of grazed surface in its path.

I fin up and over the top of the coral head, admiring a large brain coral along the top of the ridge. From very close I can make out the individual polyps that make up the coral colony. A couple of sea spiders are crawling delicately over its surface, their long jointed legs picking their way carefully over the pitted surface of the coral. On the other side of the hummock Mitch is kneeling in the sand. He reaches into his vest pocket and pulls out a cocobread wrapped in plastic. My mouth starts to water involuntarily, which is a strange sensation with a regulator gripped between the teeth. Mitch breaks off a piece, it immediately starts to disintegrate and scatter in the water. Instantly he's surrounded by a school of sergeant majors, they dash among the suspended bits of cocobread, snatching them as they pass, gobbling them down and returning for more. Mitch looks like he's being swarmed by an army of angry bees. He breaks off pieces of cocobread and hands them to some of the other divers. Amy swims in and gets a chunk. She holds it, arm outstretched, in the palm of her hand. The sergeant majors, now joined in their feeding frenzy by other little reef fish, dive bomb into her palm attacking the cocobread. I maneuver in front of her to look into her mask and I see from her eyes that she's smiling. We're both enveloped in a cloud of colorful darting fishes. Soon all of the cocobread has been devoured by the hungry hoard and they disperse to hide in the nooks and crannies of the coral.

Mitch points out across the sand flats. There's a wreck of a light twin-engine airplane resting on the bottom, I think it's a Piper Navajo. Beyond it, at the dim edge of visibility, is the forward section of a much larger aircraft, I'm not sure, but it could be a part of an old DC-

6. But we are not visiting the wrecks on this dive. We follow Mitch and soon we are swimming up to the edge of an underwater canyon. The gap across the canyon looks to be about thirty feet.

I see a subtle movement in the sand at the edge of the canyon directly in front of me. After a moment of staring at the spot in the sand, the shape of a skate emerges. It's a wide flat fish, about one-foot across, with both of its eyes on the top of its body. It hides by settling into the sand and changing the color of its skin to perfectly match its surroundings. Only by carefully looking at the spot where it's hiding can one discern its presence, until then it's virtually invisible. It's like looking at a color blindness test chart made of multi-colored dots, once you see the image it's easy to pick it out, but until you see it, it's just an unorganized jumble of dots. I fan my flipper at the skate, it swims up off the sand, flapping its wide wings and 'flies' about ten feet then drops back down to the sand. It squiggles its body flat onto the sand, sinking in about ½ inch. While doing so, the color and patterns on its body shift rapidly three or four times and then become a perfect match for the bottom that it has settled on. It literally disappears.

We swim over the lip of the drop-off. The bottom of the canyon is about sixty feet below, I feel like I'm flying. A school of blue parrot fish snake up out of the canyon heading in the direction of the coral head that we have just come from. They move in perfect unison, looking like a swiftly flowing blue underwater river.

Since we are on a shallow dive, we don't venture down into the canyon. Instead, Mitch leads us across to the other side, the crest of which rises to a depth of about thirty feet. A group of large black angel fish are patrolling a hummock on the far side of the canyon.

We swim along the edge of the canyon, a sheer wall that's adorned with Technicolor sponges, corals and sea fans and teeming with hundreds of fish. A black and white spotted moray, his mouth agape, pokes his head out from under a ledge as we pass. As we cross back over the canyon to the sand flats, I check my gauges, we're at a depth of thirty-eight feet and I have 2400lbs of air left, which is a lot.

I become aware of a loud hissing sound. I once had a regulator fail and go into free-flow when I was 100 feet under water on a dive at Isle Pigeon in Guadeloupe, so loud hissing sounds underwater grab my attention right away. I do a quick check of my gear and scan the water around me for bubbles to see if I have sprung a leak somewhere, but everything appears normal. The hissing sound continues, louder than before.

I look over at Amy to see if she's OK. She has picked up a sand dollar and is examining its underside, apparently unconcerned about the hissing sound. The bubbles rising from her also appear routine. A quick check of the divers close to me yields the same results, everybody looks normal. But the hissing sound continues unabated. I look back to Max who has been following us throughout the dive. He's on the bottom and is poking his dive knife at something that I can't see under a rock. By chance, I look up to the surface and the source of the hissing becomes clear. The underside of the surface of the sea is alive, dimpled by thousands of tiny impact splashes. It's raining very hard on the surface. I float suspended in the water enjoying the spectacle, this is something new for me, I've never experienced a rainstorm underwater before.

'CLANK . . . . CLANK' It's the sound of someone banging on their tank, the underwater signal for "LOOK AT ME!" I do a slow turn searching for the tank-banger. It's Max, he's pointing his knife, which I assume he used to bang his tank, in the direction of the group. My hunt for the source of the hissing sound has distracted me and I've fallen behind. Amy is looking back, about halfway between me and the group.

I flip my fins a couple of times to point my body toward Amy and then go into a dolphin kick, holding both fins side by side and propelling myself forward by pumping my legs hard up and down. This results in a porpoising movement, which is great for covering distance quickly underwater but can only be done for short spurts as it requires a lot of energy and air. Exerting oneself while on scuba gear is not a good idea.

Amy reaches her hand out for me as I arrive. Her eyes have a kind of scolding look to them, as if to say, *'You should be sticking close to me!'* She's right, I should be. Sufficiently chastened, I tuck up closer to the group, still keeping an eye out for the newbies.

Mitch has grabbed onto a large fish trap that's sitting on the bottom. He's examining its contents. Most of the group follows suit and soon the trap is festooned with divers hovering off it in all directions. The bottom of the chicken wire fish trap is strewn with broken coconuts and halved oranges and grapefruits. Strange bait for fish, but it works. A yellow polypropylene rope, tied to the trap, snakes up to the surface, where it's attached to a float, possibly an empty milk jug or a scrap of wood, that will bear the distinct marking of the fisherman who has dropped the trap here. There are three lobsters piled on top of one another in one corner of the trap. Swimming in the middle of the cage are several medium sized reef fish, an un-inflated puffer fish and clinging to one side is a honking big crusty blue crab.

Mitch breaks away from the fish trap and swims toward the assembly point, the dive is almost over. Just before we get there, in a gully off to the side of our path, I notice a large cloudy patch of water. At first I think that the silt that was kicked up when we congregated at the start of the dive has drifted over to the gully. But most of that should have settled by now and the cloudy area doesn't look like suspended silt, it has a kind of gelatinous quality to it.

The group gathers around the mooring point and Mitch sends them to the top two by two. Max signals to Amy and I to show him our air pressure gauges, we both have plenty left so we cruise around the bottom staying close to the mooring point as others rise in pairs to the surface. My preference is to be the last one out of the water, it means more bottom time and less time in the after-dive confusion of the de-gearing process on the boat.

I look up to the surface and see that the rain has stopped and the sun is shining. When I look back down to the bottom I see something that I hadn't noticed before. A scorpion fish, whose camouflaging is just as effective as the skate's, is on the bottom about ten feet away from me. The scorpion fish looks like a lump of barnacle encrusted rock. For defence it has a row of sharp hypodermic-like spikes in its dorsal fin which, if touched, will inject a highly poisonous and potentially fatal venom into the victim. He's sitting on the bottom facing me, his dorsal fin erect. A scorpion fish will not attack a human but it would be a serious situation if a diver or swimmer were to step on its spines. I get Amy's attention and point to the scorpion fish. She signals 'Okay' and we give him a wide berth.

Eventually, Amy and I surface and the crew aids us in getting our tanks off while we're still in the water. That done, we clamber into the boat. Everyone is now back on board except for Max and a pair of 'pro' divers. I'm still at the back of the boat while one of the pros is in the process of un-encumbering himself from all of his gear. It takes quite a while. Mitch is bent over the stern helping the guy un-clip his doo-dads and un-buckle himself from his vest. After a couple of minutes of struggling the diver bobs free of his tank and vest and Mitch hauls it aboard. "Fuckin' suicide vest," he curses under his breath as he lugs it past me to the racks in the bow.

As is normal, everybody is chatting excitedly about what was seen on the dive. I'm always amazed at what I miss. This time I missed a sea turtle and a six-foot nurse shark. I ask Max about the cloudy area that we passed enroute to the assembly point.

"I don't know mon," he says, "but it's always dere. It's a mystery of de sea."

The boat, still at anchor, has begun to roll in the swell that has come up. This doesn't agree with one of the fellows in the back. He bends over the side and unloads his breakfast into the sea. I know from past experience that puking, like yawning, can be contagious, especially if the smell of it drifts back on board. Unfortunately this proves to be the case today and one of the ladies in the back joins in the festivities and offers the contents of her stomach to the fishes.

When the gear is all stowed we untie from the mooring and head back in to the dock. Mitch puts a reggae tape on the boat's sound system and cranks it up. Still in his wetsuit, he starts dancing on the fore-deck. I stand at the front of the boat, the air rushes over my damp body cooling me and giving rise to a rash of goose bumps. The dive discussions continue as the boat smashes through the swells, and by the time we enter the little man-made cove a couple of minutes later, the six-foot nurse shark has grown into a ten footer.

The pampered treatment continues after we dock, we don't have to deal with our empty tanks. The clouds have obscured the sun again and everybody is a little chilled after the dive. There's a big barrel of warm freshwater on the dock that's there for rinsing the salt water off of the diving gear. One of the crewmen, still wet from the rainstorm, jumps fully clothed into the barrel. Max directs a sharp blast of patois in his direction and he scrambles out. But he's given me an idea.

"Let's go to the hot tub, babe," I suggest to Amy.

"That's what I was thinking," she replies.

The prude hot tub is located on a platform across from the disco patio. It's sits on top of the main swimming pool grotto about twenty feet off the pool deck. For reasons that are not clear to me, the hot tub has a glass floor. This means that people looking up from within the grotto below are treated to the sight of the bottom of people's feet in a mass of swirling bubbles. Perhaps it was designed to cater to those with foot fetishes.

We splash down into the soothing hot waters of the tub, which we have to ourselves. The elevated location of the tub provides an extraordinary view of the coastal hills and Runaway Bay. I pull Amy into my arms and gaze out over the water. Our dive this morning has been a good one.

Ocho Rios and Dunns River Falls

'Rockstone a riva battam noh kno' sun hot.'
Jamaican Proverb

We wake up to our last day on the north shore, tomorrow morning we go back to our Negrillian paradise. Our plan today is to make a quick visit to Ocho Rios, go to Dunns River falls, which is a long series of small cascading waterfalls that can be scaled, and then get back to Hedo in time for the afternoon dive.

Cliff, our driver from the trip to Nine Mile, is at the front entrance when we get there. We pile into the back of the car.

"We need to hit a cash machine Cliff," Amy says.

"No problem mi lady, der's one near de shops," he replies.

Ah yes, the shops. What would a trip to Jamaica be without the obligatory stop at the tourist traps?

"Today de cruise ships will be in Ochi," Cliff says, "we want to get in an' out as fast as possible and beat dem to Dunns."

"Good plan Cliff," I said. He doesn't realize it, but he's given me an excuse to hurry our stop at the shops.

Pulling into Ocho Rios, which is a twenty-minute jaunt from Hedo, we see that there are two cruise ships berthed at the docks. I catch Amy looking longingly at them. She worked in the entertainment department on a couple of different ships when she was younger and she has always had a yearning to get back on board.

'Ocho Rios' is Spanish for 'eight rivers', although there are actually only four rivers that pass through the area; Dunns River, Cave River, Roaring River and the Turtle River. The misnaming stems back to the mid 1600's when a Spanish force, sailing from Cuba, invaded Jamaica, which at that time was held by the English. The battle took place near Dunn's River Falls, which the Spanish referred to as Los Chorreos. According to my Larousse Spanish dictionary, chorreo means 'spurting or 'gushing', an apt description of the mouth of Dunn's River Falls. However, the English misunderstood 'Los Chorreos', instead hearing 'Ocho Rios', which is easy enough to do amid the booming of cannon and clattering of cutlass. In spite of its misnomer Ocho Rios has developed into a big bustling city, much like Montego Bay.

Cliff points out the cash machine and drops us off at the Almond Tree shops. We make arrangements to meet him in forty minutes.

Amy goes off to visit the jewelry and duty free stores and I go across the street to the craft market. Not surprising, it's very similar to the craft markets in Negril, offering sarongs, walking sticks, pipes, wicker ware and T-shirts. However, the largest of the carvings of turtles and fish seem to be much larger here, way too big to bring home on an airplane. It's peculiar, but there is an overabundance of very large giraffe carvings, which seems odd, as I have never seen one single live giraffe in all the visits that I've make to the island and the giraffe is not an indigenous species here.

I exit the craft market and I'm about to cross the road when my path is blocked by a procession of primary school children marching rank and file down the sidewalk. They're all dressed in prim brown uniforms. Their teachers have them corralled in a grid of ropes, each child penned within their own square. They pass in front of me, gazing wide-eyed at the sights, holding on to the ropes and moving as a single unit.

I catch up to Amy as she is exiting one of the high-end jewelry boutiques. A frigid blast of air-conditioned air follows her out. "Brrrrr!" she says.

"See anything you want?" I ask.

"Yeah, but I don't have twenty-four thousand American dollars on me just now."

Cliff is at our pick-up spot and we are off to Dunns River Falls, which is about two miles west of Ocho Rios on the road back to Hedo. We pull into a parking spot near the entrance gate. After bidding us a good excursion and pointing us in the right direction, Cliff gets back in the driver's seat, puts it into the fully reclined position and plops a baseball cap over his face.

We pay the entrance fee and enter the park.

"Suh! Come over heah for your shoes." A lady is waving us over to her stall, above it there's a large sign, '**Water Shoes**'. We go over. "You need to wear dese if you're going to walk de falls," she explains. Hundreds of pairs of gummy bottomed water shoes of all sizes are arrayed on the racks in her stall. I look around the compound and see that there are several other 'water shoe' stalls. People are renting the shoes, so we do the same. We put our sandals in our backpack.

From the entrance compound we join a thickening crowd that flows into a railed holding area that overlooks the exit point for the falls excursion. This tour is more organized than I had anticipated. From this point we can't really see any of the falls. Several people come up over a lip in the stream and exit onto a cement landing. I see that their clothes are soaked. There's a bank of pay-lockers nearby. We rent one and put our backpack into it.

Over the next few minutes we're moved progressively lower into a succession of holding pens that are arranged along a damp cement walkway and a series of steps that descend steeply beside the falls. At each stop we get a glimpse of a small section of the falls. The stream is approximately sixty feet across.   The falls consist of a multitude of small flat plateaus, each at a different level. On some of the broader plateaus the water collects momentarily in shallow pools before continuing its rush to the sea below.   Large boulders are interspersed on the plateaus and tree trunks and branches of various sizes are strewn at intervals across the cataracts.   The combined effect of this phenomenon is hundreds of delightful little waterfalls that step down to the sea, ranging from two to ten feet in height, over which the clear fast-running water cascades amid the constant background noise of rushing water.

At one point we are joined by a couple of falls guides who tell us to follow them for the final descent to the base of the falls. We pass under the roadway, crouching in the cramped space beneath and emerge at the bottom level of the falls, which to my surprise and great delight, is a beautiful little beach of golden sand.   There are some change facilities, picnic tables and concession stands there.

The guides instruct us to gather around them and form a circle, boy – girl - boy – girl, and join hands. Amy gives me a whimsical 'this is getting hokey' look. I have her to one side of me and an older heavy-set woman to the other.

The guide tells us that the climb up the falls covers 600 feet vertical from the beach to the exit point at the top. He also tells us that we will be climbing the falls in a single file 'human-chain' in the order that we are now in. I squeeze Amy's hand and return the look.

We're led from our gathering point on the beach, still holding hands, to the point where the falls empty into the sea. We reach the base of the falls and look up. The water gushes over three final five-foot terraces. Above that are several higher steps. The volume of water flowing onto the beach is impressive. It doesn't look like an easy climb, at least not from this vantage point. The woman beside me has come to the same conclusion and is vocalizing her concerns.

Amy and I are near the front of the line and we follow the guides to the first steps up the side of the falls. The 'human chain' struggles over the first plateau amid gestures and shouted instructions from the guides. The woman behind me loses her footing. She's saved from going into the water by myself and the guy holding her other hand, but for a moment afterward, I totter on the verge of losing my balance and falling. It's a similar scene at the next terrace. I find it difficult to climb without the use of my arms. Suddenly my lead hand is free. Amy has let go. The guy ahead of her has broken lose from the chain and is picking his own path up the falls and Amy is following him. I apologize to the woman behind me, let go of her hand and strike out on my own.

The bottom portion of the falls turns out to be the steepest. Once above the first few terraces the climb is much easier, but we still have to carefully pick our footholds in the rushing water. The gummy rubber shoes work very well, tenaciously gripping the rock of the falls. We reach a relatively placid pool and take a short break to look at our surroundings. The falls are bordered on each side by lush tropical foliage. From where I'm standing I can see bamboo, several different types of ferns, a breadfruit tree and two species of palms. Lilies and orchids are also said to bloom here.

I wonder what was it like before it was commercialized and even before that in the days of the Arawak Indians. What were the reactions of the first explorers when they came upon this place? Surely they must have been mesmerized. Did Columbus climb these terraces? I mentally strip away the streamside walkways, the manmade embankments, the signs and the people around me and for a moment I'm transported back in time. Could this be one of the reasons why the Arawaks named this place Xayamaca, the land of wood and water? It is no wonder that Dunns River Falls is considered one of Jamaica's natural treasures.

We continue up the steppes. Amy skirts around a three-foot deep pool in one of the terraces but I chose to go straight across it. The current is swifter and stronger than I had anticipated and it pushes me off balance, I topple, arms flailing, into the cool waters. I come up to the laughter of the climbers around me. To the right is a rather large waterfall, over ten feet tall. A torrent of clear water gushes out over its edge. It looks un-climbable so we skirt to the left of it. Above it is another shallower but broad terrace. In its wall is a little cave, almost big enough for a person to crawl into. I work my way over to the little cave and push my head through the water curtain in front of it. The water pours over the lip, raining powerful blows on my back. It's all I can do to maintain my balance, but it feels great and I remain there until my back is numb from the relentless pounding.

We continue our ascent, clambering over logs, wading through pools and leaning into the surging waters. After about twenty-five minutes we get to the exit point and reluctantly leave the stream. We are both soaked, me from two dunkings and Amy from retaliatory splashes brought on by her laughing at my stumbles. We retrieve our backpack, towel off and don dry clothes in the changing rooms.

The exit path from the falls dumps everybody smack into the middle of a craft market. The vendors here are Jamaica-standard aggressive. We push through the market, return our gummy shoes and go to the car. Cliff is still sleeping and he looks disoriented when I wake him.

"Mon, me hungry!" Cliff says when he gets his bearings. "You want some jerk?" he asks.

It's nearing lunchtime and after our heroic climb up the falls, the thought of jerk chicken makes my stomach wake up. "Yeah, I could eat," I reply. Amy nods.

"Good, I'm goin' to take you to one of de bes' jerk places aroun' here," Cliff promises, "My treat."

He takes us well beyond the Hedo III entrance and into the Discovery Bay area. We pull into a big roadside jerk operation, there is no better way to describe it. A tour bus and several cars are in the parking lot. A huge sign over the serving counter proclaims *'Jerk Chicken'* in enormous lettering. The facility consists of an outside circular bar, an eating area with tables, restrooms and a cookhouse. Customers place their orders and pay for them at the bar, where they are given a chit that they take over to the cookhouse. Inside the cookhouse is a large bar-b-que pit in the floor, over which is laid a grill of heavy meshing. The pit is filled with glowing embers and the meshing is heaped with pieces of chicken and pork in various stages of being cooked. Four men are toiling in the heat of the cookhouse. Two of them are flipping the meats on the grill, moving them to or from the hotter areas and periodically slathering them in jerk sauce. The other two are taking chits at the counter and filling orders. Cliff gets a mound of chicken and pork, each wrapped in tin foil. We go over to the tables and spend the next while devouring the treat.

"Dey use dried pimento wood for de charcoal," Cliff explains, answering our unasked question, *'What makes it so good?'* Cliff talks about his children and his dreams of someday owning and operating his own taxi.

He has us back to Hedo by noon, plenty of time for us to digest our feast a little and get ready for our one o'clock dive.

That evening, exhausted from our trek and dive, we fall asleep early to the gleeping of the likkle tree frogs. My last waking thoughts are of rushing waters and fleeting glimpses of lean brown bodies, clad only in loincloths, sprinting through the rain forest.

Tomorrow morning we go back to paradise.

One 'Ras Forty-Legs'

'Nyam some, lef some.'
Jamaican Saying

This morning, after a long and uneventful trip from the north shore, we check in at Sea Grape Villas, a cozy little place on the cliffs in Negril's West End.

To be more precise, one doesn't actually 'check-in' to Sea Grape. Rather, we entered the grounds via the wrought iron gate, which rang the bell attached to it, which woke up the guy who was sleeping on an old chaise lounge on the ground outside of the door of a small gatehouse. Juicy, the Sea Grape's gatekeeper and all-around jack-of-all-trades, was expecting us. He says, "Welcome home," and leads us to our villa. There are no formalities, no checking in, no credit card vouchers to sign.

"We'll look after de paperwork later," Juicy says slowly. He turns and trudges sluggishly back toward the gate. I'm left with the impression that he has a pressing engagement with his chaise lounge that he must keep.

Sea Grape, dating back some thirty years, was one of the first places in Negril to offer accommodations. It's a small property that sits directly on the cliffs, offering a wide-open view that overlooks the sea to the west, perfect for sunsets. There are three secluded villas on the grounds; named Wild Grape, Big Grape and Sea Grape. Each is cached away amid the lush tropical vegetation that covers the grounds.

Sea Grape, the original villa and smallest of the three, is the one that we will be staying in. It's a rustic, octagonal, cottage-like structure with a high, vaulted ceiling. The villa is dominated by a large, curved open area, consisting of a kitchen and a day room. There's a waterbed in the middle of the big room and two small bedrooms and a bathroom that are adjoined. The walls consist of hurricane shutters all around. I step out the twin doors that open onto a deck that overlooks the ocean. A step down from the deck is a patio equipped with a table and chairs, perfect for quiet breakfasts with the Caribbean Sea as a backdrop. There's a hammock slung between two posts.

Yeah mon! We will be comfortable here!

On a thin cross section of tree trunk, posted on a beam that supports the canopy over the patio, is a small hand carved sign that reads;

'BOB MARLEY
Slept Here 1976'

To tell the truth, that claim is the precise reason that we are here. While looking for accommodations I had come across the Sea Grape website and discovered that Bob had slept there. And that pretty well did it, although when Amy saw the sign and proclaimed, "So that's why we're here!" I denied it.

The villa is also equipped with a good stereo system, featuring a pair of massive, bashment-size speakers that sit on the loft overlooking the day room.

I delve into the big Samsonite, extract a handful of Bob Marley CDs and pop one in. The sound is good, I crank the volume up. The villa is filled with Bob's music. Proper t'ing.

The kitchen is fully equipped, albeit a little tired. After the all-inclusive pampering, we are 'roughing it' now and will have to prepare some of our own meals. To our ultimate and pleasant surprise, there is also a margarita maker, otherwise known as an electric blender.

The bedrooms are furnished with double beds and equipped with wall-mounted air conditioners. There is no mirror on the ceiling, but there is a ceiling fan over the foot of the bed. We will have to make do.

The remainder of our stay in paradise is reserved for relaxation. We haven't any excursions planned other than a visit to the beach and maybe a trip into town for provisions. However, we have planned daily snorkeling expeditions just off the cliffs in front of the villa.

"Oh Jesus! Thomas! There's a big cockroach on the wall in here!"

Amy rushes out of one of the bedrooms, her arms scrunched up to her chest. "He's huge, and he's on that wall," she points to the far wall in the bedroom. I go into the bedroom. Yes, he's a big'un alright, about two inches long, which is the standard size for tropical cockroaches. I snatch the sandal off my foot and take a lunging swat at him, but I miss and he darts away, weaving across the wall and moving at an incredible rate. He encounters the corner of the wall and stops, considering his next move. He scuttles vertically for a foot, then, making a fatal decision, he tentatively turns back toward me, moving slowly. I wait for him to move into range. He comes into my kill zone and I paste him, not missing this time. He becomes a brown splatter of his former self, in the middle of a size thirteen sandal print, and my woman feels safe again.

This is the tropics, and tropics means bugs, big ones at times. The resorts do their best to keep the rooms free of pests, but occasionally one breaches the perimeter. Then it's up to the guest to deal with them, which sometimes gives rise to opportunities for deeds of great heroics, such as the case in point.

On one of my earlier trips to Negril I came face to face with the most feared of the tropical interlopers, the dreaded 'forty-legs'. Even bug-hardened Jamaicans don't like these little beasties. Especially those who have suffered from its nasty bite, which, believe it or not, can be fatal for some people if not treated. The name ' forty-legs' has been handed down through the years from the days of British colonial rule, the British used to call centipedes 'forty-legs' and the name stuck in Jamaica.

The forty-legs that I encountered, in the bathroom of a ground level room in one of the cheaper beach-side cottages, was about five inches long and as thick as the little finger on my hand, but slightly flattened. I was getting out of the shower when I spotted him hustling across the floor. Dripping wet, I ran for my standard weapon of choice, a sandal. When I got back in the bathroom my quarry had disappeared. A creepy feeling came over me, like I was about to be ambushed. I checked the walls and the ceiling above me, not even sure if centipedes climbed walls, but the beastie was nowhere to be seen. There was only one place he could be hiding, under the skimpy bath mat on the floor. I approached it cautiously, my breath coming faster. I pinched a corner of the mat and lifted it up quickly, flicking it aside. The centipede bolted straight for me, in attack mode. I whacked the big guy hard. It was a glancing blow, striking only the rear third of his armored body. Other than changing the direction of his charge, it barely slowed him. It was as if I was battling a tiny, invincible tank. I cocked my weapon and let fly again with a mighty whack. This time it was a direct hit, and I was sure that it was lethal. The centipede wrapped himself into a tight coil and I thought that was it. A moment later I watched fascinated as the forty-legs, leaking brown juice from his hind quarters, slowly un-coiled, righted himself and then began to creep sluggishly away, leaving a trail in his path. I clobbered him twice more, two bulls-eyes. That finished him. I sat on the floor of the bathroom and caught my breath, amazed at the tenacity of the critter.

One encounter with a forty-legs is sufficient, I really don't ever want to see another one.

While on the subject of tropical bugs, let's deal with hookworms and sea lice. Hookworm is an intestinal parasite that causes mild diarrhea and cramps. Infections occur in tropical and sub-tropical climates, including Negril.　Jamaica is a Third World country and unfortunately hookworm can be a problem.　Worldwide, hookworm is estimated to infect about one billion people.　Generally, people can become infected by walking barefoot on soil that is contaminated with the hookworm larvae.　The tiny larvae penetrate the skin of the foot or the paw pad of a dog and travel through the bloodstream eventually reaching and settling in the small intestine where they develop into half-inch-long worms that survive by feasting on the host's blood. The adult worms produce thousands of eggs that are passed in the feces.　If the eggs are deposited in warm, moist and shaded soil, they will hatch and develop into larvae.　Dogs and barefoot people who walk on them can pick them up, thereby repeating the process. People who have direct contact with soil that contains human or dog feces in areas where hookworm exists are at risk of infection.　Itching and a rash appear at the site where the larvae have penetrated the skin.　Hookworm infections are cured through oral drug treatments. The obvious key to avoiding infection is not to walk barefoot in areas where hookworm is known to exist and where there is likely to be feces in the soil or sand.　Since the hookworm egg requires shaded soil in order to hatch, walking barefoot in the surf and on the beach where the sand is in full sun should be relatively risk-free.

Another bothersome condition, called sea bather's rash or itch, can be caused by so called 'sea lice'.　The rash appears shortly after bathing in the ocean.　It's caused by stinging structures called nematocysts, which form a protective barrier around the larval form of the thimble jellyfish.　The tiny larvae, approximately the size of a speck of finely ground pepper, float on the surface of the water where they can become trapped in bathing suits.　The nematocysts surrounding each larva are triggered to sting by mechanical pressure, such as when they are trapped in the waistbands and shoulder straps of bathing suits.　Over-the-counter antihistamines and topical cortisone creams are used to treat the rash.　The term 'sea lice', a colloquialism used to describe the offending pest, is a misnomer. True sea lice are actually small parasites that infect fish and have nothing to do with sea bather's rash.　Outbreaks of sea bather's rash occur intermittently between March and August, peaking from early April through early July.　Swimmers can avoid the rash by staying out of the water when the larvae are known to be present or by swimming in the nude, which isn't a problem in Negril.

One should not get the impression that Negril is teeming with parasites and nasty little beasts just waiting to pounce on the juicy flesh of arriving tourists.　I personally have never experienced neither hookworm nor sea bather's rash.　But to be informed is to be prepared and in these cases, an ounce of prevention really is worth a pound of cure.

We clean the cockroach splatter and the sandal print off the bedroom wall as best we can and unpack some of our things (all the while absorbing Bob Marley vibes), then take a stroll to check out our new surroundings.

We walk the cement pathway, carved out of the rock, that twists from the patio down to the waters edge about 150 feet distant. At the end of the path are two terraces, level areas that have been hewn out of the coral formations that make up the cliff side. The lower of the two sits about three feet above the sea and there's a swimming ladder that descends from it into the water. Here and there around the terrace, hacked into the coral, are flattened areas capped with smooth cement pads for sitting.

The view from this spot is wide open and unobstructed to the horizon. The water is crystalline, revealing a sloping bottom made up of coral and sand. I estimate the depth of the water immediately off the cliff face to be about twenty feet.

I go up onto the higher of the two terraces and stand at its edge, looking down at the surface of the water seven feet below. I stand there and stare deeply into the mesmerizing swells. The water sloshes up against the cliff face below, leaving in a blue swish as it recedes. Mother Ocean. I let myself topple off the ledge and the warm water envelops me in a splashing, silky embrace.

From my vantage point in the water I can see dozens of oblong, prehistoric looking mollusks about two inches long that cling tenaciously to the rocks at the waterline. Jamaicans call them 'sea beef', but their proper name is chiton. I steady myself with the ladder and try to pull a sea beef from its perch ('it' being the correct terminology, since chitons are hermaphrodites). Grasping its hard-ridged back as firmly as I can, I attempt to dislodge it but it doesn't budge a millimeter. Sea beef feed on the algae that grows on the rocks, grinding it off with phenomenally hard rasps that line their mouths. Apparently they can live up to 40 years, but they definitely do not live life in the fast lane; the speediest sea beef traverses a mere ten feet of rock surface per year. Although they don't look too appetizing, my old fisherman friend told me that in days gone by during hard times, a handful of sea beef would be pried of the rock and added to a pot of boiling water and grated coconut. However, I don't think that sea beef and coconut broth is a part of the current-day Jamaican diet. I once asked a beach boy if he had ever tried it and he looked at me like I was nuts.

I climb the ladder and enter the rock-walled shower stall on the high terrace. Two crabs that were resting there scuttle quickly down the wall and disappear into a hole that drains to the sea. The shower is gravity fed from a cistern located up beside the cottage. The water, which is solar heated as it sits in the feed hose that is draped along the rocks, is incredibly hot.

We go back to the villa and get some cash. Our mission is to get dinner, and jerk chicken is on the menu. The experience at the big jerk operation on the Discovery Bay road has wetted our appetites for more.

CLANK!

"What the hell was that!" Amy is looking up at the ceiling.

A sea grape pod has fallen on the corrugated metal roof of its namesake villa. It rolls down the steep roof and plops onto the cement deck. It's a sound that we will become accustomed to during our stay here.

There's a hibiscus bush growing next to the pathway that leads to the cliff road. Amy stops to admire the flowers. An iridescent green hummingbird with extremely long and slender tail feathers flits in and out of the massive red blossoms. It's a Doctor Bird, also known as the swallow tail or streamer tail humming bird, Jamaica's national bird. Unlike the humming birds that we see back home that produce a low thrumming sound when they fly, this one hovers effortlessly, producing no discernable noise. The top half of its head and tips of its wings are fringed in black and there's a broad flash of bright yellow midway across its wings. Its long swallow tail flumes droop delicately below it. This is the bird that is stylistically depicted on the tails of the aircraft in Air Jamaica's fleet. I've heard that the Doctor bird is used in obeah work, and because of this it is believed to be subject to possession by spirits, which gave rise to the Jamaican saying;

'Doctor Bird cunny, Doctor Bird hard fe kill'

The little bell on the gate to the property tinkles as we pass through. Juicy wakes up. He raises up a little from his lounge and peers at us through heavy-lidded eyes. Recognizing us, he gives a wave then drops back into the supine position.

The cliff road is a narrow, twisting pot-holed, erstwhile paved path that is barely two lanes wide. To the inland side of the road is a hard-packed dirt walking path that skirts the front of the craft and food stands that are lined up there. As soon as we cross the road and start to walk toward town along the path, a car comes to a stop beside us. The driver leans out the window, I'm expecting him to call out "Taxi?" but instead he asks us if we want to exchange money. This, of course, is totally illegal, but the roadside moneychangers will offer exchange at a rate that is slightly better than the going commercial rate. Not needing any cash we decline his offer. About thirty seconds later another car approaching from the opposite direction slows, "Taxi?" the driver asks. We decline the first of hundreds of taxi offers that we will receive along the cliff road during our stay.

We haven't gone too far when we come across a roadside vegetable stand. We select two ripe coconuts and a medium sized breadfruit. I ask the vendor if there are any jerk barrels nearby. He points down the road. "Go jus' around de corner, you'll see one not far down de road."

Jerk chicken bar-b-ques are ubiquitous along the roads in Jamaica. The telltale sign of their presence is the little plume of white smoke that wafts above them.

We trek down the road and arrive at the bar-b-que, a forty-five gallon barrel split lengthwise and mounted on a pushcart. It's tended by a lady who's turning a piece of chicken as we arrive. Beside the grill is a big plastic milk jug container half filled with jerk sauce. The lady dips a brush into the container and slaps a big dollop of sauce onto the chicken. The aroma of the cooking chicken and the jerk sauce wafts over us and I'm suddenly and ravenously hungry.

Amy and I consult as to the size of order that we should make. There are three prices posted. We reason that the least expensive, which is cheap by our standards, would be the 'meal size' for an individual, but we're hungry so we order two of the most expensive with extra jerk sauce on the side for dipping the breadfruit. The lady behind the grill goes to work chopping chicken and packaging our order. She hands us a relatively large foil-wrapped bundle, it looks about right for our appetite and I pass her the required sum of Jamaican dollars. We are about to turn and leave when she hands us another tin-foil pack. We have inadvertently ordered a complete chicken.

A dog is hanging out near the jerk stand. He looks at us, sizing us up for handouts. The dog is not threatening in any way but Amy doesn't like dogs and maneuvers so as to put me between herself and the hound. He follows us a little, hoping for a scrap, but we don't give him anything and he soon gives up and trots back to his station by the jerk stand to wait for other customers.

We walk back to the cottage accompanied by the heavenly aroma of jerk chicken. On the way I can't help but think about the old saying that warns of going to the grocery store when hungry.

This time, we get through the gate without rousing Juicy.

Back in the villa, I unpack my little radio, place it on the counter and turn it on. The Reggae Boyz, Jamaica's heroic national soccer team, are playing Grenada in a West Indies League game. Soccer, the national sport of Jamaica, seems to be on the radio a lot. At the first break in the game a commercial comes on featuring a young lady extolling the virtues of color coordinated thong panty liners. I wonder who did the marketing demographics for that spot.

I cut the breadfruit in half and put it in the oven, remembering to thank Captain Bligh as I do so. It was Bligh, of 'Mutiny of the Bounty' fame, who introduced the breadfruit and ackee trees to Jamaica. Would that the land had been so generous in return, for it was in Fort Charlotte, the military encampment that protected Lucea back in the heydays of sugar, where Bligh first met the young Mr. Fletcher Christian, the man who later led the mutiny against him.

The breadfruit, which will take about 40 minutes to bake, is a starchy fruit that grows on trees. The fruit itself is about the size of a large cantaloupe. A single, mature tree will yield several ripe breadfruits each and every day throughout the entire year, providing nourishment for many families. To me, a breadfruit tastes much like a yam, but sweeter. As it bakes it gives off an aroma that reminds me of warm strawberry jam.

Amy and I go out to the patio with half of the jerk chicken, planning to save the other half of our over-purchase for tomorrow. I unfold the foil package and place it in the middle of the table. Aromatic steam rises from the chicken. The breadfruit pieces, which I had cut up and thrown in after taking it out of the oven, have soaked up some of the jerk sauce. The chicken is cut up into diagonal chunks, the bones also chopped into pieces. This releases the flavor of the marrow and the juices into the meat. It also makes it easier to suck the marrow from the bones, an important consideration in a country where all sources of protein are fully exploited.

We begin to dine on the chicken, delicately at first, conversing between bites. But conversation soon dies out. We turn our full attention to the delicious feast, dipping the breadfruit in the sauce pooled in the tin foil and relishing each tasty morsel. The sauce is spicy hot and extraordinarily tasty. Part way into the feast, the other foil pack appears on the table. We continue, and with concentrated purpose, amid slurping, smacking and sucking sounds, work our way through the mound of chicken and breadfruit. Beads of sweat break out on my forehead.

Twenty-five minutes later it's all gone. The foil has been wiped clean of every drop of jerk sauce and a heap of bones, sucked dry of their marrow, sits in the middle of the table. I feel hot. Rivulets of perspiration run down the back of my neck. The front of my T-shirt is splattered with jerk sauce. I look at Amy, she's slouched back in her chair, her belly visibly distended. Her hands are glistening with chicken fat and there's jerk sauce smeared on her cheeks. She's wearing a contented, beatific smile.

"Hon, I think we should go for a little walk to work some of this off," Amy suggests, pointing with her chin at her belly.

"I'm with you," I said, "I just have to change." I go into the bedroom and pull my T-shirt up over my head. It's suddenly ripped out of my hands and my knuckles are beaten viciously as if by an angry schoolmarm. I duck and look up to see my T-shirt being whipped around by a madly wobbling ceiling fan. Such are the perils of a six foot two frame. I turn the ceiling fan off and retrieve my T-shirt before Amy sees it and admonishes me for my absent mind.

Mi – Deh –Yah

'If fish coulda keep him mout' shut, him would neva get caught.'
Jamaican Proverb

RUUAWK - - AAWWK! . . . .

. . . . Ruuawk - - aawwk!

My eyes pop open.

RUUAWK - - AAWWK!
(very loud, very close and from directly above)

. . . . Ruuawk - - aawwk!
(quieter, but just as strident, coming from outside)

The last vestiges of sleep drain slowly from my head. I sit up, rather clumsily, in the waterbed. In the dim pre-dawn light I fumble for the seam in the mosquito net and snake my hand through it, creating an opening through which I place my feet onto the floor.

I look into the apex of the high vaulted ceiling where the planes of the octagonal roof meet, expecting to see a large feathered creature staring down at me. I see nothing but the dim shapes of rafters.

RUUAWK - - AAWWK!

I duck instinctively. The call fills the large open room, reverberating as if amplified.

I wait for the response from outside, but it doesn't come this time.

It sounds like the call of a huge, rather upset, bird. I'm not yet fully awake and I'm perplexed by the volume of the call and my inability to locate its source. I turn on all of the lights but still can't locate the bird in the dimly lit, dark colored wooden apex of the ceiling. I open the twin patio doors, hoping that the bird will see the light and take flight to freedom.

Peering upwards, I perceive a slight movement. A small yellow delta shape moves on one of the ceiling rafters near the top. My eyes try to create a big bird out of the dark spaces behind what I assume to be a beak, but nothing materializes.

Still looking above, warily, I climb the steep ladder to the loft and creep as close as I can to the small yellow shape perched on the rafter. I peer intensely at it and slowly an image resolves.

It's a gecko! One of Jamaica's more common lizards. Its body is about six inches long and it has a long slender tail of five inches. He's looking back at me. I'm obviously not what he was expecting in return for his vocal efforts. I'm astonished that such a small being could generate such an ear-splitting call.

"What are you doing in here?" I ask him quietly.

I climb down from the loft and when I look up again I can no longer see the little yellow patch. The gecko has either skedaddled or done his chameleon thing. Whatever the case, he doesn't favor me with another serenade.

I grope for my watch on the kitchen counter and push the winder to illuminate the dial; it's 5:30am. I have a rendezvous at the water's edge in 30 minutes, so I'm thankful for the gecko's wake-up call.

The bedroom door opens a bit and a bleary-eyed head topped with a tousle of blonde hair pokes out. "Are you going?" Amy croaks.

"Yeah, see you in a couple of hours."

"What was that noise?"

" A gecko, I'll explain later . . . go back to bed."

I pass my toothbrush over my teeth, pull on my shorts, grab my hat and sunglasses and head out the door.

The sky is a lightening gray. To the east, a pink hue spills up over the trees marking the spot where another Negril morning will dawn. Venus is high in the sky and very bright, outshining everything celestial.

I make my way down the cement pathway to the water's edge. This morning the sea is slowly undulating, its surface unbroken. Even though the sun won't rise for another twenty minutes and the water is still dark, I feel the urge to jump in. But there will be no dip this morning, not until I get back from fishing.

I settle on a flat spot at the cliff edge and look out to the western horizon. My pick-up should be along soon. The air is still and cool. Occasionally the sound of a cock crowing in the distance breaks the morning silence. I sit in the quiet splendor of the pre-dawn, looking into the sea, the tranquility of the morning soothing me like a balm.

Far in the distance I hear the distinctive steady drone of an approaching outboard. I stand up and look northward along the shore. A single boat approaches, trailing a long white wake in the calm water. Aboard, I make out the shapes of two people, one standing amidships and the other sitting in the stern. That will be my fishing ride.

Joseph waves as the boat arcs toward the shore. "Yeah mon!" he calls out.

The boat noses into the cliff edge. I hop from the swim ladder onto the bow and down into the boat. Joseph offers his hand and gives me a hearty clasp. From the back, Winston nods his head in my direction, baring a snaggle-toothed grin.

The boat is a wooden runabout. By the look of it, it has been hand built from stock lumber and marine plywood. It's in decent shape, by Jamaican standards, although there is some water sloshing about below the floor decking. It's about 18 feet long with a five-foot beam. The deck and foredeck are painted red, it's sides yellow. Near the bow on each side, in tall red letters, is painted 'Mi-Deh-Yah'. About three feet aft of the name are two large stylized 'S's, complete with curlicues.

I look around the boat for fishing gear. There are no rods, no reels. What I see are two long, weathered poles, which are in fact long flexible branches cut from trees. There are four white plastic bleach jugs with fishing line wrapped around them. A milk crate sits on the deck, it contains a spool of line and a half dozen tuna trolling jigs, big hooks with plastic heads and trailing tentacles making them look like little squid.

"Do you feel lucky this morning Joseph?"

"Well," he says, looking at the sea and out to the horizon, "it looks like it could be a good day, maybe Jah will bless us today."

As we move out I spot a couple of Jamaicans snorkeling just off shore. They're trailing white floats behind them. Joseph sees me looking, "They're hunting for barracuda," he explains.

Joseph stands about six foot two. His build is lean and muscular. There are some traces of gray starting to show in the sides of his neat beard and his hairline has begun to creep back on his scalp. His dreads are well kept and hang down to about an inch above his shoulders. He's wearing a loose fitting, zip neck golf shirt embroidered with the Nike swoop, and dark cotton shorts. Joseph has a confident smile that reveals even white teeth.

Yesterday morning while I was lounging at the waterside after a dip, Mi-Dah-Yah motored up to the cliff-side. On board were Joseph, Winston and two guests who were staying at one of the other villas. They clambered out of the boat and up the ladder. They had just returned from a tour up the coast. I asked Winston if they could come back later and do the same for Amy and I. I had never seen the seascape south of Rick's Café and was curious to check it out. Winston said 'no problem' and they picked us up a couple of hours later. During the tour it became clear to me that Winston and Joseph were first and foremost fisherman. One thing led to another and as they dropped us off back at the villa Joseph said, "Mi pick you up at 6:00 tomorrow mornin', right here." Although Mi-Deh-Yah is a far cry from a charter boat, the enterprising fisherman is ever willing to supplement his income for the small burden of an extra passenger.

Joseph and Winston busy themselves setting up the trolling gear. The 40 horse Yamaha outboard pops and coughs as it idles, leaving a thin wisp of blue smoke in the still air. We drift slowly seaward. Winston retrieves two of the trolling jigs from the milk-crate tackle-box and attaches them to three-foot wire leaders which in turn are attached to the fishing line that's wound around the plastic jugs. He throws a line astern, gives the Yammy a twist and lets the line play out through his hand for about 150 feet. He stops letting the line out when he reaches a little black marker wrapped around it. He then wraps the line around his big toe. He repeats the process with a second line. We now have two lines running out over the transom.

Meanwhile, Joseph has taken the two long weathered poles and is setting them up as outriggers. The butt ends of the poles are placed into holes that have been bored into pieces of plywood that are nailed to either side of the hull ribbing. When set in position, the poles reach across the boat and extend to hang out over the opposite gunwale. The poles are lashed together where they cross amidships and lashed again where they rest on the gunwales. Strips of tread cut from an old tire keep the poles from chaffing the wood of the gunwales. The purpose of the outriggers is to allow for the deployment of extra lines that trail far out from the hull so as not to foul the lines that are set from the stern. The tips of the outriggers are equipped with quick releases to which the trolling lines are affixed. When a fish takes the bait, the force of the strike snaps the line out of the quick release and the fish is then hauled in. On Mi-Deh-Yah the quick releases are small pincers that have been hand carved out of a section of a tree branch about as big as a man's thumb. A rudimentary pulley system, rigged from a length of thick fishing line that loops through corroded fencing staples hammered in to either end of the poles, allows the quick release to be ferried in and out along the length of the outriggers. The outer lines, set to trail at about 175 feet so as not to foul with the stern lines when the boat turns, also terminate in spools wound onto big plastic jugs. I note that the stern line plastic jugs are smaller than those on which the outer lines are wound.

With the outrigger lines set, there being no rods to hold, Joseph and I each grasp a line in our hands. We hold the line lightly, so as not to lose any skin or a finger should a really big fish strike. Winston continues to work the outboard with the two stern lines wrapped loosely around his big toes.

"What are we trying to catch?" I ask.

"The Bonita tuna, kingfish, barracuda, dolphin fish and sometimes, if we're lucky, a marlin," Joseph replies.

From our vantage point on the water the splendor of the Negril cliffs reveals itself. The height of the cliffs ranges from a few feet above the water to over fifty feet south of Rick's Café. The entire cliff face of the West End is riddled with small coves and caves of varying sizes. The biggest cave, suitably, marks the coast at Negril's most exclusive resort, 'The Caves'.

We motor out to about one mile from the cliffs and turn to the east, toward the Negril lighthouse. Winston points at the water and moves his arm parallel to the shore. "This is where the ledge is," he indicates.

"This is where the tuna are," adds Joseph. We turn along the ledge and start our first trolling run.

Winston sits quietly on the transom deck, holding the outboard tiller in his left hand. He's a slight man, about 5'9, maybe 30 years old. Orange tipped dreads spill out of his oversized leather cap, falling in a jumbled shawl across his shoulders. He has a full, ragged beard. A pair of sunglasses, resting on his forehead, are lodged beneath the brim of his cap. Winston is wearing a blue pullover sweat-top, three sizes too large for him, and a pair of worn, red nylon shorts. He has a quiet demeanor but emanates the self-assurance of years spent on the water.

We head east, directly into the bright pink glow that decorates the horizon like a broad swatch of inverted bunting. Bands of clouds are stacked up there, the bottoms painted pink by the approaching sun, their tops slate gray. We sit quietly, each of us wrapped in our early morning thoughts. The motor purrs, pushing Mi-Deh-Yah through the flat water. As we pass the lighthouse the rim of the sun peeks up over the horizon, casting extraordinary beams of orange across the surface of the water. We are immediately bathed in their warmth. A frisson of goose bumps wells up across the back of my neck. I close my eyes for a moment, then open them, and let the scene before me flow into the cache of memories that I access on cold winter days.

We continue eastward, directly into the rising orb of the sun. The earth rotates, and just before the full disc of the sun breaks completely free of the sea, it trails a short stubby stalk, momentarily creating an enormous mushroom shape.

We make a wide turn back toward Negril, the eastern edges of the high clouds to the west glow, as if spray-painted in chartreuse.

There are other fishing boats out, some are trolling for tuna as we are. The boats closer to shore are pulling traps.

A tern glides effortlessly above us, turning on its swept back wings it looks as if it could fly at supersonic speeds. Winston peers up at it. The bird is fishing, its hunt for breakfast just starting.

"Do you fish with traps?" I ask Joseph.

"Yeah mon, that's usually what I do."

"How many traps do you set?"

"Well you see, I usually have about twenty-five to thirty traps, yah know. But just now I only have ten out, because I haven't got them all back out after the big storm."

"How does a big storm effect your fishing?" I wonder if I should be talking. Some fishermen don't like to talk on the boat, as they believe it can keep the fish from biting. Joseph however, seems okay with it.

"Well, it takes about two days for the ocean to settle enough to go out . . . but the water doesn't start to clear for another two days and then another two days for it to completely clear up."

"So, it stops you fishing for about a week?" I ask.

"Yeah, about a week before the sea is nice and flat," he moves his hands in a settling motion, palms down.

"How long do you leave your traps out?"

"Well, yuh see, usually about one week. I bait the traps with bread and breadfruit and it takes about a week for the fish and the sea to take away the bait. If the current is stronger, then the bait don't last that long. You have to know where to put the traps, where the fish will feed."

"How do your traps do?"

"It depends on the time of the year. In October, for about three days, is the best fishing of the year. When the fish are moving through," he waves his arms in a flowing motion, " the fish take the bait in the traps and when you pull them up you can have 100 pounds in each trap. But that only lasts for two or three days and then the fish are gone."

Winston is standing in the stern, quietly scanning the surface of the water. The dancing reflections of the sun on the silky surface of the water draw my gaze, the effect is hypnotizing.

A flying fish erupts out of the sea beside the boat. It propels itself along mightily by kicking the water with its tail fin, leaving a trail of diminishing sized ripples in the water. Once up to speed it stops kicking and glides for about a hundred feet on its outstretched fins before it splashes down. I'm surprised at how far it flies.

"They do that to escape predators," Joseph says.

"I bet it works," I respond.

"Yeah mon, except when they are trying to get away from a dolphin fish. The dolphin fish is the fastest swimmer in the sea. They follow the flying fish by watching their shadow and when it comes down, they catch it," he makes a quick chomping motion with his hand. "Yeah mon, the dolphin fish is *very* fast."

Time passes. We troll some more. When we make abeam the Pickled Parrot we carve a wide turn back to the south. I watch the lines trailing from the outriggers as they cut the water behind us. Another boat, trolling as we are, passes us about fifty yards to port, moving in the opposite direction. Joseph stands up, looking at the other boat he makes an exaggerated shrugging motion, holding his arms cocked out to his sides. The mate in the other boat holds his hand, with the index finger extended, high above his head. "Deh have one," Joseph says.

Winston points to the northwest, he says something in patois to Joseph. I make out the word 'squall'. Far away on the horizon is a dark patch of cloud with a frame of lighter clouds in the shape of a wide capital letter 'U'. Joseph says, "Not'ing to worry about."

For me, fishing has never been entirely about catching fish. Certainly I like to catch fish, but I've been on a few fishing expeditions where I've come back empty-handed. Fishermen don't like to admit it, but if pressed each and every one of them will admit to having been skunked. But as the saying goes, *'The worst day of fishing is way, way better than the best day at the office.'* So I'm happy just to be on the water enjoying the company of Joseph and Winston and if we catch fish, well that will be a bonus. However, I am keenly aware that for these gentlemen, and they are gentlemen in every sense of the word, getting skunked means going hungry.

"What does 'Mi-Deh-Yah' mean?" I ask Joseph.

"Mi-Deh-Yah?" he laughs, "it means *'I am here'*," he points down, indicating 'here', "yah know, it's patois."

Joseph pulls out a spliff, lights it up and passes it around. "Where do you live?" I ask him.

"Well, I live in the fishing village in Negril . . . yah know, beside the river near the beach."

"Between the craft market and the river, right?"

"Yeah mon, yah know it." I've walked through the tiny fishing village on a few occasions. It offers a glimpse into a lifestyle that differs starkly from the up-front, largely tourist face of Negril.

"You're from Canada?" Joseph asks.

"Uh huh, Ottawa, have you ever been there?"

"Yeah, to Toronto, quite a few times when I was younger. Had some good times there. I been to Germany and the States too, Pittsburgh. But now I like to stay here in Jamaica. Yah know, fish, burn a couple of spliffs a day . . . feel good."

"Oh yeah?"

"*Yeah* mon," he replies, with an earnest emphasis on the 'Yeah'.

A school of small fish breaks the surface to shoreward. "Bonita," Joseph says, "they're feeding, but they're too small for us . . . way too small." The fish create a traveling pattern of burbling swirls on the water. Nearby, a group of a half dozen flying fish launch themselves in formation. They splashdown fifty feet away. We leave the feeding Bonita in our wake. I'm amazed at the activity on the surface. Although we've been trolling for a while and haven't caught anything yet, there hasn't been a dull moment.

After a while, Joseph picks up the thread of our conversation on traveling and says, "But now I'm having a lot of pressure put on me to go to Chicago . . . lots and lots of pressure mon." I don't ask, but I assume it's a woman. Joseph is a good-looking man.

Winston listens to our conversation but remains quiet. He's standing up in the stern, tiller in hand, scanning the water ahead of us. "Grass!" he says, and veers the boat to starboard. We plow through an area of floating grass and seaweed.

Joseph looks concerned, "Rassclot!" he says. As a result of the turn, the port outrigger line has come inboard, Joseph grabs it and starts to pull it in with an efficient bent-over, smooth hand-over-hand motion. He retrieves the line until the trolling jig is skipping along beside the boat, clearing bits of grass and seaweed from the line as it coils up on the deck at his feet. He repeats the process on the other outrigger line and Winston does the same for the stern lines.

"Raas!" Winston says. I look ahead expecting to see more grass and then realize that, being a man of few words, Winston is expressing his exasperation at the floating grass and lack of fish while economizing on his verbiage.

A sea turtle comes to the surface ten feet to port. It's a large hawksbill. His shell is over three feet long. He examines us with a large curious eye. We watch him, no one says anything. The turtle submerges but re-surfaces five yards on. Again, he gives us a long look. Falling to stern, he dives again, we watch for him to come back up but he doesn't.

Winston and Joseph exchange murmured phrases in patois. I don't get all the words but I recognize the tone; two fishermen pondering where the fish are, wondering if they are going to catch anything.

We churn along in silence, making another turn when we get beyond the lighthouse. I think about other fishing expeditions that I have been on; the expensive boat and all of the latest high tech fishing gear. I regard the utter simplicity of the set-up that we have. For a moment I consider asking them if they would like me to send them some commercial gear, but I worry that they might take it as an insult and I demur. Then I realize that commercial gear would just be an encumbrance for them. It would corrode and break and be replaced in short order with handmade gear. I begin to appreciate the utility of their gear, it's perfect for what they are doing.

Winston mutters something, points to a few birds off to starboard and veers toward them. Joseph explains that the birds are fishing for the same bait-fish that our prey are after, that the birds are a sign that fish may be there.

A flying fish breaks the water and arcs over the stern, reaching a height of eight feet. This gets a rise out of Winston, he calls out, "Mon, he climbed," and laughs. I notice that he has the roach end of the spent spliff stuck to his bottom lip.

The sun, recovered from the effort of rising, has turned its attention to heat and the temperature is rising. We troll, running with the slow undulations of the sea. It's as if we are pushing along over soft rumples of plush velvet.

"The fish, they just don't want to bite today," Joseph says to no one in particular.

I don't answer. I consider it bad luck to talk about dry spells when in the middle of one.

"Maybe a jack dolphin came by and scared all the Bonita out to the deep," Joseph muses.

"What's a jack dolphin?" I ask.

"Oh, a lone hunting dolphin that comes in close to shore, we call it a jack dolphin. It comes in fast and hunts along the ledges in here. When that happens it scares all of the fish out deep," he points out to sea, "and the fishing is bad."

"What's your record catch?" I ask.

"One day we come back wit' eighty t'ree Bonita," Winston says from the back.

We troll slowly past a boat that is stopped in the water. The fishermen are gathering in their gear and simultaneously bailing the boat. I check the level of the water beneath the decking, it hasn't risen since we started. Mi-Deh-Yah is sufficiently seaworthy that we won't have to bail. I point to the stationary boat and ask Joseph, "Are they giving up?"

"Yeah . . . . but we're going to make another turn . . . . maybe Jah will bless us with some food, yah know?"

No sooner are the words are out of his mouth that the port outrigger line twangs out of the quick release and I feel it tug in my hand. I stand up and start to pull the line in, imitating the technique that Joseph used when he cleared the lines of grass. There's moderate tension on the line as the fish on the end of it moves jerkily further out to port.

One of the stern lines has a fish too. Winston, standing up, pulls the line in and steers the boat with his thigh on the tiller.

"You okay with that fish?" Joseph asks me. I nod, continuing to haul on the line. Then the other outrigger line snaps free and Joseph turns his attention to it.

My fish is zigging into the stern line that Winston is hauling. He gestures to me and I lift the line over his head and move to the other side of the boat. Joseph and I pull our lines in side by side. He calls out as he sees his fish deep in the clear water directly below the boat. In short order he has the fish aboard. He holds it up, dangling from the line. It's a Bonita tuna, a beautiful fish about two feet long. The Bonita has unusually large eyes for its head size, which gives it a shocked expression. It has a dark back, a faint yellow lateral band and a silver belly. I know this fish by its Florida name, 'black fin tuna'. Joseph extracts the hook from its mouth.

While watching him with his fish, I've slowed in the retrieval of the one on my line. "Keep pulling!" Winston says from the back of the boat. He doesn't want me to lose it. I haul on the line and see the fish flash under the boat twenty feet below. Six more tugs and I have it aboard, Winston lands his across the stern at the same time. Now he's smiling. We're not going to be skunked today. The three fish could be triplets, they are identical in every aspect. We admire the fish for a moment and then put them in the back of the boat, they flop wildly, whacking their bodies against the transom.

Soon all four lines are set and we are trolling again, heading north along the coast.

"How much do those fish weigh?" I ask Joseph.

"About seven pounds," he says, "a good size. But you can catch much bigger ones out in the deep water." A good-sized Bonita is a twenty-pounder and they can go as much as forty pounds.

"Grass, dere!" Joseph motions to Winston. The boat veers but in spite of the maneuver we enter into a large area of floating grass and seaweed. We make a big turn back toward Negril and once again clear the lines.

Around us, most of the trolling boats have left the water. I realize that this is our final run. We come abeam the villa and stop to retrieve and stow the gear. I dismantle the outriggers and place them lengthwise along the gunwales. Winston sees my efforts and comments appreciatively, "You're doin' de work!"

As we approach the cliff side of the villa Joseph apologizes for the lack of fish.

I respond, "Anytime you catch a fish, it's a good trip, and we caught three."

"Yes, we give t'anks for what we caught," he agrees.

We pull up in front of the villa. Amy is sunning on one of the lounges. Winston cleans the fish by making two cuts across the belly, anterior and posterior, then reaches in the forward cut and wrenches out the offal. He drops it in the water. Then he chops the head off one of the fish and fillets the body for me.

I jump ashore and wave goodbye to them. They both give me a hearty wave and Mi-Deh-Yah turns east, cutting a swath toward the fishing village.

Sand Dogs

'Every dog t'inks im self a lion in im master's yard'
Jamaican Proverb

There are a lot of dogs in Negril. All of the dogs that I've seen running on the beach, in town and along the cliff road look roughly the same; medium sized mutts, short haired, sandy colored (appropriately) with tinges of brown. The majority of them are strays. Unlike the U.S. and Canada, stray dogs and cats are the norm in Jamaica. Dogs that belong to someone are usually chained up in the yard. The stray dogs hang around in packs. They look like brothers and sisters, which they probably are. The dogs on the beach, from my experience, are happy and friendly. I've seldom heard them bark, except to one another from a distance, and of course when following the Police 4 X 4 down the beach, in which case they will raise a ruckus that would make the hounds of the Baskervilles envious.

The strange thing is, these strays aren't the bedraggled creatures that one would rightly expect for the Third World. No, these pups look very happy, well fed and contented; healthy even, especially the males, their scrotums and contents thereof dangling proudly intact.

When you think about it, the beach dogs have a lot to be happy about. Nice weather all year round, an ocean to cool off in, plentiful opportunity to scavenge food, and a large safe playground where they are free to roam as long as they behave. What more could a dog possibly want? Oh yes, for the males, open season on the bitches. Spend any time on the beach and one eventually sees a pack of these sandy colored dogs romping full speed down the beach, playfully nipping at each other as they splash through the surf. It's doggie heaven.

When hungry, the dogs will hang out near the numerous food outlets that line the beach. I watched one of them work a tourist who had just bought something to eat and was carrying it back to his lounge. The dog came slowly up to the guy, who was a Mr. Universe type with a tiny bathing suit and a hairless, oiled body. Mr. Universe shooed the dog away. The dog retreated about five feet, but didn't give up. This was repeated a couple of times, each time Mr. Universe stopped and shooed the dog away, it would retreat a little, but as soon as he turned to walk again, the dog would close the gap. When Mr. Universe got to his lounge and sat down, the dog crept up and sat down about three feet away from him. Again, 'Shoo!', followed by a retreat and a creeping advance, repeated a couple of times. Finally the dog, with his ears flat to his head, was sitting right beside the lounge.   Mr. Universe shook his head resignedly and gave it something from his plate. But that wasn't the end of it. A couple of minutes later the guy was holding up bits of food and making the dog jump for it. The dog had this happy doggy look, his ears now pointed straight up, and the guy was laughing and having a good time and tousling the dog's head.   Yeah, when you've been hustled by a true pro, you think it was your idea in the first place.

I'm not a dog lover, I could take them or leave them, but I do enjoy watching the Negril dogs frolic on the beach.   However, not everybody shares my ambivalence, there are many who just plain don't like dogs, and one of them is Amy. Not only does she not like dogs, she is deathly afraid of them. A big dog chased her when she was a kid and she was bitten by another, so her fears are not irrational. The existence of "marauding packs of wild dogs," as she describes them, is not one of her favorite Negril attractions.

This afternoon we grabbed a ride to the beach on the Margaritaville shuttle bus as it rumbled past the Sea Grape gate. It's an old school bus that has been painted a bright green and decorated with Margaritaville advertisements.

The Jamaica Margaritavilles, located on the beach in Negril, on the Hip Strip in MoBay, on the departures level of the MoBay airport and in Ocho Rios are part of the ever-expanding chain that is run by Jimmy Buffett from the States. It wasn't always that way. Initially the Negril and MoBay Margaritavilles started out as Margeuritavilles, (note the different spelling), and they were run by a local entrepreneur. Jimmy Buffett took issue with the use of the name and made the Jamaica owner an offer he couldn't refuse. They are now partners and the spelling of the name has been changed.

The Negril Margaritaville caters to the younger crowd and each night during spring break it's jammed wall to wall, road to shore with hormone-flushed, alcohol-infused, heaving, sweating bodies fully engaged in pre-coital dance and drinking rituals. Margaritaville is the closest that you can get to an American style sports bar in Negril.

It's impossible to miss Margaritaville at night.   Installed on the beach is a large set of twirling searchlights that pinwheel in the night sky over the site. These lights are very powerful and would put to shame anything that was used during the Battle of Britain.

It's hard to miss the place during the day too, a fifteen foot inflated beer bottle bobs happily in the breeze at the edge of the property.

Moored about fifty yards offshore is a large blue and yellow floating raft-trampoline. Today there is a group of rambunctious young guys out jumping on the trampoline. They're getting a lot of air, doing back flips and bouncing off into the sea, all the while yelling at the top of their lungs, "We crazy, mon!"

We grab a couple of Red Stripes at the Margaritaville bar and head south along the beach toward town.

"Oh pretty lady!" a vendor calls out from the shade of a bush. "Come over heah, let me braid your hair!" She and an accomplice, who is carrying a broken section of aloe leaf, walk out from the shade and approach us, drawing in front of our path.

"No braids today, thank you," Amy says.

"How about some nice aloe for your burn?" the other says. But Amy doesn't have a burn, after weeks in the tropical sun she has tanned to an even mid-brown. But that doesn't stop the aloe woman. She squeezes a blob of juice from the plant, grabs Amy by the arm and massages the oily gel over her shoulder and upper back.

"No . . ," Amy says and looks at me helplessly, pulling away in vain from the woman.

"Dat feels good, Hmmmmm?" the lady asks.

We continue to walk but the woman persists, following us and holding on to Amy, squeezing more aloe gel from the break in the leaf and spreading it over her shoulders.

"We don't have any cash on us," I say. Feeble attempt, I admit, but worth a try. Of course it doesn't work.

"OK . . . that's fine, thank you," Amy says, finally managing to break free from the woman's tenacious grip.

"Dat's t'ree hundred J," the aloe lady says.

"All I have is fifty, here take it." I give her a rumpled $50J note, not happy about being extorted but wanting to get on with our walk without a big scene.

"Fifty J!" the woman cries, as if I had insulted her. "It's t'ree hundred!" She sees another fifty J note in my hand. "OK, jus give me another fifty and dat will be fine."

"Sorry. Fifty, that's it, goodbye." We walk away to the moans and muted curses of the aloe lady.

"Bitch," Amy mutters, casting a look back.

Soon we pass Kuyaba, one of Negril's best restaurants. We pause and look into the open dining area. Hung around the bar are several swinging net chairs. I recall sitting in one of them, slumped back in front of one of the coolest beach bars in the Caribbean, twirling lazily with a frosty cocktail in hand.

"Remember this place?" Amy asks.

"How could I forget?" I answer.

In the years leading up to the millennium, Amy and I had talked a lot about where we wanted to celebrate the BIG event. We definitely had ruled out staying at home; that would have been too mundane. I knew all along where I wanted to be when the big hand and the little hand got together at the 12, and that was standing barefoot on the beach in Negril. However, I didn't come right out and say it. I dropped a few well-placed hints and waited for Amy to kind of come around to the same idea by herself. Eventually she did arrive at the right decision and we spent Millennium Eve in Negril and we had our Millennium Eve dinner at Kuyaba.

With all of the doom-and-gloom hype that led up to the millennium it was ironic that there was a power failure in Negril that evening. We had only just sat at our beachside table at Kuyaba when the lights went out. The entire beach went dark. This had nothing to do with the predicted millennium meltdown, it was just one of those periodic power failures that occurs in Negril. The only lights to be seen were the headlights of the cars moving along the road to the cliffs. Then some of the larger resorts got their auxiliary power units running and they lit up. But around us it was utterly dark. The wait staff put out table lanterns and lit them. It was magical and so very romantic. We ordered the four-course millennium eve special; velvety lobster bisque, half papaya stuffed with crab, jumbo pepper shrimps and crème caramel for dessert. The food, the service and the ambience were truly befitting a millennium dinner. Without the lights, everyone spoke in hushed tones. Our candle-lit dinner was accented by the soothing sounds of the sea washing up on the shore yards away.

At some point after we left Kuyaba, the power came back on, immediately proclaimed by amplified reggae music from several beach spots. It was still before midnight and the beach was packed with the biggest crowd that I have ever seen. It was as thick as the crowd in front of Bourbon Beach during a show except it was like that all up and down the beach. The air was electric with anticipation. There were bonfires, big ones, every hundred yards or so along the beach. Virtually everybody was carrying a bottle of champagne. We had ours, a 1990 vintage (the year we met) decorated with hand-painted tulips, brought down special for the event. As the hour approached the crowd grew correspondingly more festive. All around us the sounds of champagne corks popping, mixed with crackling bursts of firecrackers filled the air. For the thirty minutes leading up to midnight, the sky over Long Bay was periodically lit with 'teaser' fireworks launched from various venues along the beach.

Appleton Distilleries had set up a large raft that was loaded with fireworks and it floated, deceivingly dark and mute, about 100 yards off shore. At about five minutes to midnight, someone down near the Hedo end of the beach launched a parachute flare. It arced high up over the water, then ignited and hung under its canopy casting a bright yellow hue over the bay. It floated slowly down, leaving a lazy trail of smoke in the air. When it was about halfway down, another flare was launched followed by another a minute later.

Somewhere down the beach, somebody with a microphone was counting down. He got to about 10 seconds and pandemonium broke out, the Appleton raft came alive, launching a fusillade of sparkling rockets that burst in the sky. More fireworks were launched from several other sites along the beach. The water of the bay reflected a kaleidoscope of color. Amy slung her arms around my neck and planted a big, lingering kiss on my lips. We stood there in the crowd and held each other. The air was filled with the sounds of hundreds of popping champagne corks and cheers. I opened our bottle and let the cork fly into the water.

We had made it, the year 2000 had dawned and we were still alive!

One of the bonuses of being in Negril over New Years was seeing the many Jamaicans that came down to the beach during the holidays. New Years day the beach was crowded with Jamaicans and it was wonderful to see the children splashing and playing in the sea. As tourists we mistakenly believe that Jamaicans are always visiting the beach, but in fact the great majority of them rarely get to the ocean.

Back to our beach walk. . . . After our reminiscence at Kuyaba we turn and go north. There's a couple walking toward us. She's middle aged, white and looks European. He's Jamaican, young, good looking and well built. They walk by, we exchange nods. I glance at Amy and she returns a little grin, her eyebrows are raised but she says nothing.

Around Negril it's common to see middle-aged women tourists, mostly European and usually traveling by themselves, with younger, good looking Jamaican men, many of whom wear their hair in dreads. I know I'm generalizing and will undoubtedly hear about it (it's a sensitive topic) but for the most part (and there are many genuine exceptions) the male of the couple is a hired 'hand'. These gentlemen are referred to as 'Rent-a-Dreads' or 'rentas', the Negril euphemism for male prostitutes.

The women who accompany the rent-a-dreads are apparently

unabashed about the arrangement. You will see them and their beaus walking hand-in-hand on the beach during the day. Now, I don't recall seeing male tourists walking the beach with their hired girls. But it is normal to see the working girls with their dates at night in the bars and clubs. So, why the difference? As near as I can figure it, and I've had some help from women who have been through the scam, this is how it works.

The rent-a-dread is a slick, hard (no pun intended) working professional. Scamming tourist women is how he makes his living. In many ways his work can be likened to that of the fisherman. He sets his traps, visits his favorite spots, reads the weather. He baits, he trolls, he waits patiently. He watches for and preys on the 'green' ones; the girls who haven't had the game run on them before. Some sniff the bait and move on, some take a little nibble and decide it's not for them, but eventually, inevitably, he hooks into one.

With the working girls and their Johns, there is no façade, sex for money, plain and simple, Badda – Bim, Badda – Bis, thank you Miss. Would that it were so simple for the rent-a-dread and his Jane. But if the renta just comes out and propositions the lady, she likely gets insulted, says something like, "Not in your wildest dreams Charlie!", and then maybe slaps him for effect. So the rent-a-dread has to finesse his catch. He woos her, complements her, buys her a token drink, they laugh. It's warm, the moon is bright and high, there's magic in the air. They dance, she gazes deep into his dark, intoxicating eyes, and she falls for him. Beach love. He is so handsome and fit and so . . . exotic. And he's so different from the guys she has known. They go for a walk under the stars. Later, they have sex and it's the best that she has ever had . . . and now he has her.

The next day they meet again, he says he's a little short on cash but he's getting a big payday at the end of the week, could she spot him $50 until then? He tells her if she hangs with him he can be her personal tour guide, show her the 'REAL JAMAICA' save her a lot of money 'cause he's Jamaican and can get her the 'Jamaican rate'.

He tours her around, she ends up paying for everything, his meals and drinks. The sex is fantastic. He sees a little boom-box and a pair of shoes that he really likes, she buys them for him, after all, he is her man and this is the real thing. Her week in paradise is over but she is coming back, soon too. Could she send him a few CDs from the States? He calls collect from Jamaica and talks sexy with her. The calls cost her a fortune. Could she wire him a little cash, maybe $200? He's having some cash flow problems. And Oh!, he is looking forward to seeing her again so much!

Next time she comes down to see him she stays at a hotel where he is 'saving' her $10 a night. He tells her it's $40 a night, and he has it all set up. He says that he has to pay the bill in order to get the 'Jamaican deal'. She gives him the money, the rate is actually $30 a night. He tries to talk her into buying a car for him so that when she is in Negril he can drive her around and save her a ton of money on taxis. He could pick her up and drop her off at the airport, and it would really help him out in earning a living. It goes on and on, the pressure is relentless and the variations are endless.

A really good rent-a-dread can have many tourist girlfriends in different phases of the scam. He may also have a wife and a few Jamaican girlfriends. He schedules the visits carefully. The women actually do believe that he is theirs and theirs alone, until the scam starts to fall apart, as it is destined to. One scam victim told me that while she was visiting 'her' man he had to go to the airport to pick up some friends. He said he wouldn't be long, "Soon come!" He didn't come back for three days. She later found out that he had actually gone off to get married. She was quite piqued that she didn't even get an invitation, after all, they had been so much in love.

While on the subject, here's something that I find surprising, Jamaican men don't favor their women with oral sex. It's considered taboo. To me this seems incongruous considering their otherwise liberal attitudes toward sex. They have no hesitation about receiving oral sex (so I've been told), which is not surprising, but they do not reciprocate. I've asked Jamaican men about this and have only received vague answers in reply. Some say they just don't, it's not an accepted practice, but they can't explain why.

However, women who date Jamaican men have told me that some of the men do return the favor, but don't want them to tell anyone (it's surprising how people will confide in you when told that you're writing a book). So, in spite of the taboo some Jamaican men do 'it' but they just won't admit to 'it'. The likely exception to this is the Rastafarian who, as a vegetarian, has good reason to refrain from the practice.

It's an unusually hot morning that even has some Jamaicans commenting that it's going to be a hot day. However, there are a few dark clouds in the west and it seems to me that we might get some rain.

Amy and I agree that we need a break and commandeer a couple of empty lounges in front of Charela Inn. I'm sitting propped up, hands behind my head, watching the world go by through my sunglasses. Amy is lying flat on her stomach on the lounge, a little closer to the water, snoozing. I see them coming from the north, a pack of five happy beach dogs, tearing along at breakneck speed as if in hot pursuit of an invisible rabbit. The leaders rip right on past us, but tail-end Charlie pulls out of formation just as he's passing Amy's lounge. He circles a bit, nose to the sand, closing in on what has derailed him then begins to dig vigorously. The others notice that he has dropped out and quickly circle back to join him in his quest. Other than some loud panting and the occasional 'Huff!', this is all happening quietly. The site of the dig, unfortunately, is about two feet from my new bride's still-sleeping head. Soon all five dogs are furiously digging in the sand, and getting more excited as they do.

I don't say anything, hoping that the pack will find nothing, get bored, and move on, leaving Amy to sleep through the whole episode none the wiser. That doesn't happen because Charlie's efforts are soon rewarded, he finds something. I can't see what it is, perhaps a half-eaten hot dog. Whatever the treasure, he attempts to make off without sharing it like any self-respecting doggie should.

This immediately results in a dog-pile and an accompanying eruption of barking, snarling, biting and yelping. Amy wakes with a start as two of the mutts slam into the side of her lounge. She lets out a piercing scream and simultaneously pivots into a sitting fetal position. I jump up from my lounge, wave my arms at the dogs and give them a "Shoosh!" I didn't have to, they were already running down the beach with their tails tucked between their legs, scared half to death by the blonde-headed screeching lady. A couple of them glance back with a "What de 'ell is wrong wid 'er?" look on their faces. I sit down beside Amy and explain what has happened. A beach vendor lady who had seen the incident comes over and asks her if she's okay. Amy calms down pretty quickly and within a couple of minutes, we are laughing about it and the dogs are nowhere to be seen.

It took a little longer for her to calm down after she was bitten by a dog while we were vacationing on the island of St. Kitts. We were staying at The Bird Rock Hotel, a cozy, comfortable little place, but a long way from anything or anywhere. We had struck out on what was planned to be an afternoon of hiking and exploring. We were all kitted up; backpack, camera, bathing suits, sandals, towels, a change of socks and sunscreen. We had just left the hotel property and were proceeding up a pathway through a nearby vacant lot when a dog appeared from under a bush beside the path. It was a squat brown and black mutt with short hair. We had seen this dog around before and recognized her by the milk-laden teats that dangled from her chest. She came at us, her teeth bared, snarling, barking and snapping. She stopped short of the path and stood there. Amy let out a little yelp grabbed me and pushed me between her and the dog, one of her patented moves. We sidled slowly past the dog, who stood her ground. Once we were about six feet past her we turned and continued on our way.

I thought that was the end of the encounter, the dog really didn't seem that threatening. But I was wrong, she charged us from behind with surprising speed for a short-legged mutt. In an instant the dog had attached itself to Amy's right ankle. She yelled, "It's biting me!" and kicked at it. The dog let go and hastily retreated back under the bush. So ended our hiking expedition.

I did a quick check of Amy's ankle and saw that the top layers of skin were broken. A big neon sign that read 'rabies' flashed brightly in my head. I knew that Amy was thinking the same.

We went back to the hotel and told the attendant at the front desk what had happened. The owner of the hotel, who was there every day, suddenly appeared from his office.

"You got bitten by a dog?" he asked, concerned.

"Yes, look" Amy said, pulling her sock off to show him the teeth marks on either side of her ankle.

"What kind of dog was it?" he asked as he bent to examine the bite.

"A short brown and white one, a little dog about this big," I said, indicating its size with my hands.

"Was it a female, with milk teats?" asked the attendant.

"Yes," said Amy hopefully, "Do you know it?" We were both still thinking rabies and hoping to identify and capture the dog for tests if need be.

The owner and attendant looked at each other, paused for a moment, then both shook their heads, "No," said the owner.

We were taken to the local hospital in the owner's van. The hospital was a simple low-rise whitewashed concrete block structure with shutters for windows. The rooms were located off sidewalks in the central open-air courtyard. We waited for a while in the 'emergency' room until a doctor could see us.

She was very nice and assured us immediately, before we got the chance to ask, that there was no need to worry about rabies, as St. Kitts had been rabies-free for forty years. Amy was greatly relieved until she was told that she would have to get a tetanus shot as a precaution. Next to dogs, it is needles that she fears most.

We got back to the Bird Rock and went directly to the bar. We told one of the hotel guests what had happened and when we described the dog that had bitten Amy she said, "Oh, that's the owners dog!"

and then, as an afterthought, "You should sue him!"   She was American, so her suggestion came as no surprise.

Amy kept the socks that she was wearing when the dog bit her. In the months that followed, on the occasions when she wore 'the sock', she would spread the fabric to show the puncture holes at the ankle, garnering sympathy from all who listened to her tale.

Here are a couple of interesting facts about St. Kitts; it has one of the largest veterinary schools in the Western Hemisphere, and there are more monkeys on the island, some 40,000 of them, than there are people. Monkeys are not protected, but guns are outlawed on St. Kitts so it is difficult to control the monkey population, as they are very difficult to trap. Because they destroy fruit crops, the monkeys are regarded as pests. They are said to pick the finest mango from the tree, take one bite from it and then discard it. The southern part of St. Kitts has been laid aside as a large nature preserve and the monkeys have overrun it. We drove a rented motor bike through the preserve one day and were surprised to see dozens of monkeys sitting at the side of the road watching us go by.

One dog that Amy did get along with was a little guy named Muffin. We met him in Cuba. He was with his mistress who was one of the most eccentric people whom we have ever come across.

We were staying at a resort on the north coast of Cuba.   One afternoon we walked down the beach to get some ice cream from a beach bar. As we were standing there lapping it up, an older woman who was sitting on a high bar stool next to us said hello and introduced herself as Pamela. The smell of rum was strong on her breath and she was wavering slightly from side to side as she sat on the stool. Laying in the shade under the stool was a small black and white dog with long fur.

Pamela told us that she was from the Toronto area. I judged her age to be 65ish. She was very thin, had bleached blonde hair and she was wearing a flower print bikini with the shoulder straps removed.   Her eyes were watery-blue and her skin was deeply tanned and wrinkled all over.   Pamela was actually in very good shape, a living testament to the preservative qualities of rum. She pointed to the dog under the stool, "And that's my Muffin," she said, "he's a Shih Tzu."

"Oh, that's *your* dog!" I said. I thought it was very unusual for someone to bring a dog on a vacation to the Caribbean, let alone to Cuba.

"Yes, we travel everywhere together, and besides, I couldn't leave him back home because I'm going to be here for a month and we would miss each other too much. Wouldn't we Muffy?"

Muffy, wearing a red bandana around his neck, looked out from under the barstool panting, slobber running out from both sides of his mouth, his flat nose moist. He looked hot, I said so.

"Oh, don't mind Muffin!" Pamela said, "He's fine, aren't you Muffy?" Muffin looked up and snorted and wagged his squat rear end.

"See?" said Pamela, "Muffin's fine!"

"How did you *ever* get him into Cuba?" I asked.

Pamela pulled a ream of papers out of a plastic grocery bag and handed them to me. "I have to bring these papers with me everywhere we go in case Muffin and I get stopped," she said. I rifled through the papers. They were in Spanish and they had official looking stamps plastered all over them. "I had to get Muffy vaccinated and his vet had to write letters that I had to get translated and it cost me a lot and it took months to get approval," she said.

I believed her. From what little I knew about Cuban bureaucracy, it looked to me like Pamela had pulled off a major coup in getting Muffin into the country.

"When I got to the airport the immigration officer wouldn't give Muffin to me until I paid him another $200 US dollars," she said.

"What a rip-off," I said.

"I know, but they wouldn't give him to me and I could see him in his cage and he was crying, weren't you Muffy?" said Pamela. I looked down at Muffin, who, by the 'pity me' look on his flat furry face, seemed to understand all that was being said.

We talked some more. Pamela said that she came to the Santa Lucia area of Cuba quite often and had made friends with several Cubans. Later that week, we ran into her again at another beach bar where she introduced us to a younger Cuban man whom Amy and I assumed was her boyfriend.

After our ice cream we continued our conversation on the patio of an adjoining club. It was happy hour and a live band was playing salsa music. From the conversation I came to the assumption that, although eccentric, Pamela was rather well off, so I asked her where she was staying.

"Oh, I'm staying with some Cuban friends at Cocoa Beach," she replied. This threw me off. I thought she was going to give the name of one of the five-star resorts on the beach.

"You two should come over on Monday for lobster," she offered, "Carlos' wife will cook it for you and the price will be very reasonable."

Amy and I talked it over and since we wanted to visit Cocoa Beach anyhow, we accepted Pamela's offer.

"OK, wait for me on the beach in the afternoon and I'll come and get you," Pamela instructed, flicking the ashes from her ever-present cigarette into the sand.

The following Monday we boarded the trolley for Cocoa Beach. The trolley was actually a broken-down bus that had been converted into a people-mover. The engine and seats were removed and the roof had been cut off. Benches, tables and little patio umbrellas were installed inside and the whole thing was painted over with gay colors. It was towed around by an old farm tractor and when moving slowly down the road it looked like a mobile party, which in fact it was. Just before arriving at Cocoa Beach, we passed the little fishing village where Pamela was lodging. There were a couple of decent-looking homes there, as Cuban homes go, and we assumed that Pamela was staying at one of them. We got off the trolley and walked down to the beach. Pamela was already there, sunning, smoking and sipping on a beer. Muffin was nearby, lolling in the shade of a coconut palm. The long fur on the top of his head was tied up in a little geyser. He was still wearing his red bandana and I noticed that it had a little embroidered image of a Shih Tzu on it and above that was embroidered, 'Muffin'.

Pamela greeted us and after some small talk she said that we should follow her along the beach to her place, but to do so at a discrete distance. This was our first inkling that our lunch at Carlos' place wasn't exactly under the 'legal' column in the Cuban law book. We waited for Pamela to get a little way down the beach and then set out after her. When she got to the fishing village she turned up into the houses and we lost sight of her. We stopped at the spot between the two houses where we thought that she had cut up into the village. Still no sign of Pamela. We wandered around a bit, hoping to spot her, but the village, which was really just a single dusty road with houses on the beach side of it, was deserted. It was siesta hour.

"Pssst!" we heard from behind us. We turned and saw a man, whom we assumed to be Carlos, between two houses, signaling us to follow him. He quickly ducked back between the houses. Curiouser and curiouser. We walked to the spot where Carlos had been but he was nowhere to be seen. We found ourselves alone, standing in the heat of the midday sun on the dusty road, with visions of platters piled high with steaming lobster quickly fading. We stood there, flummoxed, scratching our heads.

"Pssst!" This time a woman, who turned out to be Carlos' wife Lilly, was crouched in the doorway a few houses down waving to us. When she saw that we had seen her, she too ducked back into hiding. We went to where she had been (or so we thought). A door stood open. We walked straight into the wrong house, much to the surprise of the family of Cubans who lived there. There were five or six of them sprawled out on a couple of beds that had been pushed together. We had walked in on the family siesta.

After some hand waving and Amy's hurried attempts in Spanish to explain why we had walked into their house, one of them caught onto the name 'Pamela' and directed us to the house next door. We apologized profusely and they were quite gracious about our mistake. We went next door and finally located Carlos' house. There was a thoroughly beaten '49 Chevy parked out front. Other than that, it was much the same as the houses of fisherman that are built along Jamaican shores, very basic.

We entered our 'dining room', which turned out to be Pamela's bedroom. Her cot had been removed and a table was installed in its place. The floor was concrete, swept clean, and the walls were bare 2 X 4 studs with clapboard on the outside. A single light bulb dangled from the open-raftered ceiling. The room had two windows with bug screens stretched over heavy-gauge wire meshing. The shutters were mounted on the inside. An old, non-functioning icebox served as Pamela's clothes closet. Stacked in one corner were Pamela's matching green vinyl suitcases. Beside them was a folded blanket where Muffin was taking a siesta. I crouched down in front of him, "Are you hot today Muffin?" I asked.

"Oh, don't mind Muffin! He's OK, aren't you Muffy? Pamela said.

We sat down and enjoyed a passable good lobster lunch with rice and fried plantain, all washed down by a couple of 8.6% Cuban beers.

As for the subterfuge, Pamela explained that it was illegal for Cubans to serve tourists in their homes. She said that there had been an undercover cop walking about when we were trying to find Carlos' house and that he had stopped her and demanded to see her papers, which she had produced. Eventually the cop had left the area and that's when Carlos and Lilly had waved us in.

We saw Pamela and Muffin a few more times before we returned home from that trip. Now whenever I hear 'eccentric' I immediately see a picture of Pamela in my mind. She's standing on a rocky part of the beach, darkly tanned, wearing a flower-patterned bikini with a hot pink baseball cap on her head. Loyally sitting at her side, wearing his red bandana and panting like a train chugging its way up a steep hill, is good 'ole Muffy.

Cliff Jumping is Dangerous

'Every man has a right to decide his own destiny.'
Bob Marley - 'Zimbabwe'

.   .   . my stomach leaps up into my chest and I feel weightless. My shorts flap in the rushing air as I plummet toward the water. I keep my eyes on the horizon for a second, then close them tightly. There's a mighty slap across my butt and lower thighs and I'm in the water, plunging rapidly toward the sandy bottom. I let go of my nose, open my eyes and release my 'boys', both thankfully still intact. My downward momentum slows, I spread my arms out and kick mightily for the surface which is way above me at the top of a column of swirling bubbles.

It seems like minutes, but seconds I later burst to the surface. I look up at the cliff edge from where I leapt. It looks incredibly high from here. A kid standing up there is peering down at me, waiting for me to clear the splashdown zone. I swim out a little and locate Amy who still has the camera up to her eye. I wave, she waves back. I'm her hero.

The backs of my thighs are stinging from the impact with the water, but other than that I'm undamaged. I kick over on to my back and float in the warm water. The sky is clear and blue and fathomless. Mother Ocean coddles me. I don't ever want to leave her embrace.

Reality chooses this moment to come crashing into my revelry. The day after tomorrow we go back to that other world. The world of snow shovels and alarm clocks and jobs and traffic. The world of responsibilities. I try to push the thought away but it doesn't work this time. I roll onto my stomach and do a surface dive, propelling myself toward the bottom until my ears scrunch. I grab onto my black coral pendant and rub it - - *'I'll bring you back.'*

Amy and I spend the rest of our time in paradise sleeping in, relaxing, laying in the sun and walking barefoot in the surf. We soak up the serenity of the early morning and the convivial hubbub of the afternoon. And we start planning our next trip.

Which raises a couple of questions, dear reader; when to go and where to stay. A Negrilophile will tell you that anytime is the right time. I would agree with that with one exception, that being the spring break. Unless you happen to be at that wonderful point in your life when you are one of the 'Breakers', I counsel you to stay away from the frat party that takes over the southern part of the beach and the cliffs from the last week of February through the third week of March. The northern part of the beach where the more expensive all-inclusives are located is, for the most part, insulated from the Breakers by the higher prices.

Where to stay, on the beach or on the cliffs? All-inclusive or non-inclusive?   Good questions to which there is no single answer, except, try all combinations.

I usually stay on the beach when visiting Negril because I like to be where all the action is, however the cliffs are very nice too, quieter and more secluded than the beach area. If you like to walk, the beach is where you should be. Walking the cliff road, while fascinating, is not conducive to relaxation.

But no matter when you go or where you choose to stay, beware, Negril will beguile you.

PNS

'When yu go a Jackass yard, yu noh fi chat 'bout big iyaz'
Jamaican Proverb

My name is Roland and I'm a Negriloholic . . . I suffer from PNS.

Many people who visit Negril on a regular basis (and there are legions) report a curious affliction that is referred to by the cognoscenti as PNS. Others call it Negrilitis. PNS is the abbreviation for Post Negril Syndrome if you have just returned from a trip to Negril, or Pre Negril Syndrome if you have planned a trip and are suffering through the seemingly interminable time period before you actually board the airplane.

Please don't snicker, I am not joking. PNS is not to be taken lightly.   Some people are immune to it, but if you have a predisposition, you *will* be afflicted.

PNS symptoms vary depending on the person and the severity of the affliction. Here are some common symptoms;

- Can't stop thinking or dreaming about Negril,
- Sudden, deep cravings for jerk chicken,
- Unusually persistent morose feelings after returning from a trip to Negril,
- Depression and anger when looking at snow and miserable weather (I suffer acutely from this),
- Inexplicable grinning and feelings of euphoria when a chance reference to Negril or Jamaica is encountered,
- Insatiable yearning to talk about Negril to friends and acquaintances. (People will smile politely and nod their heads, but as soon as you aren't looking they'll roll der eyes and 'kiss teet' behind yu back.)

Unfortunately, although treatment is available for the symptoms, there is only one cure, moving to Negril, which realistically, is not an option for the vast majority of PNS sufferers. Here are some of the things that will bring relief from an acute attack of PNS:

- Look at photos taken while in Negril.
- Examine your Negril souvenirs (some women have children by Jamaican men, now that's a memory that lasts a lifetime).
- Get support, it's out there. Talk to someone about Negril, preferably someone who has been there and is a fellow sufferer. I talk to Amy, but she isn't afflicted with PNS, so I don't get the

same level of relief as I would commiserating with another sufferer.

- Read a book about Negril, like this one. Another book that I recommend is 'Banana Shout' by Mark Conklin. Reading books about Negril will provide solace until you finish the last page, but beware that the immediate aftereffect can be devastating.

- Search the internet for Negril websites. One of the best is www.negril.com (run by a fine American ex-pat named Rob Graves who lives in Negril). Here you will find lots of information about Negril that can be picked over with relish. There is also a message board that is frequented by hundreds of fellow PNS sufferers. Some are in the extreme dependency stages, feel sorry for them and offer your support and condolences. Residents of Negril also post messages on the board. Chatting with them is very good for PNS and they are also good sources of information for planning the next trip.

- Listen to reggae tunes, especially Bob Marley, every day. This works for me, it's like an IV drip of anti-PNS-biotics with the added benefit of the message in the music.

- Plan a trip to Negril. This is an effective treatment, which will convert your Post Negril Syndrome into Pre-Negril Syndrome, the less virulent version of the strain. Depending on the severity and stage of development of your PNS, the recommended trip dosage ranges from a minimum of one week per year for early-stage PNS on up to permanent residence for the severe and advanced stages. But beware of this treatment, it is addictive and expensive. My personal dosage has gradually crept up to four weeks per year. Pray for me.

- Write a book about Negril. This book represents one full year's treatment for PNS.

A PNS attack can strike at any time and with varying severity. The Post Negril Syndrome attacks that occur during the weeks immediately following a trip are the worst. They fade in intensity in equal proportion to the fading of one's suntan. But they never entirely go away, like a suntan that leaves freckles.

The oddest occurrences of PNS are those that happen when on vacation at a place other than Negril. I've heard reports from people who, when visiting another Caribbean island, spend their entire vacation wishing they were in Negril instead.

Now, at first, I thought this was merely an exhibition of bizarre and perhaps compulsive behavior, until it happened to me personally while vacationing in Las Vegas. I was okay until day two of a four-day stay. Doing just fine, taking in the sights, losing money, enjoying the 100-degree heat (but no ocean to plunge into). Amy and I were walking down the Vegas Strip when PNS snuck up and slapped me in the face. I was accompanying her to the 'Fashion Mall' (actually, I was dutifully in tow, reluctant, dragging my feet). We were about halfway there, passing Harrah's Casino when my ear caught the faint strains of reggae wafting out from a little entertainment area bedside the hotel. *'chuka... chuka,... chuka'.* The familiar PNS twinges began, I NEEDED to get closer to the music, I needed my fix, something to scratch the itch.

"Uh, Hon, I'm hot and my feet hurt and I really don't want to go to the mall... how about I hang out and wait for you here?" I pleaded. *'chuka...chuka...chuka'*

"Is that reggae I hear?" she said, lifting her head a little and turning her ear toward the beat.

"What. . . huh, reggae?"

"OK, I'll see you back here at 1:15 – 1:30." Ah, it's a tough hand that is dealt to one who lives with the chronic PNS sufferer. So I pecked her on her sweet, understanding and slightly perspiring lips and walked into a very enjoyable hour of reggae with innovative use of the steel drum. I didn't catch the name of the band, but they said they were from Kingston. The lead singer said the Strip needed some reggae and they were here to provide it. They played a couple of Bob Marley tunes and saved my life.

So, naturally, I sat there and listened to the music and thought about Jamaica and Negril. I thought about when I was going to go back and I made a mental list of the things I wanted to do when I got there. Here it is;

- One evening, I want to take a flashlight and sneak up on one of the big toads that live under the buildings near the beach,
- I want to see if I can catch a glimpse of one of the little gleeping tree frogs that sing at night,
- I want to go to Little Bay and spend some time at Bob Marley's seaside cottage,
- And I want to go to YS Falls and swim in behind the falling water curtain and poke my head out through it,
- I want to go for a long walk on the beach on a hot day with the sun pounding down on my back, sipping on a cool Red Stripe as I go,
- I want to jump the cliff at the Pickled Parrot and then walk all the way down the road into town to the roundabout,
- On the way to town, I'm going to stop at Tiny's bar and have a drink there and stay until the sun goes down,
- And Cuba's is on the way too, so I'll stop there and I'm going to have a big bowl of the best conch soup in the world,

• And I'm going to hunt down my old Jamaican fisherman friend, and ask him how the crab migration was this year,

. . and that's only the start of it.....

. . . BOING! . . .

The band is saying that they will be back in twenty minutes and I'm back in Vegas, my Negrillian daydream broken. The desert sky is cloudless and the sun is high and hot. I feel good, rosy all over, like I've just had a shot of Appleton. The PNS has been sated and has slunk back into its bolt-hole. I've had an unexpected dose of reggae and a cool beer, and I've thought about Negril for the first time in several days.

I see Amy coming back from her shopping expedition. She has a Neiman-Marcus bag in her hand and a smile on her face.

I'm smiling too.

Walk Good

You think it's the end, but it's just the beginning.
Bob Marley – 'Want More'

 This book was written almost entirely in the studio of my home in Ottawa.   It's a comfortable room, decorated in a Caribbean motif and adorned with memorabilia acquired over many trips to the islands.

The Rasta-Lion that I got near the Pickled Parrot is hanging on the wall. He's dreadful . . . he's wonderful. Each time I look at him, in my mind's eye I see Junior holding him high above his head and calling out, "I LOVE YOU!" I told Junior that day that I would give his Rasta-Lion a good home and take care of it. I have, and now I love it too.

The worn-down alabaster conch shell that I picked up in front of The Beachcomber is sitting on a shelf and beside it, proudly displaying its creamy pink chamber, is a perfect conch shell (but that's another story). Irie, the fish carving who attended our wedding, sits atop an armoire. From his high perch he looks down, mouth agape, on all that pass, his body permanently twisted into a sharp turn.

The note from the bottle that Amy and I cast into the sea made it back to us two weeks after we got home. A couple from Alberta found it washed up on the shore near Beaches. We had hoped it would float on the ocean for years, eventually landing on a beach in Africa, in fact its journey covered only two miles.

These are my Jamaica touchstones, the things that bridge the time between trips.

Since I started this book Negril has evolved a little. 'Wild Thing', the party boat, was taken by Hurricane Michelle. But she has been replaced and the beat goes on. And, Miracle of Miracles, the road from MoBay to Negril has been finished! I never really believed that it would happen.

So, my tale is ended, thank you for reading it and sharing some of my memories with me. Maybe I'll see you on the beach sometime. Look for me meandering in the surf with a Red Stripe in one hand, a conch shell in the other and a contented smile pasted across my face.

Walk Good, mi friend.

Roland Reimer
Ottawa, Ontario
June, 2002

Jamaican Patois, Colloquialisms and Proverbs

Some Jamaican Patois and Colloquialisms

Although patois can never be learned from a lexicon, a small sampling is presented here to give a sense of the richness of the language and its roots in the Jamaican culture. Jamaican patois comes in many dialects and derivatives, the deeper one goes into the backcountry, the thicker and more arcane the dialect. As is the case for every language, one must live it to learn it.

Babylon – Represents all that is bad in society, big bad business, corrupt politicians and police. The system, or in the Jamaican vernacular, 'the shit-stem'.

Ball-edd – (bald head) a straight person or a person without dreadlocks, one who works for Babylon.

Bammy - a pancake that is made out of cassava that has been grated and squeezed to remove the bitter juice.

Bashment – a big party with much loud music, a dancing party.

Big Bamboo – The Jamaican term for the penis, also the name of a song that extols the virtues of the Jamaican man's penis.

Big Ups - hearty congratulations.

Blood Claat! – the universal Jamaican epithet, a variant is Raas Clot, and also, Bumba Clot, which can mean someone who has had his partner cheat on him.

Bredren - one's fellow male Rastafarians

Cool Runnings – a salutation that is usually used at the time of departure on a long journey. It means have a good and a safe trip.

Craven Choke Puppy - someone greedy who wants everything but when they get it, they can't manage it.

Cuss, Cuss – a loud argument or brouhaha with lots of swearing.

Caan't – can't, as in "Me caan't nyam all dat!" (I can't eat all of that!)

Darkers – sunglasses.

Downpressor - an oppressor of the people.

Dread – an ambidextrous word, can mean a person with dreadlocks, a serious thing, a dangerous person, or can be used as a verb, an adjective, a salutation, an expletive or an exclamation.

Dreadlocks - hair that is neither combed nor cut (but is kept clean).

Duppy – a ghost.

Dutty – dirty.

Every t'ing cook an' curry. - Every thing is OK, there's nothing to worry about.

Fe (Fi) – 'to' as in 'Have fe go.' 'a fe' as in 'Have to.' 'fe dem' as in 'their'.

Fiah – Fire

Galang bout yuh business. - Go along about you business.

Ganja – marijuana.

Gwaan go maas. - Go and cool off your temper.

I an' I – for Rasta's 'I and I' replaces 'me', 'you', 'they' and 'us'. Rastafarians look upon these terms as divisive. The communal 'I and I' embraces the self and the divine JAH.

Irie – Originally, this was used by Rastafarians to mean "I free", meaning free from repression and Babylon. When one's mind is not taken hostage by the Babylon system one is "I-free", the pronunciation gradually evolved to Irie. Now 'Irie' generally means all is well. It is used as a salutation, as a description of a feeling, 'I feelin' irie'. A positive affirmation, good vibes.

I-tal – Rastafarian for Vi-tal. vital, organic, natural, wholesome; refers to way of cooking and a way of life.

JAH – The Rastafarian God figure. Jah is believed to be a contraction of Jehovah. Jah Ras Tafari, Haile Selassie, King of Kings, Lord of Lords, conquering Lion of the Tribe of Judah; Rastafarians revere Haile Selassie, ex-emperor of Ethiopia, as the personification of the Almighty.

Kiss me neck! – An exclamation of surprise.

Kiss teet. – To kiss one's teeth or to cluck to make a noise of disapproval, dislike, or disappointment.

Licky-licky - fawning, flattering, obsequious.

Likkle - little.

Macca - thorns.

Mash it up. - A huge success.

Mash up - To crash, to break or ruin.

Me bleach hard lass night. - I partied straight through the night.

Niyabinghi – a tribe of East African warriors who resisted colonial domination, a type of drumming, a large Rastafarian spiritual gathering, a certain type of orthodox Rastafarian.

No problem. – evr'y t'ing is cool mon.

Nuff Respect – as respect for others is a very important tenet in the Jamaican culture, 'Nuff' respect is like saying 'lots of respect to you'.

Nyam – to eat.

Obeah - a practice brought from African by slaves pertaining to matters of the spirit and spirits, spells, divinations, omens and extra-sensory perception.

One love - A parting phrase, an expression of unity.

Pinckney – a child, children.

Raggamuffin – a Jamaican ghetto dweller.

Rude bwoy - A criminal, a hard-hearted person, a tough guy.

Sensemilla, Sensie - popular, potent, seedless, un-pollinated female strain of marijuana.

Skank - to dance to reggae music, to move with cunning ulterior motives.

Spliff – a marijuana cigarette.

Walk good. – Walk safe roads and may all your travels be rewarding.

Whafedoo. - We'll have to make do with what we have, or we'll have to deal with the situation.

Why yu fe galang so? - Why must you behave in such a manner?

Ya nuh see? - You don't see?

Yu dam lagga head bud. – As in 'You stupid jackass!"

Some Jamaican Proverbs

Jamaican proverbs consistently counsel patience, forbearing and respect for others. This is a small sampling of some of my favorites. As you will see when reading them, there is much old wisdom conveyed by these simple truisms.

Alligator lay egg, but 'im noh fowl.
(The alligator lays eggs, but it isn't a fowl.)
     Things are not always what they seem.

Bad fambly betta dan empty pigsty.
(A bad family is better than an empty pigsty.)
     It's better to have a bad family than no family at all.

Bucket wid hole a battam have no business a rivaside.
(A bucket with a hole in it has no business at the riverside.)
     Unless you are perfect, mind your own business and don't criticize others.

Bug blanket mek man sleep late.
(A thick blanket causes a man to sleep late.)
     An over-abundance of luxuries causes one to become complacent and to take life's blessings for granted.

Chicken merry, hawk deh near.
(The chickens are merry, the hawk is near.)
     Every silver lining has its dark cloud and even in the happiest times one must still be watchful.

Cotton-tree no know how him bottom stan' im no call breeze.
(If the cotton tree doesn't know how strong his roots are it doesn't call for a breeze.)
     Don't call trouble unless you are sure you can cope with it.

Cuss-cuss noh bore hole a mi skin.
(Cursing doesn't bore holes in my skin.)
     Words cannot hurt me.

Dawg no howl ef im ha bone.
(A dog doesn't howl if it has a bone.)

Şatisfied people don't complain.

De olda de moon, de bryta it shine.

(The older the moon, the brighter it shines.)

> With age comes wisdom.

Deaf ears give story-carrier trouble.

Rumors don't circulate when people don't listen to gossip.

Every day bucket go a well one day de bottom will drop out.

(Every day the bucket goes to the well, one day the bottom will drop out.)

> Things wear out, literally and figuratively.

Every day yu goad donkey, some day he kick yu.

> Don't be misled into thinking that the weak will not fight back if continually goaded.

Every dog t'inks im self a lion in im mastah's yard.

(Every dog things that he's a lion when in his master's yard.)

> People are always confident in their own surroundings, such may not be the case when they are thrown into other environments.

Every jackass t'ink im pickney a racehorse.

(Every jackass thinks his children (pickney) are racehorses)

> Parents are often overly expectant of their child's capabilities.

Eat wid de debil but gi im long spoon.

(Eat with the devil but give him a long spoon.)

> Give yourself room to maneuver when engaging in dangerous practices.

Geti-geti no want it, and wanti-wanti can't get it.

> Those who have don't want, and those who want can't get.

Hog say, di fus water 'im cetch 'im walla.

(The hog says, the first water he sees, he's going to wallow in it.)

> Make best of the first opportunity that presents itself.

In Jamaica, if it's nice you do it twice.

> Not so much a proverb as an axiom by which people live.

I no come to hear about how horse dead an' cow fat.

> Cut out the crap and get to the point.

If fish coulda keep him mout' shut, him would neva get caught.

> No explanation required.

It hard fe keep out de debil, but it wus fe dribe him out.

(It's hard to keep out the devil, but it's worse to drive him out.)

> It can be difficult to stay out of trouble, but it's more difficult to extract from it.

If yuh cyann fight Bushman tek way im bush.

(If you can't fight the bushman, take away his bush.)

> There are more ways than the obvious to accomplish a desired goal.

If you got you han inna debbil mout, teck time draw it out.

(If you've got your hand in the devil's mouth, take time to draw it out.)

When immersed in problems or trouble, be very careful in withdrawing from it.

If yuh neber wear boot, yuh wi neber feel de pinch.

(If you never wear boots you never feel the pinch.)

Until you've been in a situation you really have no idea of the consequences.

Johncrow feel cool breeze.

There are people who, like Johncrow (a buzzard), will jump at any opportunity that arises from someone else's misfortune.

Lang road draw swet, shaat cut draw blud.

(Long road draws seat, short cut draws blood.)

Taking what appears to be the easier, shorter path, may in fact turn out to be the more difficult.

Man noh dead, noh call 'im duppy.

(The man's not dead, don't call him a (ghost) duppy.)

As long as someone is still in the game, don't dismiss their potentials.

Man noh done cross riva, noh fi cuss alligator long mout.

(If a man hasn't done crossing the river, he shouldn't curse alligator long mouth.)

Don't cuss those who can block your path.

Mi com yah fe drink milk, mi noh com yah fe count cow.

(I come here to drink milk not to count cows.)

More action! Less talk! Let's get down to business!

Monkey mus' know weh 'im gwine put 'im tail, before 'im order trousiz.

(A monkey must know where he's going to put his tail before he orders trousers)

One must know one's self before doing what others are doing.

New broom sweep clean, but de ole broom know de corner.

(The new broom sweeps clean but the old broom knows the corners.)

The old and experienced don't miss the not so obvious.

Noh care how boar hog try fi hide under sheep wool, 'im grunt always betray 'im.

(Don't care how the boar tries to hide under sheep wool, his grunt always betrays him.)

It doesn't matter how much of a disguise someone puts on, eventually, their true character will surface.

Noh put yu cap whay yu cyan reach it.

(Don't put your cap where you can't reach it.)

Don't live above your means.

Not ev'rybody brotfast ready same time.

(Everybody's breakfast isn't ready at the same time)

Don't envy those who are enjoying success, your time will come.

Nyam some, lef some.

(Eat some, leave some.)

Indulge, but put aside for tomorrow (harder times).

Ole fiyah tick easy fe ketch.

(Old fire sticks are easily re-kindled.)

Old battles or old loves are easily re-entered.

Rockstone a riva battam noh kno' sun hot.

(A rock sitting on the river bottom doesn't know the heat of the sun.)

If you are in a sheltered situation, you don't really know what hardship is.

Sorry for maga dog, maga dog turn round bite you.

(Sorry for meager dog, meager dog turns around and bites you.)

Hasty acts of charity can produce less than desirable results. Someone that you help may show no thanks and may even scorn you.

Too much callaloo, mek peppa-pot stew bittah.

(Too much callaloo makes the pepper pot stew bitter.)

Too much of a good thing, can spoil everything.

Trouble no set like rain.

Unlike the dark clouds that herald bad weather, trouble comes without warning.

The higher the monkey climbs the more him expose.

No explanation required.

The gal come wine up on me.

The woman danced up and put the make on me.

Tis a foolish dog, bark at the flying bird.

Don't get worked up about things over which you have no control.

We run t'ings, t'ings noh run we.

(We run things, things don't run us.)

We are masters of our own fate.

Wha no good fe breakfas no good fe dinnah.

(What is no good for breakfast is no good for dinner.)

What's bad is bad, time will not change it.

Wha sweet a mout' hat a belly.

(What is sweet in the mouth is hot in the belly.)

What tastes sweet in the mouth can burn the belly.

Water more than flour, time tough.

When making a dumpling, water is plentiful but flour is scarce, times are hard.

When cotton-tree tumble down every nanny-goat want fe jump over.

(When the cotton tree falls, every nanny goat wants to jump over it.)

When the mighty fall the weak rush in to take advantage.

When rat like fi romp 'roun' puss jaw, one diay 'im gwine en up inna puss craw.

(When the rat likes to romp around the puss's jaw, one day him going to end up in the puss's craw.)

When one flirts too much with danger, soon he or she will get hurt.

When water trow weh i' cyan pick up.
(When water has been thrown, we can't pick it up.)
    What's done is done, you can't turn back the hands of time.
When yu go a Jackass yard, yu noh fi chat 'bout big iyaz
(When you got to the jackass's yard, don't chat about big ears.)
    Don't criticize others in their presence.
You don't miss the watah 'til da well run dry
    No explanation required.
Yu mek yu sail too big fi yu boat, yu sail wi capsize yu.
(If you make your sail too big for your boat, your sail will capsize you.)
    Don't get involved in things that are too big for you.

ISBN 155369871-1